D0216984

A Gentle Guide to Research Methods

Pine Bluff Jefferson County Library
200 East 8th Ave.
Pine Bluff, AR 71601

A Gentle Guide to Research Methods

Gordon Rugg and Marian Petre

Open University Press

Open University Press
McGraw-Hill Education
McGraw-Hill House
Shoppenhangers Road
Maidenhead
Berkshire
England
SL6 2QL

email: enquiries@openup.co.uk
world wide web: www.openup.co.uk

and Two Penn Plaza, New York, NY 10121-2289, USA

First published 2007

Copyright © Gordon Rugg and Marian Petre 2007

All rights reserved. Except for the quotation of short passages for the
purposes of criticism and review, no part of this publication may be
reproduced, stored in a retrieval system, or transmitted, in any form,
or by any means, electronic, mechanical, photocopying, recording or
otherwise, without the prior written permission of the publisher or a
licence from the Copyright Licensing Agency Limited. Details of such
licences (for reprographic reproduction) may be obtained from
the Copyright Licensing Agency Ltd of 90 Tottenham Court Road,
London, W1T 4LP.

A catalogue record of this book is available from the British Library

ISBN-10: 0 335 21927 6 (pb)   0 335 21928 4 (hb)
ISBN-13: 978 0 335 21927 8 (pb)   978 0 335 21928 4 (hb)

Library of Congress Cataloging-in-Publication Data
CIP data applied for

Typeset by RefineCatch Limited, Bungay, Suffolk
Printed in Poland by OZ Graf. S.A.
www.polskabook.pl

The McGraw-Hill Companies

Contents

List of Figures

Preamble

If you scorn to build cities, to sail ships, to settle the wilderness, to master the secrets of prehuman knowledge, then what have you achieved?

(*Night Winds*, p.68)

So there you are, facing the prospect of doing some research of your own. You've read the books about research methods, and have dutifully attended the lectures and training courses on research methods, and you're still feeling lost and confused. You're not sure of the difference between Popper and postmodernists, or between structuralism and symbolic interactionism (and you're not sure whether it makes any difference or not); you don't know how much data you'll need to collect, but you have a vague belief that more is better than less; you have occasional attacks of panic about what will happen if somebody else discovers the answer first, or if you get something wrong. You're not sure where to start, and you are resolutely not thinking about what you'll do after you've finished, because you have too much to think about right now. If you're feeling that way, you're in good company, because most researchers feel that way when they start their careers. This book is intended to help you out of that feeling, and into a better state of mind.

It's intended for students whose research involves studying human beings or collecting information from human beings. That's a broad field: it includes, for instance, social geographers, and computer science students getting their software evaluated by users. It also includes research studying human beings via the artefacts that they produce, such as analysis of texts. Although fields such as literary criticism are well established and have their own ways of doing things, there's plenty of scope for introducing some new ways of tackling most fields, and we hope that this book will introduce readers to some fruitful new approaches to their own areas. Having said that, this book is not intended for physical sciences such as geology, metallurgy, nor for physics, mathematics and the like, which involve a quite different set of research methods; similarly, it's not intended for disciplines such as music which study human artefacts in their own right rather than as an insight into their makers, nor for descriptive disciplines such as history. We have considerable respect for those fields, and the reason that we've excluded them from our scope is simply that they do things so differently that they would require different books from this one. From this point on, unless otherwise specified, when we talk about research we'll be talking about research which involves human beings somewhere in the field of study.

This book does two main things. It outlines the big picture of research – what research is, how it fits into a career, how it fits into the world. It also describes a lot of the nuts-and-bolts details – classic contingency plans; things to remember when tabulating your data; how to treat your informants properly. It illustrates all of this with examples, some of which are real (for realism) and some of which are fictitious (to spare the innocent, and some of the guilty). For the fictitious examples, to spare potential embarrassment we have used people, places and institutions culled from science fiction and history.

We've covered topics in varying degrees of depth. Where a topic is well covered by easily located literature, we've given a quick overview and moved on. Where a topic is either not well covered by existing literature, or where the relevant literature is difficult to find, we've gone into more detail. We've also focused more on topics which everyone is likely to encounter, such as data collection methods, and less on topics which will only affect some readers, and which are already well covered in the literature, such as inferential statistics. There's also the issue of length: covering everything in the same level of detail would have doubled the size of the book, so we've reluctantly had to say much less about statistics than we would have liked.

On that practical note, we'll end this preamble. We hope you find this book helpful, useful and a Good Thing.

Acknowledgements

Amid such a mass of small letters, it will not seem surprising that an occasional error of the press should have occurred. I trust, however, that the number of such errors is small; and I am confident that the generous, the learned, and the experienced (and it is their good opinion, and theirs only, I am anxious to obtain) will not deny me their kind indulgence.

(Forbes's Hindustani Dictionary, p.iv)

We're grateful to the people who helped with this book, and to the students and colleagues who have, whether advertently or inadvertently, introduced us to many new learning experiences.

We're particularly grateful to Sue Gerrard for her help with the preparation of the manuscript.

Introduction

The structure of this book: research design, data collection and data analysis • Taught degree projects: what they are, things to watch out for, and practical points • PhD second studies: what happens when your first study changes your plans • Strategies and principles: demonstrating excellence, exploring territory rather than trying to prove a hunch, avoiding trouble, and learning from the wise • Choosing a topic, or cups of coffee, easy pickings and blaming others • Departments, systems and supervisors: how to behave like a professional, get a good reference, and avoid needless trouble • 'How do I get a good mark?' – things that can send out the wrong signal, and how to avoid these • Academic writing: why it's different from other writing, and how to do it well

> . . . *certain subtle points which may or may not lend a hideous and incredible kind of rationale to the apparent chaos.*
>
> (*At the Mountains of Madness*, p.53)

The structure of this book: research design, data collection and data analysis

This book begins with a section about student projects and PhDs, since these are likely to be the reason for many readers opening this book in the first place.

If you're already familiar with these topics, or they don't apply to you, then you can cheerfully skip that section.

The rest of the book is divided conceptually into three main bits. The way that these three fit together is that the research design determines the overall structure of your research; the data collection methods are for gathering the data within that structure, and then the statistical analysis is for making sense of that data. Research design and statistical analysis are both fields which have well-established frameworks. Data collection has previously been something of a Cinderella in comparison. Everyone has agreed that it's important, and there's a lot of published material about the individual methods used for data collection, but there's previously been a significant lack of a systematic framework to guide researchers in their choice and use of the appropriate method for their needs. We've tackled this by introducing a framework, and by including a set of chapters systematically covering a range of techniques, which you can use independently of the framework if you wish.

That's simple enough in principle, but in reality, if you have any sense, you'll bear the statistical analysis in mind when choosing the research design, and will also bear the data collection methods in mind when choosing the statistical analysis and the research design, so that you don't waste time collecting bad, pointless data. For instance, you might discover that using a particular statistical test to analyse your data will mean that you only have to use two-thirds as many subjects as the test you originally intended, but you'll need to collect the data using a particular type of scale in order to use that test. To use another example, you might realise that your best strategy is to do a demonstration of concept with a single case study as your design, with a little-known data collection technique to demonstrate your point, and with only qualitative analysis. In both cases, you gather less data, and you also do a better job of the research. As usual, it's wise to do some homework, stop when you hit diminishing returns (i.e. the point where you're not finding much that you haven't already found) or start feeling lost, and then take advice from someone knowledgeable about this area.

Closing remarks

The style of this book bears various similarities to that of our previous book, *The Unwritten Rules of PhD Research*. We've deliberately used informal language for clarity and readability. We use a completely different style when writing academic papers, so you shouldn't even momentarily consider writing up your own work in the same style as this book.

We've assumed that you will also read more specialist texts where appropriate – our aim is to give you a solid overall grasp of the big picture and some important nuts and bolts, not to give you specialist knowledge of, for instance, how to do analysis of variance. We've pointed towards further reading, rather than trying to produce a prescriptive bibliography.

We've included anecdotes to illustrate our points; all these anecdotes, however improbable, are true unless otherwise stated (even the episode with the mole on the dual carriageway). We've changed the names of sinners, but retained the names of the virtuous (though giving first names only, so they can deny any involvement if they're feeling embarrassed or modest). We have also started each section with a quotation, to brighten what might otherwise be a solidly worthy chunk of morally improving prose.

Taught degree projects: what they are, things to watch out for, and practical points

The outside world, of course, knew of our program.
(*At the Mountains of Madness*, p.21)

The next few sections are intended for students who are reading this book because they're about to do a taught degree project, with one tangential section for PhD students. If this doesn't apply to you, then you might prefer to skip ahead. If it does apply to you, then it's highly advisable to understand the background context to projects before you start planning your research.

The System, in its infinite wisdom, requires most students to do a piece of original independent research at some point; for PhD students, this is the main purpose of the PhD, whereas for students on taught courses, it's just one more bit of the course. If you're an undergraduate, it usually happens in your final year; if you're a Master's student, then it usually happens after the taught modules. There are many similarities between the issues involved in undergraduate and Master's projects; there are also some significant differences, which is why we've written this section, to reduce the risk of your running into problems inadvertently.

A surprising number of students don't know the big picture, so here it is. It's pretty simple, though the details vary between departments:

- You choose a topic for your project.
- You are equipped with a supervisor.
- You research your topic, taking advice regularly from your supervisor.
- At the end of the project, you write it up as a dissertation.

If your project is boring and/or badly done, everyone involved tries to forget about it as quickly as possible. If your project is interesting and well done, you can use it as a stepping stone to your goals – for instance, if you want a career in academia, your project could be a route to a PhD. It can also get your foot in the door of an organisation where you want to work.

The project normally has to be an original piece of research. This usually means that it involves a reasonable amount of primary research, as opposed to just secondary research. There's more about these concepts elsewhere in this book, but in brief, primary research involves your finding out something which nobody knew before; secondary research involves your finding out what other people have already discovered about the topic. As usual, each university, faculty and department tends to have its own view of how all this should be interpreted, which is why we use words such as 'usually' a lot. Your primary research isn't expected to result in an earth-shattering discovery; it's just intended to demonstrate that you know how to carry out an adequate piece of primary research.

The administrative procedures, general concepts and project topics in your department may be almost identical between undergraduate and Master's projects. However, this does not mean that the resulting projects are expected to be much the same, and this can lead to problems if you go from a first degree to a Master's degree in the same topic, and fail to realise that you're now playing a different game with different expectations. Quite what the expectations are, however, is an interesting question, and can lead to considerable debate when course teams meet. In brief, the further through the academic system you go, the less you are expected simply to quote The Truth™ from the textbooks, and the more you are expected to show capable independent thought. There's the further complication that historically there's been a tension between Master's degrees viewed as an advanced version of the corresponding undergraduate degree, and Master's degrees viewed as something different from an undergraduate degree: a common example in the past was 'conversion' Master's courses.

All very well, you might think, but why should I care? You might care because these past debates have influenced the form of present-day projects, and because you might inadvertently stray into unpleasant territory if you're not careful, like some innocent ramblers wandering on to a battlefield from long ago, whose flowered meadows still harbour the deadly relics of those distant conflicts, waiting to spike you on their sharp bits.

One common example of this is different marking criteria for undergraduate projects and for Master's projects in the same field. The Master's projects will be expected to show more 'masterliness' than the undergraduate ones, and there can be extensive debate about what is meant by 'masterliness'. It is inadvisable to involve yourself in that debate. It is much more advisable to find some things that would definitely be construed as showing 'masterliness', include them, and let everyone including yourself get on with their lives without needless hassle. As a rough rule of thumb, anything showing more theoretical sophistication, or a mature understanding of the field as a whole, or reading of advanced literature on the topic, is likely to help show 'masterliness'. Conversely, a tattily presented bit of work whose bibliography consists of a textbook and three internet URLs is unlikely to impress anyone with its maturity and sophistication.

That's a brief summary of the background context. The next subsection gives some advice about your enemies on an undergraduate or a Master's project. It's important to know about these because if you don't you can blunder into trouble unwittingly, regardless of how clear your conscience is and how hard you work.

Knowing your enemies

Typically, supervisors are not impressed if they think that you are doing the minimum possible amount of work on a topic. If you give the impression of harbouring such thoughts, then your supervisor will become less sympathetic towards you. It's a cliché, but a true one, that you get out of your project what you put into it, and it's your job, not anybody else's job, to put that in. There is also often the belief that there's one right answer to every question, with all the other answers being wrong. If you give the impression of thinking this on your project, then it won't stand you in good stead – you need to show that you're capable of handling at least some areas where your chosen discipline hasn't yet reached consensus.

If you're a Master's student, then one of your main enemies is the final year undergraduate student. Undergraduates who have come straight to university from school have had only limited experience of the world, and are therefore typically not strong on thoughtful, insightful, mature analysis of a problem, its context and its significance. If you're doing a Master's project, then it's a good idea to include something which allows you to demonstrate that you can think like a sophisticated grown-up.

The topic of grown-ups brings us on to another enemy, namely the practical person from the outside world. There is much to be said for the outside world, but the thing to remember is that if you're doing a degree, then you are being examined on how much you know about the topic of the degree, not how much you know about the outside world. A classic version of this in computing-related disciplines is the project that tackles a problem which is important to someone in the real world, but which fails to demonstrate any evidence of learning anything on the course. There are related problems, such as claiming that academic writing is a load of nonsense, and that business English is much better. This betrays severe cluelessness about the nature and purpose of academic writing, and usually leads to an unhappy outcome. If you've entered academia from the outside world, and you don't know why the academic world does something the way it does, then the wise thing to do is to find out by asking someone knowledgeable at a suitable time (as opposed to asking angry rhetorical questions about it in a lecture, and ignoring the answer). There are usually sound reasons, but they sometimes take time to explain; if you ignore sound reasons in any field, then you are simply asking for trouble.

The last generic enemy that we'll discuss here is the person with internet access. The world is full of bright people with internet access. Most of them are perfectly capable of hacking together a plausible looking document on pretty much any topic, from websites that they've found via a Google search. There are various problems with this approach to secondary research (apart from the age-old problem of plagiarism, which is likely to be detected, and to result in a humiliating fail). One of the main problems is that this approach is typically devoid of any critical assessment of the quality of evidence, particularly in relation to hotly debated topics. A related problem is that it frequently produces a hideously oversimplified account, through missing or ignoring the grown-up texts which tackle the realities of the problem. A classic extreme example of this is the number of people who believe there's a serious case that the Egyptian pyramids were built by aliens; there are a lot of websites promoting that argument, and very few which explain the much less glamorous, but much more solidly based, reality. At degree level, you need to demonstrate that you're capable of sophisticated analysis of the appropriate evidence. Naive Google searches are not a good way of demonstrating this.

The next subsections describe some problems that are particularly likely to happen specifically to undergraduate or specifically to Master's projects.

Common problems for undergraduate projects

Undergraduate projects typically run through your final year. So what? So the hand-in date then typically comes near the end of your final year. This may not seem terribly significant until you consider the relative dates of Easter and of the hand-in deadline. You could discover that your supervisor (and potential respondents, if you've left your data collection too late) will be taking some well-earned holidays just at the time when you need them most. Unfair? If you can think of a fairer solution, then the world would be grateful. Claiming that lecturing staff should not have holidays at Easter is not a strong argument.

Common problems for Master's projects

Master's projects typically start near the end of the academic year, and run through the summer vacations. If you've read the section about common problems for undergraduate projects, then you have probably guessed what's coming next. The hand-in date for your Master's projects may coincide with the time when your supervisor heads off for the wilderness holiday in Antarctica that they've been looking forward to since they booked it last November, and which gives them the only fortnight in the year when they are away from their office for more than five days at a time. It may also coincide with a time when the undergraduates head off to have fun over the summer, leaving you without a convenient supply of human subjects for your work. Claiming that academic staff and undergraduates should not be allowed to have summer holidays is not the strongest of arguments. Maintaining a good relationship with your supervisor and working out a plan for how to synchronise the stages of your project with their holidays is a better strategy.

Another common problem for Master's students occurs when the department has lingering disagreements about the nature and purpose of your Master's degree. There are often disagreements about the relative balance of vocational and academic components in the project, and also about the type of vocation for which the project is intended to prepare you. So, for instance, one member of computer science staff might think that a computer science MSc should prepare students for a job as a programmer (and should therefore require all MSc projects to contain some programming); others might think that it should prepare them for a job in some area of computing, including areas which do not require programming (and should not, therefore, require all MSc projects to contain some programming).

A similar problem occurs when a discipline overlaps with other disciplines – so, for instance, both computer science and marketing departments might teach e-commerce. If your project appears to be at the edge of your chosen discipline, then it can run into arguments about whether or not it demonstrates the relevant skills – for instance, a computer science project which focused on the marketing aspects of e-commerce might run into problems, whereas a computer science project which focused on the software aspects of e-commerce probably wouldn't. This is unfortunate, because cross-fertilisation between disciplines often leads to very interesting results. One simple way of reducing this risk is as follows. You can begin the introduction of your dissertation with an opening line which is a paraphrase of: 'An important problem in X is Y', where X is your discipline, and Y is a problem which is clearly part of your discipline and not of another discipline. This clearly locates your project within your discipline, not in debatable territory at the edge of it. You can then talk about how a possible solution comes from discipline Z. That makes it clear that you're based in your own discipline, and are simply seeing whether something from another field can help that discipline. This strategy is not guaranteed to work, but it does reduce the risks. In case you're wondering, the reason we advise using a paraphrase is that if you use the precise words that we used, then cynical markers who have read this book will immediately wonder whether you're using those words because you're a problem case and a possible heretic from some other discipline who has also read this book, and who is trying to conceal their aberrant tendencies.

Sordid practicalia

Whether you do an undergraduate or postgraduate project, the administrative procedures will probably be much the same. There are sections on these later. An important thing to remember about procedures and practicalia is that you can make life a lot better for yourself if you (a) work backwards from the end point and (b) look at things from the other person's point of view. So, for instance, if you do this for the hand-in date, you realise that a lot of other students are going to be descending on the binders and the photocopiers at the same time, so there might be queues; aiming to hand in a couple of days early might be a good idea. Similarly, if you know your supervisor's going to be away for the first two weeks of April, you can work around that by using those weeks to get something else done. It's particularly useful if you think about the end product of your project from someone else's point of view, such as a potential employer. Anyway, that's about it for this topic – on to the next.

The next section is intended for PhD students who have just finished one study, and have realised that they might need to change their original plans for their second study. It's also relevant if you're a new PhD student wondering what to do for your first study. If you're doing a taught course, then you don't need to read the next section.

The section after that explains the key principles underlying research; it uses some extended metaphors which we return to repeatedly throughout this book. Once you've grasped those principles, everything else should make much more sense.

PhD second studies: what happens when your first study changes your plans

He had had a terrible experience and had made a terrible discovery which he dared not reveal to his sceptical colleagues.

(*The Case of Charles Dexter Ward*, p.144)

So there you are, well into a neatly planned PhD, undertaking your first study, having carefully remembered all of the things that lesser mortals might have overlooked, and well on track (or at least somewhere near there). What happens next? What happens for many students is that their first study produces interesting and unexpected results which suggest that the original research plan needs to be changed. What do you do? One obvious answer is to talk to your supervisor. That's true and sensible, but it still leaves the underlying question: do you plough ahead with your original, neatly planned design, or do you change your plans? Sometimes the first option is right; sometimes, the second. If you and your supervisor decide to change course, then that gets you into some interesting problems, which is why we've written this chapter. Some of the problems are administrative. The System is not keen on radical changes of direction in a PhD, so some elegant wording may be needed. Other problems are to do with the research itself.

Sometimes your first study suggests that your second planned study was asking the right question, but needs a discreet change within the same overall framework (for instance, a different method for data collection, or a different subject population). That might involve quite a bit of effort, but no radical change in overall direction. Other times, your first study may suggest that your second planned study was asking the wrong question altogether. That's a much more profound change. For instance, you might have started off tackling something which looked like a purely technical problem, and then realised that it was in fact a social or a political problem, not a technical one. A classic example of this comes from the earliest days of statistics, when the Prussian cavalry were investigating why some units suffered more deaths through kicks from horses than others, which looked like a problem with different horse management practices between units. However, the analysis showed that the distribution of fatalities across units was just what would be expected if the fatalities were random events distributed across units in a purely random manner – i.e. a proper explanation of this problem depended on understanding statistics, not on understanding horse management.

As this example suggests, the change of focus may be a pretty drastic one. This is good news if you get things right – you might produce a major breakthrough. It can, however, be correspondingly bad news if you get things wrong; you can end up looking like a half-baked idiot. What sometimes happens is that a PhD student who has spent their formative years immersed in one approach suddenly discovers another, and becomes an embarrassingly enthusiastic convert to the new approach. True believers of this sort are often unaware of the underlying complexities of their new faith, and go round peddling a naive version of it (since the very fact of their being new converts means that they have not had time to master the full intricacies involved). If the student persists in this approach till the end of the PhD, then there's a fair chance that the department will appoint an external examiner who is an authority on the relevant approach, and there's also a fair chance that they'll not look kindly on vapid outpourings.

If your first study suggests that a radical change of direction is needed, then how can you tell the best route? In practice, your supervisor is likely to give you safe advice along the lines of 'let's just get through this PhD without too many changes, and then follow that idea up properly afterwards'. You can always plant a flag on the idea via a conference paper or equivalent, and you then have the rest of your life to follow up that idea, without the risk of screwing up your PhD.

That should make it clear that we're not advocating sudden, drastic changes in the direction of your PhD. Conversely, though, it would clearly be silly to persist with an original plan which has been superseded by events, so if this has happened to you, then you might want to think about ways of changing some aspect of your original plan to make it a better fit with reality. You might, for example, decide to use a field study rather than a controlled experiment, or you might decide to use card sorts rather than a questionnaire, or you might want to use an argumentation-based representation rather than tables to show the results of your content analysis. This book is intended to give you enough information to identify some sensible options, which you can then investigate in more detail.

Right, on to some similes for what research is really about.

Strategies and principles: demonstrating excellence, exploring territory rather than trying to prove a hunch, avoiding trouble, and learning from the wise

We profited by the excellent example of our many recent and exceptionally brilliant predecessors.

(*At the Mountains of Madness*, p.14)

The normal student's reaction to an impending project is to adopt the ostrich position and hope that the whole business will go away. This is an understandable reaction, but not very helpful.

A more productive approach is to work backwards from where you want to be. Do you want fame, or fortune, or a virtuous life of worthy achievement, or what? Once you know this, you can start working backwards from your goal, and figuring out how to use your project as a stepping stone to move you in that direction. If, for instance, you're doing media studies and you have decided that you really want to work for Porsche, then you might consider doing a project looking at media depictions of Porsche. You will then be able to approach Porsche, telling them what you are about to do, and ask them whether they would be interested in seeing your results. Since this is in essence free market research for them, there's a sporting chance that they'll express an interest, which then gets you a foot in that door. (This particular example will probably stop working about a week after this book is published, since unimaginative Porsche-loving students will probably follow this specific recipe in large numbers and alienate Porsche forever, but the underlying principle remains sound.)

Much the same principle applies if you want to go on to a high-flying career. If your project produces findings that are accepted and used in your field (for instance, if they're written up as a journal article), then that's an indicator that you are capable of significantly good things. Most students aim too low and underachieve, usually because they don't know what they're capable of and because they don't know how to achieve that potential. This book is intended to help with that problem.

If you're a normal human being, you may well be painfully aware that you're not sure what you want to do with your life; in that case you can craft a project which keeps your options open. That's a bit more complex, but still perfectly routine, and leads on to the next stages in the process, which involve three important metaphors, namely cabinetmaking, cartography and cockroaches. Cups of coffee are also involved, but we'll discuss that later. Once you have a better idea of where you want to end up, then you can start deciding what sort of project can help you move in that direction – the sections on doing the preparatory reading and on choosing a project topic are particularly relevant to this. It's highly advisable to seek, and listen carefully to, advice from knowledgeable people at each stage. You may have some idea where you want to go, but you probably won't know the best way of getting there. Anyway, on to the principles of cabinetmaking, cartography and cockroaches, as well as the invaluable cups of coffee.

Cabinetmaking

Back in The Past, apprentices learned their craft for several years, and were then examined to see whether or not they were ready to become fully qualified master craftsmen. If you were an apprentice cabinetmaker, you would be required to produce a cabinet, which would then be examined by a group of master cabinetmakers to see whether you could do all the things required of a master. If you had any sense, you would make sure that your cabinet included every sophisticated feature that you could think of, so that there was no doubt about your ability. If you didn't demonstrate your ability adequately, then you were cast into outer darkness. It's much the same with projects: your project is your cabinet, and it's your responsibility to make sure that you include evidence of relevant skills in it. If you produce the equivalent of an MFI flatpack, then the judges will have no way of knowing whether or not you can make cabinets, and will give you a mark which reflects that absence of evidence (i.e. somewhere between a borderline fail and zero, depending on just how clueless you have been).

Another handy concept which relates to this principle is the concept of the toolkit. If you're an expert cabinetmaker, you'll probably have a large set of cabinetmaking tools, each of them useful for different purposes. Some of them will allow you to do things easily which would be difficult or impossible without them. Part of your expertise as a cabinetmaker consists of knowing about lots of different kinds of tool, so that if you're called upon to do some particularly tricky task, you know what tools will let you do it efficiently and brilliantly; part of your credibility as a cabinetmaker involves having those tools ready for use. If you can demonstrate your knowledge of several different types of fretsaw, for instance, you'll have a lot more credibility than if you appear to know how to use only one type of saw.

It's a good idea to consider your choice of topic from the viewpoint of cabinetmaking. Does your intended topic give you the chance to demonstrate a suitably wide and impressive range of skills, or does it restrict you to demonstrating only a few skills that everybody else knows? Anyone can do a mediocre internet search, read some books, do a badly designed questionnaire survey, and speculate in an uninformed manner about the implications of their painfully mediocre findings. This is also a consideration when it comes to applying for jobs – what sort of project will make someone choose you in preference to a bright school-leaver? From both points of view, you need to show solid skills that untrained members of the public do not have. This leads us on to the second invaluable principle.

Cartography

Another classic error is to set out to prove something rather than to investigate something. Imagine that you're a sixteenth-century explorer trying to raise funding for a journey of exploration. Imagine further that you tell your prospective sponsor that you will find Eldorado; that you receive the funding; and that you then find nothing but swamps and jungle without a hint of gold. You might at this point find yourself thinking about what happened to Sir Walter Raleigh, who reported a similar lack of promised findings to his sponsor, and who was executed for his failure. He had the excuse that his objectives were actually set for him by a capricious monarch, rather than being ones he would have chosen if he had any option; you have the advantage of not starting off out of favour with a capricious absolute monarch (though some readers will probably have unworthy thoughts about their supervisors at this point). Anyway, returning to the main plot, Raleigh would have been in a much happier position if his objective was simply to map an agreed area, and to report on what he found there. That was what Cook did for much of his career, and nobody complained when he produced detailed maps showing that vast expanses of southern ocean were utterly devoid of features: for a sailor, knowing where there is no land for miles is an important bit of information, and in academia, knowing that a topic is a dead end is very useful as a way of avoiding wasted time.

All very well for long-dead sea dogs sailing the Spanish Main, you might be thinking: how does this translate into contemporary research design? One way relates to methods. In the old days, the first stage of exploration would often involve explorers with machetes hacking their way through dense undergrowth, notebook and pencil in pocket. The result of this would typically be a set of sketch maps drawn from whatever vantage points were available. Some of the information would be quantitative, involving measurement – 'about five leagues wide' or 'too deep to wade across'. Some would be qualitative, involving the types of thing present: 'dense jungle' or 'range of hills' or 'here be dragons'. The maps would be imperfect and incomplete, but at least they'd give you some idea of what was over the horizon, and of whether you'd found a modest island or a mighty continent. Subsequent explorers would fill in the gaps with some basic surveying tools and produce moderately accurate maps; if someone decided to build a town or stake mining claims, then they would bring in theodolites and measuring chains, producing extremely precise maps.

It's similar in research. Someone discovers a new area of research, and hacks around in its undergrowth for a while, armed with the equivalent of a machete, a notebook and a sweaty shirt. This might translate into participant observation or unstructured interviews in some disciplines, or digging a trial trench in others. If the area looks interesting enough, then a fresh batch of researchers arrive, with tools that will give more accurate results, perhaps via field experiments; if it's really interesting, then the equivalent of theodolites will appear, in the form of controlled experiments.

Why, you might wonder, don't people start with controlled experiments and cut out the preliminaries? For the same reason that you don't begin exploration with theodolites and measuring chains: these are comparatively slow, and you need to decide whether it's worth investing time and effort in getting so much detail about a small part of the terrain when you don't even know what's over the next hill. The machete and notebook may be imprecise, but they give you a pretty good overall idea of the big picture fairly fast, which then allows you to decide which places merit more detailed investigation.

So, that's cabinets and cartography; you might by now be wondering whether the bit about cockroaches will be unpleasant, but don't worry, it isn't. It's about staying out of trouble, which cockroaches mastered long ago.

The cockroach principle

Some topics and some areas are just asking for trouble. Sometimes the trouble is equivalent to a conflict-ravaged land waiting for someone heroic to step in and sort things out, whatever the cost to the heroic person. More often, the trouble is equivalent to a deep and glutinous mud pit, waiting to swallow would-be heroic types weighted down with shiny, very heavy armour. Before you get too keen on tackling something that looks virtuous and necessary, it's a good idea to ask yourself what a cockroach would do in this situation. The answer is that cockroaches didn't out-survive the dinosaurs by looking for trouble. Normally a cockroach would leave the rescuing of ravaged lands to someone who has already rescued at least one small to medium-sized province and who knows what they are doing. At this stage of your career, you should concentrate on developing your skills, so that when the day comes to ride into that conflict-ravaged land, you know what you are doing, and don't end up in a mud pit instead.

At any given moment the world of research intersects the human world in a way that provides enough mud pits to satisfy a legion of wetland ecologists. Anything involving politics, religion or sex is usually a good way of getting much further into the limelight than any sane cockroach would contemplate for an instant. Each age has its moral panics and folk demons, which usually relate to religion, sex and politics; often the moral crusades of one generation appear naive and painfully bigoted to the generation which follows. Pointing out such regularities, or pointing out split standards and rank hypocrisy in your society, may well be an exposition of truth, but these truths are already well known in the relevant research communities, and having them as your research topic runs the risk of you featuring in a tabloid newspaper headline and being publicly vilified before you're ready to take on that role. Topics like this need to be researched by someone, but you need to be careful about just what topic you're tackling in what way at this point in your career.

There are also topics which are a Bad Idea, on a scale meriting capitals, for other reasons. One perennial favourite involves the scope of your intended work. Undergraduates normally design projects that would tax a good Master's student; Master's students in turn favour projects which would scarcely fit into a three-year PhD; while PhD students incline towards research goals which would fill the rest of their working life. Something like 'discovering why students make mistakes, and finding a solution to this' is probably a bit too ambitious, for example. A closely related Bad Idea is to tackle something which has already been shown to be impossible (for instance, setting out to devise a perpetual motion machine). There is a school of thought which argues that they laughed at Galileo and Columbus; that's true, but on the same principle, they also laughed at a large number of jesters and clowns. Received wisdom is quite often wrong, but if the error was obvious enough for a student to find easily, then you need to ask yourself whether it's significant that none of your many predecessors was able to find it before you.

That gives you some idea of how to view research topics from the cockroach point of view, but there are also other factors which need to be considered from this viewpoint, such as choice of supervisor, which leads on to the next important issue, namely coffee as a means of learning from the wise.

Cups of coffee

Cups of coffee are so important that we used them as the cover illustration for our previous book. Why? Readers familiar with life will know that there are things which it is very useful to know, but which nobody in their senses will admit to in writing. Information of this sort is passed on informally, by word of mouth, often over a cup of coffee away from prying ears. An informal chat, off the record, with a suitable member of staff, is something that can be enormously helpful. It can clarify organisational politics, or give you useful leads, or help you make sense of career planning. This needs to be done with tact and discretion, since nobody in their senses is going to tell you the full, sordid, unvarnished truth about their department or their colleagues, but they may well give you some useful hints in what they say and in what they significantly fail to say. If you pick the brains of a suitable member of staff well before you choose your project topic, then this can make all the difference in terms of how your project will turn out. Who is a suitable member of staff? If you're not sure, start with an approachable one, and ask them who would be suitable for what you have in mind. You'll need to have different conversations at different stages of your project; sometimes they'll be with your supervisor, and sometimes they won't, but the principle remains sound. It also remains sound in later life, where good communication networks can make all the difference.

Anyway, that's enough for the moment on these topics. The next section deals with choosing a good topic – how to avoid easy-looking options which will waste your time, and how to find a topic which will help you towards what you want from life.

Choosing a topic, or cups of coffee, easy pickings and blaming others

So it's true that you plan to supplement Nentali's 'Interpretation of Elder Glyphics'?

(*Night Winds*, p.273)

Once you have some idea where you want to go, and what sort of project will help you move in that direction, you will need to choose a topic for your project. This section describes some ways of identifying good topics, explains what constitutes a 'good' topic, and also describes some pitfalls to beware.

Departments vary widely in their approach to projects. Some departments produce a list of projects which have the blessing of the department's System, and expect you to choose one of these; others leave you to choose your own; still others use a combination of the first two methods. If you're confronted by the Approved List, and none of them really suit you, then you may choose to use some low cunning; if there's an element of choice, then the situation is more straightforward. We'll deal with the straightforward case first, and come back to low cunning later.

Before that, though, some words of hope and warning. Some projects have the potential to be turned into commercial products which will make the worthy student rich. This might sound like a glittering prospect, and it is. However, this takes you into the realm of Intellectual Property, patents and copyright. The law in these areas is complex, and is still changing. If you're thinking of going down this route, then there are two things you need to do:

1 Check with the projects co-ordinator about your institution's policy on this
2 Don't mention it to anyone else, since that might count as putting your brilliant idea in the public domain, and therefore make it impossible for you to patent the idea.

It's an important topic, but because the situation is so fast-changing, and because most cases are unique, we won't say more about it in this book.

Cups of coffee again

If you're bright, reasonably competent, and have good social skills, then you can go a long way towards choosing your topic by having a cup of coffee with the right member of staff. Most departments have at least one person who is a projects buff, just as most have at least one person who's sound on stats, and one who's sound on the literature back to 1842, and so on. If you have a chat with the person who's good on projects (who is not always the one who's in charge of organising the projects), and explain to them what you want to do with your life, then there's a good chance that they'll suggest something helpful. It's worth remembering that you know what you want from your life (well, to some extent at least), and that they know about ways of getting there; they've been in the profession for longer than you, so they'll know all sorts of ways that you'd never have thought of. It's a good idea, from the viewpoint of tact and diplomacy, to have done some homework first. The homework shows that you aren't simply expecting someone else to do all the thinking for you. How do you do this? One sensible way is to find one sensible starting place in the literature.

Easy pickings

There's a literature on most subjects imaginable, and this can be used to find a good project topic quickly and easily. (Identifying which topics are good, and for what reasons, is another matter, but more on that later.) Clueless students work almost completely from the internet. Students with a clue are aware that there are academic journals, which clueless students usually don't bother to read. Suppose that you're interested in people's attitudes to computer-based crime. It's a popular topic, so you'll need to differentiate yourself from hordes of uninspired individuals. A good way of doing this would be to look up a recent journal article on the topic, read it, and re-read in detail its 'conclusion and further work' section. This will, as you might expect, include some suggestions for further work that needs doing in this area. You are now in a position to approach a suitable member of staff, to tell them that you've just read Young & Green's article on cybercrime in the *International Journal of Criminology*, and to ask whether Young and Green's suggestions about attribution theory in perceptions of cybercrime would be a suitable starting point for a project. This is a much stronger position than telling the same member of staff that you've looked at some websites about computer crime and decided that this would be a really cool topic. With any sort of luck, you can now have a productive chat with that staff member about suitable topics. They might make it clear that they disagree with Young & Green's approach, but that isn't a problem for you: reading that article is your ticket into the conversation which can steer you towards a better topic, so it's not been a waste of your time.

A brief note to PhD students. The 'ripping off the "further work" section' strategy is usually a good one for Master's students and undergraduates. It's not so straightforward for PhD students, since the 'further work' section is where shrewd researchers stake their priority claim on something that they haven't done yet, but which they will quite possibly have already done by the time the journal article appears in print (because of the lead time on journal articles). For students on taught courses, this isn't likely to be much of an issue, but for a PhD student concerned to stake their own claim to originality in an area, it's something that requires thought. This is one where your supervisor, or a member of staff working in that field, can be helpful in terms of finding out whether or not the author has done that further work yet, or plans to do it in the foreseeable future.

What happens if there isn't a suitable member of staff to advise you about your possible project? That's a worrying sign, because in that case, who would be able to supervise you? If there isn't a suitable supervisor around, then it may be worth rethinking your topic, to see if there's another topic which would suit you reasonably well, and for which you could find a suitable supervisor.

Anyway, back to doing the homework before you speak to someone suitable. Doing homework is an invaluable skill and will stand you in excellent stead in later life. There's also the consideration that you'll need to learn the relevant skills anyway sooner or later while doing your project – you can't build your entire career on cups of coffee with other people. Doing your homework involves identifying a suitable topic on the basis of intelligent information gathering, without substantial input from other people. For this, you'll need to have a good idea about what's happened in a given field, what's happening there now, and what's likely to happen next. A good way of getting an overview of what has happened already is to find a review paper and wade through that. What is a review paper? It's a paper reviewing significant developments in the field since the last review paper (usually about 10 to 15 years). Review papers are typically written by major authorities in the area (so they know what they're talking about) and typically mention all the most significant papers in the area, so you know what the main reading is. They're very useful for identifying gaps, i.e. topics within that field which haven't been researched adequately so far (a good starting point for a project). They're an invaluable resource, and surprisingly few students have ever heard of them. How do you know that something is a review paper? Usually the title begins with something like 'Review article' or 'Review paper' followed by a colon and the subtitle; sometimes it begins with something like 'A review of . . .'.

Blaming others

The advantage of working from a review paper, or from a good recent paper which you use as a foundational paper, is that you can quote them for the key assertions on which your work is based. If, for instance, you begin by saying: 'There appears to have been surprisingly little research into the role of attribution theory in computer games (Smith 2005)' and the Smith paper is a major review article, then you can scarcely be blamed if it turns out that there is a little known but substantial body of work on just that topic. This is particularly useful when you're trying to point to a gap in previous research coverage: it gives you a strong case against a cynic who claims that you simply haven't managed to find the right literature. Writing 'A Google search on these keywords produced only 28 hits' is like wearing a neon sign saying 'I'm clueless and don't even know how to do a literature search', but citing a good review paper is a very different strategy. Much the same principle applies to using the same research design and methods as were used in your foundational paper:

you get a set of brownie points for doing a proper replication or extension to the original work, and you're also covered against accusations that the design or methods had faults.

Suitability and sanity

Whatever the method you use to get to the choice of topic, you need to assess the suitability of your intended project. This includes questions such as the following:

- Is it the right project to act as a stepping stone to your life goals?
- Does it let you display the right cabinetmaking skills?
- Would a self-respecting cockroach tackle this topic?
- Is it feasible with the resources and skills that you have?
- Is there a disastrous risk lurking beneath its placid surface?

It's very tempting to choose a topic because it looks easy. The risk is that it would actually be easy for anyone to do, in which case it's hardly likely to impress anyone when you've finished it. A wiser strategy is either to do a topic which is easy for you because of your prior knowledge, but which would be difficult for anyone else, or to do a topic which is difficult for anyone including you. Both these strategies leave you with a set of demonstrable skills which can help you move on towards your goals.

You will probably be able to say what you want to do with your life (though you may not: the final section of this book, about planning your later life, may be useful in that case). For the other questions, your best strategy is to read the relevant bits of this and other books, and then, once you've done a respectable amount of homework, have a cup of coffee with the right person and take advice from them.

Low cunning

The section above assumes that you will have some freedom in your choice of topic. What happens if The System expects you to choose a project from the Approved List, and gives no apparent room for choice beyond that? In this situation, you need to use a certain amount of tact and lateral thinking, as well as low cunning. Telling the department that it's hidebound and wrong, or that Rugg and Petre recommend a different approach, won't get you much sympathy from the department, or from us, respectively. A better starting point is to sit down and look at things from the department's point of view for a moment. There's probably a reason for the use of the Approved List. It probably involves reaction to painful experiences in the past, where students have done something disastrously horrible on their own initiative. More optimistically, it may involve good experiences from using an approved list: the positive side of the approved list is that any projects on it are likely to be sound, and to have been thought through by someone who knows what they're doing, which is not always the case with the projects that students generate on their own. There are two main ways of tackling things within this framework. One is to have a quiet, tactful word with an appropriate member of staff well before the annual list is published, and see whether a project fitting your interests can be put on to the list. This will require some careful thought to make sure that your lovingly crafted project isn't then brutishly allocated to someone else; we leave the handling of this as a further opportunity for you to practise tact and diplomacy skills. The other way is to see whether an existing project topic can be modified in the direction that you want. This has obvious advantages if a suitable project exists, but is trickier if one doesn't; it's also not always clear which projects can be modified in a suitable direction and which can't.

Whatever approach you use, it's worth considering things from the department's point of view, and the supervisors'. Many things make more sense from that perspective, which is the topic of the next section.

Departments, systems and supervisors: how to behave like a professional, get a good reference, and avoid needless trouble

. . . for they knew the tendency of kindred eccentrics and monomaniacs to band together . . .

(*The Case of Charles Dexter Ward*, p.253)

The process of doing your research will bring you into contact with The System in its various forms. As a PhD student, you have to deal with entities such as the Postgraduate Degree Research Board, or whatever it's called in your institution. Whatever your level in the academic food chain, you will have to deal with your department, its procedures and your supervisor. Often these dealings are straightforward and have a happy ending. Often they are apparently straightforward and have an unremarkable ending which is not actively bad, but which is passively bad – you achieve something which is okay, but which is short of what it could have been. This is a particularly pernicious problem because it tends by definition to go unnoticed. Most students underachieve for various reasons, and we hope that this book will help at least some students to improve on that situation.

Dealings with The System can also be actively bad, for various reasons, which is what this section is mainly about. Sometimes they are bad because The System is bad – you have a supervisor from the lower reaches of hell, or your department has done something monumentally silly with its new procedures and turned you into collateral damage. More often, however, problems arise either because the student has done something really silly, or because the student has not adopted suitable strategies for dealing with an imperfect world. Many of these problems make more sense if you view things from the point of view of the department and the supervisor, which is what we will describe next.

It's important to remember that universities are different from schools. The core function of a school is to educate children. A university, in contrast, does not have a single core function; it has several core functions, some of which are complementary to each other, and others of which are conflicting. One obvious example is research: departments are assessed on the quality of their research, with high research ratings being rewarded by increased income. High research ratings also bring other advantages, such as being more attractive to high-calibre staff looking for a new job. Degree courses are just one of the things that departments do, and if you're a high calibre researcher, then every hour you spend lecturing is an hour away from your research (and is also accompanied by several hours of preparation time, exam time, etcetera, making the cost to you much higher than it might look to an innocent student). The higher the status of your department, the more the staff will be pulled in several directions because of factors such as these.

Departments also change through time. For example, a department might decide to structure one of its courses so that graduates from that course are eligible for accreditation with some prestigious outside professional body. This has obvious advantages, but can also bring disadvantages – for instance, it might mean that student projects have to fit prescribed criteria. That's an example of proactive change; at least equally common is reactive change, where the department changes in reaction to some hideous episode in the past which should never be allowed to happen again, such as the time that Dr West encouraged all those projects on barnacle reproduction. After such episodes, departments will be understandably twitchy if a student unaware of the past happens to suggest a project topic which stirs dark memories. Departments also often change in a mixture of proactive and reactive behaviour – typically by minor tweaks to procedures from year to year, to build on things that went well last year, and to improve things that didn't go so well.

Departments also have a moral, professional and legal obligation to maintain standards of various sorts. At its simplest level, this is an obvious Good Thing. There are, however, less obvious levels which regularly lead to problems for naive or clueless souls. No organisation in its senses will announce that it ignores its own procedures, or that some of its staff are incompetent. If you have had problems with your supervisor or your department, then there are smart ways to handle them, and clueless ways to handle them. If, for example, you appeal against a low mark for your project on the grounds that your supervisor was a shambling, incompetent caricature of what an academic should be, the department might privately agree wholeheartedly with this assessment of the supervisor in question, and might have been trying to get rid of the individual for years, but there is little likelihood that they will say so in public, so such an appeal would be doomed to failure from the start. If, on the other hand, you have a discreet word with the projects officer early in the project, and provide them with a reasonable-sounding argument for changing supervisor with no loss of face to anyone involved, then the chances of success are much better. In an ideal world, you'd never be in this position in the first place, but it isn't an ideal world, and an important principle in life is learning what battles to fight, what battles to refuse, and how to tell which category a given battle falls into.

There are similar issues from the viewpoint of your supervisor. Supervisors were not put on this earth for the sole purpose of getting you a good mark for your project. Supervising you is a pretty minor part of their life, which might account for perhaps half an hour per week of their time. At a practical level, they have a lot of more important things to be getting on with. At an ethical level, your project is your responsibility, not theirs – their role is to give you supervision, and it's up to you whether you make good use of it or not.

One important thing about supervisors is that your project supervisor will often be one of your referees when you go job hunting. Most references these days are pretty anodyne, because of the legal problems associated with any other sort of references. A reference saying: 'This student gained an Upper Second Bachelor's Degree' and nothing more is of no real use to you – the subtext to the potential employer is that you're so unremarkable that the referee couldn't think of anything actively good to say about you. It's worth thinking about what raw material you can give your supervisor to help them write a glowing, non-anodyne reference for you. For instance, have you paid attention to common professionalism, such as always turning up to supervision meetings at the agreed time, and giving advance warning if you're unexpectedly unable to attend a meeting? Most potential employers specifically ask referees about your punctuality and attendance, but few students realise this. At a higher level, have you shown initiative and good sense in your work, or have you done the minimum possible, and grudgingly? At a still higher level, have you done anything remarkable, such as getting a publication out of your project, or doing your project in collaboration with a major player in the field? All of these are things where working well with your supervisor can make life a lot better for both of you.

A closing point: some students attempt to do their projects without contact with their supervisors. This is discourteous, because it implies that they know better than the supervisor, and also because the supervisor will have to spend time going through the time-consuming process of checking what has happened to the student, in case they have ended up in hospital after a car crash (yes, that sort of thing does happen, and the checks take a lot of time). It's also a reliable recipe for failing. If you don't get on well with your supervisor, try to learn the professional skills needed to get along at least tolerably – they'll come in handy later in life, when you have to deal with line managers. If that doesn't work, then try a tactful word with the projects officer to see whether you can change supervisor.

To end on an encouraging note, it's worth remembering that departments and supervisors like seeing students do well: even the most misanthropic of staff are aware that student successes reflect well on the supervisor and department as well as the student. If you use some initiative and sense, then you can improve your chances of pairing up with the right supervisor for you, and of doing something that will benefit you both.

The next section is a brief digression about various common ways in which students send out unintended wrong signals, and how to avoid these.

'How do I get a good mark?' – things that can send out the wrong signal, and how to avoid these

The macabre direction of his interests had earned Opyros a shadowed reputation among the intellectuals and academics of his audiences. Thus literary fame escaped him – though notoriety did not.

(*Night Winds*, p.99)

You get a good mark by doing a good project. That raises the obvious question of what counts as a good project in the first place, which is what this book is about. A point worth remembering, while we're on the topic, is that asking academics about how to get a good mark is usually not a wise move, since it implies that all you're interested in is the mark in itself, rather than in understanding the discipline that you're supposed to be learning. Next time you're on a fly-by-wire aircraft, you might want to consider whether you would feel happier knowing that the software was written by someone whose student life was focused on getting a good mark, or one whose student life was focused on learning all there was to know about writing software well. If you do good work, and make sure it's visibly good via appropriate cabinetmaking, then a good mark will normally follow.

On the subject of cabinetmaking, there are some ways of gratuitously losing marks which are worth mentioning. One classic is simply to forget that you're making a cabinet, and to omit any visible indicators of excellence from your assessed work. Another classic is to ignore the guidelines about presentation format, which will lose marks, needlessly antagonise the marker, and send out a signal that if you're clueless in this respect, then you'll probably have done something clueless elsewhere as well. A third classic is to pour needless blood into the water, i.e. to make silly, classic mistakes which have the same effect on markers as the scent of blood does on sharks. If you're not sure what constitutes blood in the water for your discipline, then it's advisable to find out as soon as possible.

It's also useful to know your enemies, namely people who do things which could cause you unnecessary grief and woe. Usually this happens because you inadvertently do something that makes you look like one of these enemies, and which then smears you by association. The rest of this section contains some remarks about potential enemies and about how to differentiate yourself from them.

Your enemies

As usual, those who share the same belief that downloading a batch of dubious articles off the internet and then doing a questionnaire survey will constitute a hot piece of research. We'll discuss the methodological flaws in this belief later. For the time being, you might want to try envisaging an interview panel deep in deliberation about the candidates: more specifically, you might want to imagine one of the panel saying: 'Wow, did you notice that one of them did a Google search for previous work, and then did a questionnaire survey? That's impressive.' You might then like to think about the implications from the viewpoint of cabinetmaking.

A useful tip, when planning a piece of research (or an interview strategy, come to that) is to write down a sensible, obvious plan on a sheet of paper, and then draw a line through it with a thick red pen. The initial sensible, obvious plan is a starting point for planning, not the end point. Everyone else will probably think of the same obvious starting point, particularly if it looks easy, so it's a good idea to re-examine this plan and to ask yourself how you could do it visibly better. For instance, anyone can hack together a tatty questionnaire or do a Google search. Not many stop to ask whether a questionnaire is the appropriate method of data collection for what they want to do, and equally few stop to ask whether there is more to literature searches than Google.

A very different enemy is the True Believer bearing witness among the ungodly. They may be an evangelical postmodernist in a resolutely empirical department, or a resolute empiricist in a postmodernist department; the essential point is that they are convinced that they are right, and that anyone who disagrees with them is wrong, and needs to be converted. This position has all sorts of psychological benefits; for instance, if everyone tells you that your research is a pile of garbage, then you can tell yourself that they're only saying that because they're foolish persons, which is a lot more comforting than confronting the possibility that your research really is a pile of garbage. Sometimes the True Believer is even right. There is, however, a time for all things: a time to be born and a time to die, a time to be right, and a time to be sensible so that you can get through this stage of your education and emerge with a bit more credibility when you start to nail your thesis to the department door. (There's also sometimes a time to realise that you were worshipping at the temple of a false god, in which case you're likely to end up feeling rather glad that you showed some sense in your choice of research design and didn't get into a needless wrangle about it.)

We've taken a somewhat flippant view of True Believers here. As should be clear from other sections of this book, we believe that ethics and principles are deeply important in research. There's a difference, though, between sticking up for your principles and going round asking for trouble regardless of the circumstances. Returning to knowing your enemies, you may not consider yourself a True Believer, but you need to beware of inadvertently looking like one. This is something where you need to understand the ideology, politics, and so forth of your department – some bristle at any mention of surveys, others at any mention of case studies, others again at any mention of inferential statistics. There will also probably be feuds within your department, with some staff members locked in a decades-long bitter wrangle about some topic or other. As usual, your best bet is to do a bit of homework, look at what sort of work has been well received in your department in the last couple of years, and then tactfully pick the brains of someone approachable and knowledgeable. There's a time to stand and fight for your beliefs, but there's no point in standing and fighting for them before you've learned how to use your weapons or put your armour on.

The last enemy that we'll mention here is the no-nonsense person from industry. These often have considerable experience of doing what they consider to be research, and insist on applying the same approach to their research in academia. Somewhere along the way, their view will come into collision with reality, though whether or not they will learn anything from the collision is another question. The problem here is that the term 'research' is used in at least two quite different senses. One sense is primary research, which is highly valued in academia; the other is secondary research, which is also highly valued in academia, but is different. Failure to understand this distinction often leads to a project which consists of a poor literature report (as opposed to a literature review, described elsewhere in this book) and/or a survey. Surveys are sometimes an appropriate research approach, but they're only one approach among many, and if they're the only one you know about, you're heading for trouble.

If you're from industry and are tackling a degree, then it can be hard going, since it's unlikely that anyone will explain to you just why academia does things the way it does. This can be intensely frustrating – for instance, you might write a report in what you consider good, clear plain English and then receive a dreadful mark with some incisive comments about your writing. There are a lot of areas where academia and industry can learn a lot from each other, but the rich rewards are hidden in a particularly noxious swamp, and that's a different story. If this problem rings bells with you, then you might find it useful to pay particular attention to the sections of this book that relate to cabinetmaking, so you can at least avoid sending out the wrong signals, even if some of the reasons remain obscure. On that encouraging note, we'll end this section, and proceed to the next.

The next section is about academic writing. Academic writing is different from other forms of writing. There are good reasons for this, but usually nobody explains these to students, leading to needless grief for all concerned.

We explain the underlying principles of academic writing, and how to send out the right signals in your writing.

Academic writing: why it's different from other writing, and how to do it well

But since the scoutie-allen, the partan, the clokie-doo and the gowk seemed not to convey any precise idea, he followed them with the Linnaean names; Stephen did the same . . . and from this it was not great way to Latin descriptions of their more interesting processes.

(*The Fortune of War*, p.61)

In most of the world, good writing is defined in pretty much the same way: clear, simple, focusing on the essentials, in plain English, and interesting. Not so in academia. Why does academia have a different perspective? There are various reasons, some rooted in scandals of the past, some in simple practicalia, some in systems and selection pressures. We'll start with 'clear and simple'.

Clear and simple language

Academic writing varies between disciplines, but whatever the discipline, there is little risk of its preferred writing style being described as 'simple'. There are various features which bring complexity, such as the use of citations in the text, the use of technical terms and the use of grammatical constructions rarely encountered in the outside world. Many students take the understandable view that if they produce text which is not cluttered with these apparent obscurities, they will produce text which is clear and simple and therefore good. This is a particularly common view among trainee teachers, who are trained (among other things) to produce simplified descriptions of topics for teaching to schoolchildren. It's also common among people from a business background, who are used to producing clear, concise reports. Academia, however, proceeds from a different viewpoint, for two reasons.

The first reason makes sense the moment that you imagine yourself in the position of someone marking 60 PDG-101 courseworks. For the coursework, the students have been asked to demonstrate their knowledge of inclusive design in public information materials. They have just spent most of the semester learning about the law on discrimination, the psychology of design, design principles, presentation of public information materials, and numerous other topics; they have been taught all sorts of things that they had never heard of before, and have worked till late at night getting to grips with the topic. They know what proportion of males are red-green colour blind; they know about several types of visual impairment, and several scales for assessing readability of text. You are expecting to see coursework which reflects this hard-won knowledge, and you have a neatly tabulated marking scheme which allocates marks to each topic which they mention. You pick up the first coursework, and you are confronted with a page of clear, simple English, telling you true and relevant things that any intelligent person on the street would know, but failing utterly to mention any of the specialist knowledge that is the whole point of the module. What evidence do you have that this person has learned anything at all on the module? Following on from that, what evidence do you have that this person, if asked to do the same task as part of their first job after graduation, would produce something that followed legal guidelines and that would be fit for purpose? The answer to both questions is not one that will improve anyone's day.

The conclusion is pretty simple: if you're writing academic text for assessment, you use it to demonstrate your detailed knowledge of what you are supposed to know. How do you do that? Technical terms and references to key relevant texts are a good way to start, which takes you back to the sort of language that we started from – academic language with lots of technical terms and references in it.

There's a second reason for academia taking its own perspective on whether 'clear and simple' should be favoured. Imagine that you're a researcher, doing some background reading to find out what's already known about a topic. You find a paper describing some highly relevant work, with surprising findings which would have far-reaching implications for your own research if they were correct. However, the paper fails to give you some crucial bits of information about how that work was carried out. You write repeatedly to the author, who is snowed under with teaching, and after several months you get a reply, with an apology that the article didn't contain that information, but explaining that the author left it out, because they wanted to keep the article clear and simple. Would you come away from this interaction impressed by the professionalism of that author? Probably not, and rightly so. In practice, this particular scenario is pretty rare, since few sane academics would use the excuse of 'wanting to keep the language clear and simple'. You do quite often, however, encounter articles which don't give you all the information that you need, and the experience is not much fun.

Focusing on the essentials

Focusing on the essentials looks like a good thing, but also runs into problems very quickly. When you're doing academic writing, you're usually being pulled in two directions. One is towards keeping the word count within a specified limit. The other is towards explaining, or at least mentioning, all the relevant factors. In the context of assessment, you're mentioning the relevant factors to show that you know about them, and to get marks for them. In the context of being a professional researcher, you're mentioning them partly as a useful courtesy to the reader, so they know what reefs to watch out for on this stretch of coastline, and partly to demonstrate your own mastery of the topic to potentially hostile parties, such as journal reviewers, and promotion committees who might one day be reviewing your work. In this context, mentioning only the most relevant topics is suicidal – you'll produce something that looks like a simplified version for teaching to the first years, and nobody would take it seriously even if it did somehow get past the conference or journal reviewers. What you need to do instead is give most attention to the most important topics, but mention the other relevant topics as well, giving them less coverage. This isn't just about self-promotion; it's a convenient shorthand that allows readers to assess swiftly whether you really understand what you're writing about, or whether you're an amateur who doesn't properly understand the topic. Skilled writers of academic English can send out most of the relevant signals of mastery within the first couple of sentences of an article; skilled readers will appreciate this, and will also appreciate the passing references to relevant literatures which they had not previously considered.

Plain English

Ironically, academic English was originally intended to make communication simpler and easier. In fact, it does achieve this, though that isn't immediately obvious until you consider the alternatives. Up till a couple of hundred years ago, Latin was widely used as a learned language for various sound reasons. One reason was that it was international – it was spoken by intellectuals across the western world, which meant that a finding could be spread without encountering difficulties from language barriers. Another was that it was relatively uniform, without many regional variations or much change over time. This meant that you could read something several centuries old, and be able to understand it. Given that your background reading in many topics can take you back a century or more, this was more useful than might first appear.

The problem with Latin was that it had to be learned, which was a significant problem if you were a bright child from a poor family without access to good education. Some might get scholarships, but most wouldn't, and that could exclude a significant portion of the community from learning. From the Renaissance onwards there was an increasing tendency for people to publish in their native language; when the Royal Society was founded in England, in the reign of Charles II, one of its aims was to encourage publication in plain English.

The trouble is that everyone has different ideas of what constitutes 'plain' English. A Scottish naturalist might consider that referring to a 'whaup' was plain English, but the term would be meaningless to most English naturalists, for instance. Much the same goes for useful analogies: British readers often encounter problems with American sporting analogies such as 'out of left field', and American readers encounter similar ones with terms such as 'on a sticky wicket'.

Even if you manage to resolve these problems, there are problems with the terminology itself. If you are a car mechanic, and the customer tells you they saw smoke coming out of a funny-shaped metal bit in the engine, you are unlikely to find that particular bit of plain English very useful. In order to get anywhere in a field of research, you need to have an agreed terminology, so that everyone understands what everyone else means by the same term. There are usually nowhere near enough ordinary English terms to describe the things that you are dealing with, regardless of your field of research, so you and your fellow researchers will have to invent new terms whenever you discover something new. You will also need to use these terms correctly. If you use a vague term on the grounds that it's plain language, this won't be much use to anyone who needs precise information.

Interesting

This is a term sometimes used by academics of a sadistic tendency when speaking to students. Academics are very wary of interesting writing, and with good reason. They're much more keen on interesting ideas and findings, and tend to like interesting ideas and findings presented in a dry, rather boring way. Why? The answer lies in assorted scandals of the past.

The core concept in research is finding out about things. If you find out interesting and/or useful things, then your work is well received. If you claim to find something and numerous colleagues spend large amounts of time following up your work, only to discover that your alleged findings don't bear any relation to reality, then you will be shunned, or worse. If you actively commit fraud, then you will probably be sacked, and vilified in the international scientific press; you will quite probably never be employed in research again. No, we're not exaggerating; precisely this has happened more than once.

The early years of research as we know it were dogged by charlatans, some of whom were conscious frauds, others of whom genuinely believed in what they were doing. A classic example was Mesmer, who claimed numerous findings about mesmerism which if true would have revolutionised science. Under closer examination, however, his claims fell apart. By that point, though, he was a rich international celebrity. There have been numerous other scams and scandals, and they are likely to continue for the foreseeable future.

A consistent trend in such dodgy work is that the perpetrators are publicity hounds, who use the media to spread colourful and impressive claims about their work, and then gather fortune and glory until they are debunked. The result of this is that experienced researchers are very wary of anyone who appears to be making overstated claims. There's a strong tradition of saying words to the effect of 'Come on, let's see the data'. In principle, if what you're saying is worth listening to, then that should be self-evident from your data; any competent reader should be able to work out the implications for themselves. In some fields, particularly in the sciences, there's an established writing style of deliberate understatement, in which the degree of understatement in your writing works in deliberate juxtaposition to the importance of your findings. A classic recent instance was the way in which the solution to Fermat's last theorem was presented at the end of a highly technical mathematical proof several hundred pages long, and phrased as if the solution were a passing afterthought. Shrewd researchers quite often use this strategy deliberately as a means of demonstrating their mastery; shrewd researchers are also aware that if there is a major error in their work, then it is likely to attract fewer insults if they have presented it modestly than if they have presented it via a major international press conference.

Summary

In most of the world, good writing is defined in pretty much the same way: clear, simple, focusing on the essentials, in plain English, and interesting. In academia, good writing is defined in terms of being accurate, complete, precise and trustworthy. Clarity and simplicity are valued, but are desirable by-products, not the sole focus. Focusing on the essentials is valued, but is only part of the story. Plain writing is valued, but has a specialised meaning. Interestingness is something which should come from the work itself, not from the language used to describe it.

Often, an apparently minor bit of wording will send out strong signals to the reader. These signals may be good, bad or ambivalent. Usually there are functional reasons for these interpretations. For instance, a particular phrasing might suggest that you have completely misunderstood a key concept in your field, which would raise questions about what else you didn't understand. A statistics student who didn't realise that 'significant' had a precise, specialist meaning, for instance, would soon encounter trouble. Conversely, another phrasing might concisely suggest that you had read the advanced literature on a topic, not just the standard student reading, which would suggest that you were showing promise.

A closing thought is that many students don't realise that the use of references in academic writing is very much a functional tool, not an ornament. There's an entire section on this elsewhere in this book. It's another skill which makes life much easier once you understand it. On that cheering note, we'll conclude this section, and move on to the next chunk of the book, which gives an overview of what research is about.

Doing a good project: summary

- Work out what you want the project to give you, and what skills you particularly want it to showcase.
- Do an initial literature search and identify some interesting topics.
- Identify a potential supervisor and have a cup of coffee with them.
- Firm up the initial project idea, making sure that it tackles an interesting question in a way which will give you interesting outcomes whatever you find.
- Take advice about scoping the project – better to do something smaller well than something bigger badly.
- Think about the follow-on from the project (publication, links with potential employers, further degree, etc); if there isn't an obvious follow-on, then this suggests that you could design a better project.
- Do the detailed literature search for this topic – identify references for the underlying problem, for the seminal article, for milestone articles, and for a foundational article.
- Plan the project, working backwards from the hand-in date, and building in contingency time (spare time in case something goes wrong).
- Meet your supervisor regularly; take the initiative, and listen to their advice.
- Write up some sections early on, so you can get feedback on writing style.
- Think explicitly about what indicators of excellence you can build into every stage of your project.
- Show drafts to your supervisor and learn from their feedback.
- Be meticulous about presentation, particularly the formatting of your references section.
- Show the final draft to your supervisor well before the hand-in date.
- Be patient; remember that the more you put in, the more you get out; keep a sense of perspective and don't overwork. Better to work smart than to work hard but pointlessly.

1

About research

Research: introduction to the nature of research, and types of research
• Research questions, and the nature of evidence: deciding what type of
question to ask, and how to handle the various types of answer • Mud pits
and how to avoid them: things that go wrong • Isms: necessary
assumptions, dubious assumptions, and being caught in crossfire
• Searching the literature: why, where, what for and how • Research in
society – agenda, context and the like: things we take for granted, and
things that can cause you trouble

> *. . . the prose chroniclers, who are less interested in telling the truth than in*
> *catching the attention of their public, whose authorities cannot be checked, and*
> *whose subject matter, owing to the passage of time, is mostly lost in the unreli-*
> *able streams of mythology.*
>
> (*History of the Peloponnesian War*, I, 21)

Research: introduction to the nature of research, and types of research

Research involves finding something new. 'New' may simply mean 'new to
everyone', or it may simply mean 'new to you'. That's a major distinction,
and one which leads to a lot of misunderstandings, particularly for people
entering academia from industry. The first of these meanings, 'new to everyone', is usually known as *primary research*. The second, 'new to you but not to

everyone', is usually known as *secondary research*. So, for example, if you consult the timetable to find out the time of the last bus home on a Sunday, that's secondary research. If you count the number of types of bird at your birdtable on Sunday morning, that's a modest piece of primary research. They're different things, and they both have their uses. So, for instance, if you don't fancy a long walk home in the rain late at night, then secondary research into the time of that last bus will be pretty important – but only to you (or to someone else in the same place and time with the same travel needs). Secondary research is also very important when you're doing the preparatory work before some primary research, since it vastly reduces the risk that you will simply reinvent the wheel through not knowing what has been done before. Again, the importance of the secondary research is pretty specific to the one doing the preparatory work, and the secondary research doesn't take on wider importance until the primary research is realised. Secondary research traditionally involved a lot of time in libraries, though now it's increasingly likely to involve a lot of time on the internet.

Although secondary research is very useful for numerous purposes, it doesn't usually lead to breakthroughs in human knowledge (for instance, discovering the cause of diabetes, or finding a better way of teaching people with dyslexia). So, although secondary research is *useful*, it's usually primary research that answers the *important* questions, the ones that other people also want answered. Breakthroughs usually come through primary research, which is why primary research is so highly valued in academia and in fields tackling big unsolved problems. Student projects in universities are therefore usually designed to assess how well you can do primary research, and are often viewed as practice for a PhD if you decide to follow an academic career.

Your department's projects handbook (if it has one) will probably refer to this in passing, using some phrase such as 'original piece of research'. This is usually understood by the academics to mean 'primary research', but may be misinterpreted by students to mean 'my own personal bit of secondary research'.

Just to confuse matters further, some disciplines (ranging from history to business studies) have a well-established tradition of using such extensive secondary research that the resulting combination of findings can count as primary research – although each bit of information is not new to the world, that particular assemblage of those bits gives an overview which nobody had before. In some of these disciplines, such as history, the results often count as brilliant primary research by any criteria; in others, the results may be more debatable. Often, the assessment has to do with how important the question (and proposed answer) is to other people, whether the secondary research has revealed or clarified something of interest in the research community. If you're not sure what the situation is with your department, then find out as soon as possible, preferably in a tactful way which suggests that you have a clue (for instance, by looking at some distinction-level dissertations from the previous year or two – much longer ago, and the criteria may have changed).

Machetes and magnifying glasses: research focus

So, research is about exploration in the pursuit of knowledge. First there's the machete stage; its purpose is understanding the basic geography and layout, assessing the lie of the land. The questions at this stage tend to be 'what' questions about what's there.

The next stage is the more detailed maps. The questions at this stage are not only about what is observable, but also 'how and why' questions about how the land is configured and why that results in swamps to the south.

Finally, there's the theodolite stage, with 'how accurate' questions, about which bits of the map need to be corrected and how to achieve that fine detail.

This recalls a famous quotation from Sir Eric Ashby, to the effect that, although we like to think about research in terms of great cartographic expeditions hacking our way through the jungle with machetes, more often 'research is crawling along the frontiers of knowledge with a hand lens'. The vast majority of research activity concerns questions of minute precision, the sort of detail that hones theory and drives controlled experimentation. Measured precision is what characterises the Ordnance Survey map and distinguishes it from the swiftly hand-rendered sketch in the field notebook. Each map has its time, its purpose, and its place in the process.

Why, you might wonder, don't people start with controlled experiments and cut out the preliminaries? For the same reason that you don't begin exploration with theodolites and measuring chains: these are comparatively slow, and you need to decide whether it's worth investing time and effort in getting so much detail about a small part of the terrain when you don't even know what's over the next hill. The machete and notebook may be imprecise, but they give you a pretty good overall idea of the big picture fairly fast, which then allows you to decide which regions merit more detailed investigation.

Types of research (an important bit)

Within primary research, there are various types of research, such as case studies, field experiments and formal experiments. Most students get lost in the big picture of this, which is why we're having a go at it here. The next subsections look at types of research ranging from the equivalent of machete-and-notebook exploration through to millimetrically accurate surveys with theodolites and measuring chains.

Describing things: what are the entities?

When you're Out There with your machete in your hand and your notebook in your bag, trying to make sense of the surroundings, one of the first things you need to decide is what categories to lump things into in your sketch maps. Some are pretty easy – rivers and mountains are pretty much the same wherever you are, for instance. Others are more difficult. 'Forest' might at first sight appear an easy one, but it isn't: European forests are very different from tropical rain forests and from cloud forests, for example, and within tropical rain forests there's a big difference between high canopy forest and secondary growth in terms of how easy it is for you to move around. As a result, you'll need to work out which categories to use in your sketches and notes. This will probably be completely qualitative – you're saying what kind of things you're seeing, but you're not trying to quantify and measure them.

It's much the same in research – you can do useful work just by describing something that hasn't been described before. The splendid Anna, for instance, investigated which criteria people actually used to prioritise tasks, as opposed to the criteria advocated in the textbooks, and found some fascinating things. That didn't require numbers, just categorisation and description.

Readers with archaic tastes will probably already have guessed that this maps quite neatly on to mediaeval scholastic questions such as 'quae sunt entia?' but we'll refrain from venturing down that particular route.

Counting things: the utility of rough measures

Although you can do useful work just by categorising, describing and sketching, there's a limit to the usefulness of this approach. Imagine that you have returned, sweaty and mudstained, from the hinterland, notebook and machete in hand, and you're sitting in the captain's cabin, describing the types of forest and swamp to the captain. Sooner or later you're likely to be asked questions such as approximately how broad and deep a particular swamp is. You could, if you felt so inclined, treat this as a sordidly plebian question, and expostulate at length about the socially constrained nature of measurement, or about the simplisticism inherent in the assumption that one can draw a clear limit to the edge of something like a swamp, but this is unlikely to gain you much respect. A captain of the old school might respond by having you keelhauled for being a smart alec; a captain of the new school might coldly suggest that a rough set or fuzzy set formulation might resolve those particular problems, and then ask whether, for instance, the swamp appeared to have any parts too deep to be waded through. Categorisation can be complex, but fortunately there are some sophisticated literatures relevant to this, so if you have any lingering anxieties, you might be reassured by reading up on them; there's a bit more about this in the section on knowledge representation.

In field cartography, you can do a lot of useful work with some basic arithmetic; it's much the same in field research, where you can do a lot of useful work by putting some approximate numbers on to things. In the case of Anna's work on criteria for prioritising, for example, an obvious step was to count how many people used each of the criteria.

We'll return to this issue later in the book, in the statistics section, since there's a whole set of statistical tests which you can apply to results of this sort – simple counts of how many things fit into which categories.

Planting coffee bushes: systematic change

Both the approaches above (describing things, and doing some basic counting) are good, solid approaches. They have their limits though. They just describe things as they are; they don't tell you anything about possibilities for change. Suppose, for instance, that your expedition discovers a new variety of coffee bush growing in the highlands, whose beans produce coffee tasty enough to render a regiment of fusiliers speechless. You realise that this might make your fortune, and you decide to try setting up some plantations in a more geographically convenient location. At three of the locations, the seedlings die ignominiously; at the fourth, they flourish and prosper, and soon produce you with enough income to endow a chair in comparative osteology at a leading university.

What you have done in this example is to try changing something and to see what happens. In three cases you get one result, and in the fourth, you get a different result. This shows you that it's possible to grow the new variety of coffee somewhere away from its native valley, and also gives you some rough numbers about how often the move will be successful. A lot of applied research is done in just this way: you try something out in a natural setting, and see what happens. The something may be a new method of training staff, or of scheduling tasks, or educating people; for each of these, you'll need to identify different things to tell you what effect, if any, has occurred. If you do this in just one setting, it's usually called a case study; if you do it with a sample of more than one, it's usually called a field experiment.

If the things that you measure consist of discrete categories, as in the previous approach which we described above, then you can probably apply the same sort of statistics based on how many things fell into which categories. If the things that you measure consist of scales (for instance, the height of the seedlings, or the weight of beans per bush) then you can use a different set of statistics, but that's another story, described in the next subsection.

Moving earth around: systematic manipulation of factors

Sticking with the coffee plantation example for a moment, the field experiment of raising seedlings in different settings was able to tell you that the bushes could be grown away from their native valley, but it couldn't tell you what made one location suitable and the others unsuitable. This is an obvious problem: for example, what would you do if your one and only plantation was menaced by coffee blight? You might be tempted to list the factors which the suitable location and the native valley had in common, with a view to identifying a suitable location for a second plantation, but that would probably be a long list; most of those factors would probably turn out to be irrelevant, and how could you tell which the relevant ones were? This is where controlled experiments come in.

What you could do is to change the factors in a systematic way, and see which of them made a difference. You might wonder, for instance, whether it was something about the soil that made a difference, or something about the climate. What you could then do is ship some samples of soil to several places with different climates, and then plant seedlings at all of these. If all the seedlings planted in the same soil flourish regardless of climate, then that's a pretty strong hint that soil is a relevant factor. This in turn raises more questions, such as what it is about the soil that makes a difference, and you can tackle these questions in just the same way. (For example, if you wonder whether it's something to do with bugs in the soil, you could try growing some seedlings in sterilised soil and others in unsterilised soil.)

The key thing about this approach is that you're identifying a factor which might make a difference, and systematically varying it in some way, while keeping everything else the same. This allows you to exclude possibilities in succession, and thereby narrow down the set of possible answers. If you do this correctly, then the answer is pretty obvious. You might, for example, give your respondents either a scenario where someone is described as female, or a scenario which is identical except that the person is described as male, and see what differences (if any) you get in the responses. If there are systematic differences between results from the male and the female scenarios, then the only plausible source of these differences is the wording of the scenarios, since everything else in the study is consistent – if you randomised whether each respondent received a male or a female scenario, then there's no other systematic difference between the two conditions which could explain differences in the findings.

For some research of this kind, you measure the results by counting how many things fall into each category (for instance, how many seedlings fall into the 'died ignominiously' category versus the 'grew and prospered' category). More often, though, you'll be measuring something on a scale (for instance, the height of the seedlings at various ages, or the weight of beans on each bush, or the temperature at which you're growing the seedlings). If what you're doing to the seedlings consists simply of increasing values for one factor systematically and seeing what happens on another factor (for instance, increasing the temperature at which you raise the seedlings, and seeing what that does to the height at various ages), then you can probably analyse the results using statistical tests of correlation. If what you're doing to them consists of putting them into separate batches, and measuring something about each batch (for instance, the batch grown in peat and the batch grown in loam, and measuring the height of the seedlings every week) then you can use a third family of statistical tests, which deal with measures of variance. We'll return to this in more detail in the statistics section.

Identifying the things to measure, and the appropriate scale or equivalent on which to measure them, is technically known as *operationalising your metrics*, and is a Good Thing. If you can get the hang of identifying metrics which bear some relation to reality, and ways of measuring them which allow you to ask and answer powerful questions, then the research world lies at your feet.

That concludes this set of extended analogies and metaphors. The next section discusses the nature of evidence. Research is about answering questions; before you get too far into asking questions, it's a good idea to know what types of answer are possible, and which type of question goes with which types of answer.

Research questions, and the nature of evidence: deciding what type of question to ask, and how to handle the various types of answer

Doubt of the real facts, as I must reveal them, is inevitable; yet, if I suppressed what will seem extravagant and incredible, there would be nothing left.
(*At the Mountains of Madness*, p.11)

This section is in some ways the most abstract, and in other ways the most concrete, in this book. Either way, it's also the most important: if you understand research questions, and the nature of evidence, then the rest of how research methods work follows from that.

What you're doing in research is answering questions. To answer a question, you need to have an answerable question – and one worth asking. You also need to understand what an answer might look like, which means you need to have the appropriate type of evidence to provide the answer. What kind of evidence you need depends not just what your question is but also on what sort of answer you want: what sort of evidence will be *good enough* to satisfy you (and your sceptical research community) in the context in which you asked the question in the first place.

One thing to keep firmly in mind when doing research is that you're not looking for evidence to support your hunch. What you're doing is looking for evidence which will answer your question *one way or the other*. The trouble with reality is that it tends to make much better sense with hindsight than with foresight, so nailing your colours to a hunch is a recipe for ending up sooner or later being publicly wrong. Good research is about asking good questions, not about gambling on what the answers might be.

Remember the cartography principle: the wisest policy is to set out to produce a map of what's out there, not to try to find a land of gold, jewels, honey and other things conspicuously absent from the lives of most students. The subsection on penguins (below) expands on this theme in more detail.

So, what does suitable evidence look like? That depends on the type of question that you're trying to answer. As often, a useful strategy is to work backwards from the end point. Imagine that you've been wrestling with the debate about how much of human behaviour is determined by genes and how much by environment; imagine further that through brilliant research you have found the answer, and that the proportions are 42 per cent and 58 per cent respectively. Once you've finished celebrating, what can you do with that information? Come to that, what exactly does that information mean? Phrased this way, it's not exactly a very helpful answer, and you start realising that it would be better to have started from a more useful phrasing of the question.

An example of this is hassles affecting secretaries. Secretaries get a lot of hassles in their lives, and there doesn't seem to have been as much research into this as there should have been. So, you might decide to do some research into the hassles affecting secretaries. It's tempting to rush off and start doing some data collection, but it's wiser to pause and imagine that you've found the answer, in the form of a great big list of hassles. So what? What will you do with this information? The answer is that you can't do much with it in this form. One way you might want to use the answer is to prioritise the hassles, with a view to doing something about them. For that, you'll need to gather information about the priority rating which each hassle has, which is a subtly but importantly different question from your initial one. Some further thought will remind you that some hassles will be easier and/or cheaper to fix than others, so you'll also need to gather some information about this. In addition, some digging around in the literature might get you thinking about whether there are hassles which are so insidious and pervasive that the secretaries just accept them as an inevitable part of life, and don't bother to mention them. These are obviously worth investigating, since the secretaries' belief that they're inevitable might well be wrong, but they'll probably require data collection via something other than interviews or questionnaires, since both these methods are bad at detecting taken for granted knowledge of this sort. Your options would include using observation to build up a list of hassles; using reports to get some insights into the hassles; using laddering to clarify subjective or technical terms that the respondents use when describing the hassles; collecting quantitative ratings or rankings for each hassle; and using scenarios or case studies to work through possible solutions to the highest ranked hassles, and the knock-on effects of these solutions. That's just a few – there are plenty of other ways of tackling different aspects of this set of questions.

So, in summary, a useful strategy is to imagine that you've found the answer to your initial question, and to ask yourself what you can do with it. A more refined version of this strategy is to draw the question as a box, and draw a line out of it for each of the logically possible answers. You should be able to write beside each answer 'this answer is interesting because . . .' and you should also be able to say what you will do as a result of this answer. If you can't do this for one or more of the answers, then you're gambling time, effort and reputation. Even if you're lucky with your hunch, this will not help your reputation as a researcher (or your mark) since it will be clear from your research design that you've asked a flawed question and made one lucky guess. Examiners view such sins in much the same way as driving inspectors view learners who overtake on blind bends on the hunch that there's nothing coming: you may be lucky on one particular occasion, but nobody in their senses is going to give you a driving licence, or hire you as an HGV driver, if you have such habits.

Penguins

One of the games we sometimes use in our research methods classes is called 'Penguins'. The core concept is pretty simple. Each student is given a folded sheet of paper. On that paper is written the name of an entity, which may be a real, living human being (such as the current prime minister), or a historical or fictitious human being (such as William Wallace or Sherlock Holmes respectively), or something very different (such as a penguin). Each student then has to tell the class five pieces of evidence supporting the proposition that the entity on their piece of paper is a real, living human being. If their entity really is a real, living human being, then the student has to give moderately strong, but not conclusive, evidence for this proposition. So, for instance, if your entity is a penguin, you might use supporting evidence such as 'My entity walks upright'. If your entity is the current prime minister, you might use evidence such as 'My entity frequently appears on television'. After each student has presented their five pieces of evidence, each student is allowed to ask one other student a question, provided that the question is not: 'Is your entity a real, living human being?' At the end of this process, the students vote on each student's case in turn, to see who has come up with the strongest argument.

It's a game that is easy to run, and which can be pretty entertaining with a good bunch of students, but it teaches some deep lessons. One is how easy it is to put together a plausible set of supporting evidence for even the most wildly untrue assertions. A second is how easy it is to produce an unconvincing account by focusing on the wrong issues. Another is how difficult it is to ask precisely the right question to get you the information that you need. For example, a question such as 'Could you use a telephone?' would exclude a penguin, but would also exclude a real, living human being if the entity on the paper is a Trappist monk under a vow of silence. Unfair? No, just an example of a difficult case, and if all you could tackle was easy cases, then research would be a lost cause from the outset.

Asymmetry and infinity

So, for pretty much any proposition there is a large set of possible supporting evidence. We could make the extreme claim that for any set of facts, there is an infinite number of explanations which are consistent with those facts (yes, we know about the debates about what constitutes a fact, which is why this chapter is here – we'll return to that question later). Does this mean that all explanations are therefore equally valid? Before answering that question, you might want to have a go at a different one. There is an infinite number of even numbers, such as 2, 4, 6, 8 and so forth: does this therefore mean that all numbers are even? If you think that the answer is 'yes', you might want to think about numbers such as 1, 3, 5, 7; you might also be interested in some gold bricks which we are offering for sale at a very reasonable price. The resolution to this apparent paradox leads into the mathematics of infinity, an area which doesn't involve as many hard sums as the non-mathematical might fear, but which does involve some pretty interesting concepts. In brief, there is an infinite set of even numbers; there is a different, but also infinite, set of odd numbers. Those of you who like interesting concepts might like to ponder the existence of another infinite set, containing prime numbers, which is just as infinite as the first two, but less densely packed.

Anyway, returning to our plot, there is an asymmetry of explanations; for any given event, there may be an infinite number of explanations consistent with the facts, but there is also an infinite number of explanations which are not consistent with the facts, and which may therefore be excluded as untrue. So, how can you decide whether or not a particular explanation is demonstrably untrue, and how can you choose between those explanations which are consistent with the facts?

If we now look at the explanations consistent with the facts, we will usually find that they vary in their neatness of fit. The normal convention in research is to adopt the simplest explanation which maps on to the most facts most neatly; as you might expect, this leads to debate about which explanation fits this description most accurately from among the candidates. This approach is also the basis of the classic approach known as falsification: you propose an idea, test it out as hard as you can, and see whether any of the tests show it to be false. If not, then it's a candidate for an adequate explanation, at least until a better one comes along. Thus, the outcome of the classic theorise/test process (the 'hypothetico-deductive model') is *not* a proven theory, but rather a theory that hasn't yet been disproven.

Social construction

One thing to remember about evidence is that some aspects of it are social constructs and others aren't. The proportions vary. In the physical sciences, for instance, heat is clearly something which exists independently of human belief systems – there were hot things in the universe long before the first hominids wandered across the world, and there will probably be hot things long after the last hominid is dead. The systems which we use to measure heat, though, are social constructs: the instruments are based on what humans can perceive or can imagine perceiving. At the other end of the spectrum, concepts such as 'bravery' or 'good taste' are found in most human societies, but are pretty much entirely human creations, which are mapped on to different behaviours and different abstract concepts by different societies. Even when there's reasonable consensus about an area, it's normally necessary for human beings to adopt a simplified version of it, since the human brain couldn't cope with the information load of trying to handle every specific instance and bit of evidence relevant to an issue.

For instance, we could examine the 'fact' that Drake commanded the English fleet that fought the Armada. The reality is more complex; the fleet was actually commanded by someone else, so at first pass you might claim that this 'fact' is wrong. (For brevity, we'll ignore other issues such as whether it's the first or the second Armada that's in question.) If you dig a bit deeper, though, you find that the official commander was a nobleman appointed largely on grounds of seniority, to keep the other captains under control, and that he reached an explicit agreement with the lower ranking Drake to the effect that Drake would give him recommendations about what do, which he would then follow. At this level, the 'fact' is actually right. Which is true? That depends. It depends on what level of detail is appropriate for your needs, and what your needs are – different purposes will have different needs. If you're researching the role of the aristocracy in sixteenth-century warfare, then the issue of who was technically in charge of the fleet is the important one – if it had been Drake, this would have been a surprising departure from usual policy. If you're researching sixteenth-century English naval tactics, then the key issue is who was making the decisions, not who was technically in command.

So, where does this leave you? It leaves you imagining that your fairy godmother has given you The Answer, and that you're working out what you'll do with it. If you're not going to do anything different as a result of knowing The Answer, then there's probably not much point in asking the question (apart from a few cases where you're checking that a rare risk isn't lurking on the horizon). The answer may take various forms. Sometimes it will be purely qualitative – an explanation, or a list of things. Sometimes it will be a causal model with some numbers in it. Other times it will be a number or a set of numbers.

Once you know what form The Answer will take, then you can start working backwards and figuring out what sort of research design, data collection technique and analysis methods will allow you to ask and answer the relevant question. What might these be? These are covered in the rest of this book. Some of that coverage is via detailed and erudite explanations; some of it is via anecdotes and stories of previous projects. One handy tip, on which we'll close this section, is to look for stories about previous projects which answered the sort of question that you want to answer: they're likely to give you some useful ideas about where to start with your question.

The next section deals with some classic things that go wrong in research. These are often a result of asking the wrong type of question, or of not knowing how to handle an answer (which is why it follows the section on the nature of evidence). Others are the result of nuts and bolts coming undone.

Mud pits and how to avoid them: things that go wrong

'I've fallen into a mammoth trap . . . All I really need to make things perfect,' he reflected bitterly, 'is a mammoth.'
The ground shook.

(*The Walls of Air*, p.157)

Oscar Wilde once remarked that the only thing worse than being talked about is not being talked about. That maps surprisingly well on to the two main types of research mud pit. The first type is when you do something so dreadful that it is spoken about for years to come, around the research equivalent of campfires deep in the forest, as a tale of nameless horror. The second type is when you do something so boring or pointless that even our talent for analogies, metaphors and similes gives up the unequal struggle. We'll start by looking at the second type first.

Boring, pointless research

It's very tempting, when time comes to choose your research topic, to go for something easy, on the grounds that you've already suffered enough and that you want to do something safe. So, you hack together a safe-looking little questionnaire about a fashionable topic, get back some replies, and write up the safe-looking results. No surprises, no challenges; no evidence that you've learned anything in the course of your long, expensive education, no evidence that you have any capacity for initiative or for independent thought. A colleague of ours calls this 'stamp collecting'. The collection makes no contribution beyond its mere existence. Not exactly the strongest position from which to embark on the next stage of your career. A useful principle is to think about the 'so what?' question. Say you've discovered that the majority of participants in your gadget design study like blue mouse buttons better than pink mouse buttons: so what? Does this finding contribute to a coherent theory of aesthetics, or is it just a gee-whiz finding, without any further significance? Who is it useful to, besides the gadget manufacturer buying plastic dies? If you can't answer 'so what?' or the companion question 'who cares?', then you need to avoid asking that research question in the first place.

Does this mean that you should go for risky research? No, quite the opposite. The phrasing in the previous paragraph was about 'safe-looking' rather than 'safe'. Safe research, paradoxically, involves asking questions and using methods which are not immediately obvious. If something's obvious, then it doesn't offer much scope to display your genius. A much better strategy is to ask your research question in such a way that, whatever you find, your results will be interesting and useful.

A neat example of this is the excellent Carmel. She was looking at people's perceptions of internet banking. The obvious thing to do was to use a questionnaire and ask people what they thought about internet banking. That had already been tried by large specialist companies, so the likelihood of her finding something that they hadn't was slight. Instead, she used a scenario-based approach, so that she could compare her findings to those from the surveys already described in the literature, and assess whether scenarios had any advantages. Whatever she found, it would be useful, mapping a little bit of territory which hadn't been explored before. That would have been enough by itself, but she also added a twist. The scenario described how Chris had some money and wanted to decide where to invest or save it. Half the scenarios asked the question: 'What advice would you give him?' The other half were identical except that they used the words: 'What advice would you give her?' That one word of difference produced fascinating differences in response. The advice to the female Chris was about nice safe places to save the money where she wouldn't lose it in a stock market crash; the advice to the male Chris was about great ways of taking a few risks with investments which could make a lot of money if all went well.

It's also possible to produce no findings at all, usually through ignoring the Three Ignoble Truths. These are discussed next.

First Ignoble Truth: hardware breaks and software crashes

This is pretty self-evident. A surprisingly high proportion of previously reliable machines will decide to break at the most inconvenient moment possible, often in a way that makes you look incompetent or dishonest (for instance, by developing an intermittent fault that the technicians can't replicate or fix, the week before your work is due in). A surprisingly high proportion of students omit to do regular backups, and then have bad experiences when their data is wiped out by a virus or system crash the day before the work is due in. A more subtle version is when your data are subtly corrupted because of a fault in the hardware or software, producing plausible-looking but utterly wrong data. It's always a good idea to budget in some time for handling equipment failure, checking your data, and so forth. It's also a wise idea to make sure you have arrangements in place for repairing or replacing defective equipment.

Second Ignoble Truth: resources are never there when you need them

This is a subtler problem than the previous one, since it can take many forms. Sometimes the resources are predictable, such as binders for the final copy of your dissertation – pretty trivial, but still capable of making you look like a right idiot if you haven't realised that there will be a lot of other people trying to get their dissertations bound at the same time as yours. More often, they'll be things that have been beneath your radar, like a quiet place in which to do your data collection, or a decent bit of kit to record the sessions, or specialist advice from the member of staff who has been researching that area for the last

20 years, and who has gone off for a three-week holiday in Alaska when you desperately need advice about a crucial, esoteric bit of your research design. One resource which frequently isn't there is spare time: most student research ends up short of time at the end. It's a good idea to plan to finish a fortnight before the due date, and plan backwards from that step by step: you know how fast you write, so you can work out how long the final parts of the write-up will take you, which gives you the date by which your data analysis must be done, and you can find out from your supervisor and your pilot sessions how long the data analysis will take, which tells you when your main data collection must be finished, and so forth. This is where good research design is invaluable; it can dramatically reduce your data collection times and data analysis times (down to a few hours for collecting the entire data set, and a couple of days to analyse it, for some types of research).

Third Ignoble Truth: people fail to deliver, get sick and die

A lot of research depends on human beings, whether as subjects, as technical advisors, as supervisors, as sources of access to materials and subjects, and so forth. All of these people have lives of their own, and will have a perverse tendency to view their own problems as more important than yours. Some of your research subjects will turn up late, or turn up with their ability to perform a task restricted because they have been bitten on the thumb by a mole they were rescuing from the dual carriageway, or fail to turn up at all because the boiler blew a gasket in the middle of January so they had to stay in for the central heating engineer. It's advisable to look at things from their point of view: how much of their time are you asking for? How convenient is the timing from their point of view? Why should they want to help you in the first place? Most research is dependent on the goodwill of others, and if you're in that situation, then you should be appreciative of whatever support you get. An issue which may affect you if you're dealing with an outside organisation via a contact person in that organisation is that people change jobs quite often, which can leave you in a tricky position if your contact person leaves and is replaced by someone less helpful. In an ideal world, the contact person would warn you well in advance and arrange a smooth handover, but in reality this doesn't always happen, especially if they leave because of fallings out with their line manager. If you're dealing with an outside organisation in this way, then it's a good idea to talk to your supervisor about fallback plans.

Tales of horror

There are many ways of getting things actively wrong in research, but in the case of students' research, there's one line which usually crops up somewhere in that campfire retelling of the tale. That line is: 'Then we found out that the student had . . .' or its counterpart 'Then we found out that the student hadn't . . .'. The subtext is that the student did something, or failed to do something, without the supervisor being aware of the situation. A typical example is the student who sent out a long, badly designed questionnaire to numerous organisations without taking advice from the supervisor first. The questionnaire failed to produce anything useful, and made the student, the supervisor and the institution look pretty silly in the eyes of a large number of outside organisations. The worst research is usually carried out by students who vanish from sight for months on end, and hand in something which their supervisor has never seen.

If you meet your supervisor regularly, and plan each stage of the research together, then the likely outcome is that your work will at least be adequate, and will probably be significantly better than if you worked in stubborn isolation. In a worst case, if you inadvertently do commit some hideous mistake, but you did the deed with your supervisor's knowledge and agreement, then The System is likely to treat you much more understandingly. Most departments, in such (admittedly rare) situations work from the position of asking what a reasonable student would do when given that advice by their supervisor, and calibrate their marking accordingly. For instance, if you have done something improper with your statistical analysis, on the advice of a supervisor who was having a bad day, then the department will probably make due allowance for that advice (assuming that it didn't involve something that any competent student would be expected to know anyway).

The next section is about something which can lead you into nameless horror, but which is also necessary, namely ideological underpinnings of research. On the one hand, research is not a Spock-like activity with a single Right Way of doing things: all research is based on underlying assumptions. On the other hand, some sets of assumptions are a bit dubious, and some are the topic of venomous feuds, so if you have any sense you'll stay out of the crossfire.

Isms: necessary assumptions, dubious assumptions, and being caught in crossfire

'But tell me, though, how would you deal with the Dualists?'
'By the prescribed formula for any heresy. They should suffer impalement, their bodies left for night beasts and carrion birds.'
(Night Winds, p.272)

The academic world is permeated by words ending in 'ism'. Most, but not all, of these refer to schools of thought. Examples include structuralism, postmodernism and symbolic interactionism. What are these, and why should you care? We'll answer the second question first, on the grounds that it's fairly easy to answer; the first question evokes some strong images of nailing soup to a wall. There are two main reasons why you should care about isms. One is the cockroach principle; you can blunder into isms unwittingly, like a cockroach venturing into what it thinks is a nice quiet room, only to discover that none of the humans in the house go in there because it's full of aggressive spiders. Another nobler reason is that many isms are a good thing which you need to know about. Why the aggressive spider metaphor? (Arachnophobics might like to know that we won't use that metaphor again in this section, so they can read on.)

The reason goes back a step or two, into the nature of knowledge. Some things in research are pretty straightforward. You write a bit of software to add up some numbers; either it adds them correctly or it doesn't, but either way there's not much scope for debate about the outcome. At a more grandiose level, you design a new type of mobile phone, and it either functions as a phone or it sits there as an inert heap of plastic and metal. The underlying technology may be complex, but the outcome is clear and unambiguous. In other areas, though, outcomes are not clear and unambiguous. Crime is one example among many. Suppose that someone sets out to prove that a traditional outdoor upbringing with plenty of hunting, fishing and shooting will keep children away from crime. It's a pretty safe bet that someone else will point out in response that it all depends on what you mean by 'crime', which is a social decision. Society decides where the line is between gratuitous cruelty to animals and legitimate sport; you can't run the decision through a bit of equipment which gives you an objective answer on a nice digital readout.

Similarly, in some disciplines the subject matter has some blindingly obvious natural divisions which give you a blindingly obvious way of structuring your categorisation of the field. In zoology, for instance, multicellular animals pretty obviously fall into distinct types, with only very small numbers of debatable cases, so the clearly distinct types are an obvious starting point; in astronomy, solar systems consist of various chunks of matter doing things like moving round a sun, which gives you another obvious starting point. In other disciplines, though, there isn't any obvious natural division, and it's up to you how you want to structure your model of your field. Some models will give you interesting, productive insights; others will give you nothing that you didn't have before; others again will fall somewhere in between.

If we turn to crime once more, then there are various starting points. One is to look at how society chooses to categorise crime, and to focus on the processes of categorisation and labelling. Another is to argue that regardless of what we label as criminal behaviour, there has to be something driving people to flout whichever societal rules happen to be in force rather than obey them; this argument can lead to fields such as criminal psychology and medical models of causes for criminal behaviour (such as damage to the frontal lobes of the brain). This gives us three schools of thought already. There are also methodology-based schools of thought; for instance, you might sensibly argue that to understand crime properly, you need to study it from the criminal's perspective as well as society's, which has led some sociologists to go undercover among gangs, for instance. Which of these is the right answer? All and none of the above – it isn't a case of one containing all the truth, and the others being wrong. They're doing different things in different ways, so trying to compare them directly is like trying to compare a grapefruit and a lawnmower.

Extending the process a bit, you get into questions such as what research is, or what it is for, or what the nature of evidence is. Again, all of these are societal constructs. This doesn't mean that, for instance, the laws of gravity are an arbitrary social convention – if humanity were to be wiped out overnight by an infestation of triffids, gravity would continue to behave just as before. It does mean, though, that societal factors make some forms of research more prevalent than others within a given society.

The risk in this general area is that you will drift into wibblespace and start producing vacuous, navel-gazing nonsense. A popular example in philosophy is the school of Last Tuesdayism. This is a school of thought which argues that the whole universe, complete with records, memories, fossils, etc., was created last Tuesday. The school is unfortunately fictitious, as far as we know, but that does have the advantage that we're unlikely to be sued for libel when we use them as an example. If the school did exist, it would probably (human nature being what it is) soon develop schisms between rival groups, such as those who believed that the universe was created last Tuesday morning, and those who believed that it was created last Tuesday afternoon. There is no evidence which could allow anyone to judge between the two arguments, since both are equally congruent with all available evidence, but that never stopped people from arguing on the basis of faith in other areas, and it certainly doesn't stop people from arguing about isms, which is why you need to beware of 'isms' from the cockroach point of view.

Many disciplines – probably most, possibly all – are riven by debates between rival 'isms'. Sometimes these are legitimate and proper academic debate; sometimes they're more like the ultimately pointless and vicious civil wars described by Thucydides; sometimes they're like an irritating child complaining about not having enough pocket money while you're soaking wet in near-freezing temperatures trying to fix a burst water main that has wiped out the central heating on New Year's Eve, with no prospect of an emergency plumber for the next four days. What you do not want to do if you have any shred of sense whatever is to give the inadvertent impression that you belong to an 'ism' which is viewed as the irritating child by those who will be marking your work. They may try to be professional about recognising that there are legitimate differences of opinion within their field, but there's no point in testing their professionalism unnecessarily, and there's even less wisdom in counting on it. So, it's a wise idea to find out about the main schisms in your field, and to avoid sending out any signals associating you with something that you don't believe in.

What if you do happen to believe that a particular 'ism' is The Truth, and that your department is populated by gratuitously ignorant benighted heathens?

Well, you might want to think about that cockroach, and about the theology of just wars; if you don't have any reasonable chance of winning this particular battle, then it's better to save your energies for another day when your chances might be better, and to reduce needless effusion of blood at the present. If you're a passionate postmodernist in a department of empiricists, or vice versa, then you might want to think about ways of demonstrating cabinetmaking skills which don't involve needless confrontation or needless abandonment of principle – there will probably be topics which allow everyone to get on with life with face preserved all round.

There's also the consideration that you might realise, with the passing of time, that you were worshipping at the temple of a false god. The religious analogy is actually quite a good one, since what often happens is that otherwise sensible people who have grown up within one tradition (such as empiricism or postmodernism) suddenly discover a diametrically opposite tradition and embrace it with the fervour of a born-again evangelist. Like many born-agains, they often embrace a naively simplified version of the faith, with prominent fervour and lack of judgement, in a way which embarrasses those members of the faith who have had time to think it through and to come to a reasoned, sophisticated understanding of what it is really about. So, for instance, born and bred empiricists may discover postmodernism and then loudly preach a naive version of it to everyone in earshot, to the embarrassment of everyone in earshot. This is not a good strategy for your first bit of research, since it will by definition fail to show many cabinetmaking skills, and will display you in an equally bad light regardless of whether your examiners happen to agree with you or not – examiners are usually well aware that their job is to assess your ability to make cabinets, regardless of the particular style of cabinet you happen to favour.

We discard the subject, and move on. The next section is a nuts and bolts section, picking up a theme that we discuss repeatedly throughout this book, namely searching for information. Most students don't get much tuition in this, and in consequence waste time and/or miss important information. We discuss how to search, what to search for, and where to search.

Searching the literature: why, where, what for and how

He was heard to cry out in a high, terrified fashion upon entering his library.
(*The Case of Charles Dexter Ward*, p.238)

Any idiot can type a search term into an internet search engine, and many idiots do. The typical internet query is about 2.4 words long and has about a 14 per cent chance of failing because it contains a mis-spelling. Pretty much anyone can do that type of search. So, how do you do a more professional search?

The answer involves understanding why you do a literature search. There are several reasons for the literature search and for your subsequent literature review. These include the following:

- Explaining to the reader what the problem is that you're tackling.
- Explaining which approaches have been tried before.
- Explaining why they failed (otherwise it would be solved and no longer a problem).
- Explaining what your approach will be.
- Explaining the background to your approach (previous work, etc.).

A key aspect of this process is that it needs to be comprehensive and systematic. If you're explaining which approaches have been tried before, and you miss two of the main ones, then that sends out a signal that you do sloppy work. This is not the sort of signal that will endear you to anyone. It also brings the strong likelihood that you will reinvent the wheel and make it square. Conversely, if you do a thorough, intelligent literature search, you will send out a signal that you are an intelligent, capable professional; you will also end up with a project which will find out something interesting. So, how do you do a thorough, professional literature search? There are various components to this process which include:

- what you search
- what you search it for
- how you search it.

The following subsections discuss each of these in turn.

What you search

The novice student knows about the tools of books and the internet; the expert researcher knows about books, the internet, journals, conference proceedings, ephemera, bibliographic databases, and more. Knowing about these things gives you several advantages. One advantage is that you know how to get a quick, trustworthy overview of a field. Another is that you know where to look for the most accurate, comprehensive and sophisticated descriptions of previous approaches. A high proportion of this material isn't on the internet.

What you search it for

There are various reasons for searching these sources of information, as described earlier. One reason is to get a quick, trustworthy overview of a field. Suppose, for example, that a kindly member of staff has listened to your account of what you would dearly like to do for your project, and suggests that

Bayesian belief networks might be just the thing for you. How do you proceed from there?

A good first step is to read an introduction to the topic. Good places to look for introductions include encyclopaedia articles and book chapters. Tackling a complete book about Bayesian belief networks at this point would get you into too much detail too soon; however, a chapter about the topic in a more general book would probably be at the right level. This is somewhere where the internet can be useful – online encyclopaedias or online introductions (for instance, in a university's online lecture notes) can give you a quick result. Cynical supervisors often advise their students against quoting these initial sources, since they can make you look like a naive amateur, and advise you only to quote the more advanced sources. Shrewd, cynical supervisors often advise their students to quote these sources with the verbal equivalent of a superior sniff: for instance, 'It is widely stated that X is true (e.g. Smith 2004), but the reality is somewhat more complex (e.g. Phibes 2005)', where Smith is the introductory source you found on the internet, and Phibes is the journal article you found a bit later. This has the advantages that you don't need to throw away a reference that you spent time reading, and of explicitly differentiating you from the unwashed multitudes, though if you do use this approach, you need to do so with reasonable care, since otherwise there's the risk of looking like a pompous brat, which is not the best of signals to send.

If the topic looks like what you need, then you need to move beyond the lightweight introduction for the interested general reader, and on to the grown-up stuff which gives you the full, complex truth. One good way of doing this is to find some review articles. Review articles review what has been done in a field over the last 10 to 20 years (typically starting where the last decent review article ended). They are typically written by heavyweight academics specialising in that field. They're not always easy reading, but they are typically crammed with descriptions of the main approaches which have been tried, and the main articles about them. They're usually called 'review articles', and many publications index them as such. You can also try searching the internet for them – for instance, a search on 'review article Bayesian belief networks'.

Review articles are typically published in journals, and are unlikely to be on the internet (though you may find references to them there). To obtain a copy of the article itself, you will probably either need to search the shelves of the library, if your library has that journal, or to order it on inter-library loan, if your library doesn't have that journal. A point of warning: it's extremely irritating to find a reference to a promising-looking review article, order it on inter-library loan, and then be told that the details you have provided are wrong – that there is no article of that title, by that author, in the issue and volume of the journal that you have specified. This is often due to the original source having mistyped some of the details (e.g. claiming that it's in volume 23, issue 4, instead of volume 24, issue 3), and is usually fairly easy to fix, but it wastes time and is very frustrating. This is why academics get so picky about how you lay out the references in your own dissertation: if you're sloppy about it, then it suggests that you might perpetrate the loathed 23(4) error.

Another good place to look for an overview of the field is in the introduction section of a recent journal article on the topic. At this stage, you may not understand the main content of the journal article itself, but you can look through the introduction, and see what it says and which articles it quotes. If you do this for several articles in the same field, then you will start spotting regularities – that all of them mention the 2001 Poole & Bowman article, for instance, and describe it as a landmark article. You'll also start to get a feel for how they tackle things – whether they're heavily mathematical, or data driven, or based on abstract models, or something else.

Once you've got a reasonable overview of the field, if it looks like the right one for you, you can now move on to tracking down the key articles. The key articles will probably have been published in journals; some of these journal articles may also be available on the internet, since many authors now post their journal papers on the web after a decent interval because of copyright law, but most won't. In the old days, you would track them down via paper indexes, which was about as much fun as it sounds; now there are specialist databases containing details of journal articles in most academic disciplines (for instance, the main psychology journals are indexed on PsycLIT). University libraries subscribe to a range of these databases, and as a student you will be able to access at least some of them for free. Many of these databases contain not just abstracts, but also the full text of the articles, which makes life much easier for you. Often, though, you will need to order articles via inter-library loan.

Institutions vary in their generosity; inter-library loans can become expensive in large numbers; the loan process takes time. From your reading so far, you should be able to identify about half a dozen key articles, which you will need to read particularly carefully. They fall into various categories.

Seminal articles are the ones which first introduce a concept to the world, or at least introduce it to a field where it was not known previously – for instance, Lotfi Zadeh introducing fuzzy logic to the world, or John Maynard Smith introducing game theory to evolutionary ecology. You read and cite these partly to show due respect, and partly to show that you have done your homework thoroughly right back to the start. Naive researchers and dim cynical researchers often don't go back more than 10 to 15 years in their literature searches, on the grounds that anything older will be out of date; better researchers are aware that bright cynical researchers often recycle old ideas under a new name after a decent interval (about 20 years, usually) and that bright ethical researchers often find a useful new way of applying an old concept to a current problem.

Milestone articles are similar to seminal articles, except that they mark a place where research in a field made a significant advance, or took a marked turn in a particular direction. Examples of this include the introduction of fuzzy control theory, a development of fuzzy logic, and of stochastic game theory in evolutionary ecology. You need to read and cite these for the same reasons as seminal articles.

Straw man papers and example papers are pretty much what they sound like. The straw man is an argument that you set up so that you can demolish it (usually a weak argument that you need to mention because some people believe it, and which you demolish so you can show that you do know about it and that you do know why it's fallacious). Example papers are papers which you use as examples of something – for instance, you might say that there has been extensive work in your field using a particular approach, and then give three or four typical examples. Many researchers use these as a way of getting some easy brownie points for papers which they read and which they subsequently decided to be of little real use – by citing them as example papers, at least a researcher can get some merit out of having read them, even if they weren't much use for anything else.

The last main category is the foundational article. This is the article that you are using as your starting point – the giant on whose shoulders you are standing. You can use more than one foundational article, for instance, by applying a concept from one field (the first foundational article) to a problem in a second field (the second foundational article). The key point is that you are using this article as the foundation on which your own research is built. It therefore needs to be a good article (as indicated by the quality of the journal it's in, and the status of the author's previous publications, etc. – your supervisor should be able to help here). You will therefore need to read it thoroughly and carefully. It will offer various goodies. Its introduction will contain an overview of the area, and the key references, reducing the risk of your missing any yourself. Its 'further work' section will contain useful ideas for further work, one of which might well be the basis for your own project. Its 'method' section, by whatever name it is called, will contain a detailed description of what the author did; you can legitimately use exactly the same method yourself, and apply it in a different way or to a different problem (making sure that your dissertation explains exactly what was from the foundational article, and what is your own work). If the article doesn't meet these criteria, then you need to ask whether it's suitable for use as a foundational article. Once you have a good foundational article, then one effective strategy for your project is simply to test one of the suggestions in the 'further work' section of that article. If the suggestion works, then you write it up from the viewpoint of 'Wow, Smith suggested this and it works' (though don't use that precise phrasing); if the suggestion doesn't work, then you write it up from the viewpoint of 'Hmmm, Smith suggested this and it doesn't work'. Either way, you've found something useful that other people would like to know about, and you have a sporting chance of being able to write a follow-on paper of your own to submit to the same journal, if you do your project well enough.

How do you find a good foundational article? Sometimes you'll be given a recommendation for one – for instance, your supervisor suggests one. Other times, you'll be interested by the work of a particular author that you meet in your literature survey, and you track down a recent article by that author which fits the bill. Sometimes, you'll just stumble across one while browsing – there's a lot to be said for browsing, if you use it together with a deliberate search strategy, as opposed to using only browsing. Browsing alone runs the risk of missing key literature, but it does give you a chance to find something useful by serendipity.

Anyway, that's a brief summary of what to search, and what to search it for. The remaining issue is how to conduct the search in a professional, efficient manner that goes beyond the naive 2.4 keywords.

How you search

Most search engines are based on the same underlying principles. If you know what these are, then you can search much more efficiently.

One principle is the keyword. This is the word that you type in, and that the system searches for. Some bibliographic databases are indexed using a limited set of keywords; some let you search not only the indexed keywords, but also the full text of the articles themselves. Each approach has advantages and disadvantages, which space prevents us from describing in detail; in brief, indexed systems allow more systematic searches, but limit you to the terms used in the index, whereas full text searches let you search for any term you like, but don't give you such a systematic overview of what is and isn't in the database.

Another principle is Boolean searching. This uses a very small set of concepts, such as AND, OR and NOT (usually written in uppercase, for historical reasons, but meaning what they appear to mean). Most search engines hide the details of this from you in the normal setting, but allow you to use Boolean searches in the 'advanced search' option. In brief, searching with AND will only find records which contain all of the keywords you specify; searching with 'OR' will find records which contain one or more of the keywords you specify. 'AND' searches usually find a smaller number of records than 'OR' searches, but usually have a higher proportion of relevant records within them. 'OR' searches usually find more records, but usually have a higher proportion of irrelevant records. So, for instance, if you're trying to find records about the mathematical topic of game theory, searching on 'game' AND 'theory' will find only records containing both 'game' and 'theory' but searching on 'game' OR 'theory' will also find you huge numbers of records which are just about games or just about theories, but not about game theory. It's well worth investigating the 'advanced search' features and the help facilities for them; if you're prepared to invest some time, and if you approach it systematically, being able to use these features is a valuable professional skill. You might only need it on a few occasions, but on those occasions it will make a significant difference.

So, on to inverse frequency weighting. This sounds complicated, but the basic concept is very simple. For most searches, there will be relevant records which don't contain all the keywords you specified. This is why most systems use Boolean OR unless you tell them otherwise; they're erring on the side of giving you a larger number of relevant records, even if they're accompanied by more dross. The system could simply present the resulting list to you in some systematic form, such as alphabetical order or most recent first, but this isn't very satisfactory – there are obvious advantages in first showing the records most likely to be relevant, and then showing them in decreasing order of likely relevance. How can the system do this?

One way is to weight them by how many relevant keywords they contain. If you type in four keywords, then the system can show you first the records that contain all four, then those containing three out of four, and so on. This means that if you type in several keywords, rather than just a couple, then the first records on the screen are more likely to be relevant than if you only typed in a couple; conversely, the last records on the list are more likely to be irrelevant grot, since they will be picking up just one keyword each.

Another way of prioritising the records is by how specific the keywords are: the more specific a keyword is, the higher its weighting, and the more vague it is, the lower its weighting. One way of doing this is to count how often each word occurs in the system's records and calculate a weight using the formula $1/n$, where n is the number of times a word occurs; a word occurring in 1,000,000 records will have a weighting of $1/1,000,000$ and one occurring in 1,000 records will have a weighting of $1/1,000$, which is a thousand times greater. The system then prioritises the output list so that you see the records with the highest weightings first.

So what? So, the more specific the terms you put in, the more likely you are to get a high proportion of useful records rather than irrelevant grot. By a fascinating coincidence, some of the most specific terms are technical terms and authors' names – precisely the same things that get you brownie points when you include them in your writing. How do you know which terms to use and which authors to use when the whole point of the search is to find out about them? The answer is that you bootstrap yourself up. You do this in the following way.

Your initial reading or suggestion from someone over coffee will have given you at least one or two relevant keywords. For instance, if someone suggests using repertory grids, then you have 'repertory grid' as keywords, so you can type that into a search engine and see what comes out. Next, you scan a few relevant-looking records, and see (a) what technical terms keep cropping up and (b) who the main researchers seem to be in this area. You write down the technical terms, the researchers' names, and any other specific terms that look useful (such as names of journals that appear to publish a lot of material on this topic). You then work systematically through this list. So, for instance, your first list of words from a search on 'repertory grid' will probably contain the term 'Personal Construct Theory' and the name of George Kelly. Your next search might now be on 'repertory grid Personal Construct Theory Kelly', and should find a lot of relevant records.

Once you have a fair idea of the main concepts in the relevant field, you're in a position to start investigating the specialised part of the field most relevant to you. For instance, if you're interested in using repertory grids to investigate carers' misunderstandings of clients' values, the initial search should have found something about exchange grids, where you get someone to complete a grid as if they were someone else, and compare the results with those from a grid which actually was completed by the other person. You can now search for previous work on using exchange grids for this very specific purpose, and you might find a couple of articles where people have done precisely this. At this point, you may well be able to use one of these articles as your foundational article. If you do this, you can also look up other publications by the author of the foundational article, to see whether there are other useful ideas that you can include in your own design.

It's tempting to stop searching completely at this point. What is wiser is to use this as a starting point, but to do further searching periodically throughout your project, as further issues come to light – for instance, you might run into practical problems with the methodology, and find some useful pointers in the literature about ways of handling them. You'll also find further searching useful when you write the discussion section of your dissertation. Most projects turn up some unexpected findings; most good projects turn up something unexpected and interesting, and you'll need to read a different set of literature to make sense of it. As usual, it's not wasted effort; wise students add continuously to their references as they go through (but they also make sure that they have a good enough grasp of the main underpinning literature before they get started on the project proper).

Summary

At the end of the initial search, you will be able to answer the following questions. By yet another fascinating coincidence, they provide the underlying structure of a solid introductory section for a dissertation.

- What is the problem that you are tackling?
- Why is it an academically significant question worth doing a project on?
- What are the main things that have been tried before? (And what has been tried that not many people know about?)
- Who tried them?
- Why didn't those approaches work?
- What are you going to try that's different?
- Where did you get that idea from?
- What evidence is there to suggest that this might work better?
- If it doesn't work, will that finding be a useful, significant absence, or will you just look like an idiot?

If you can't answer all these questions, then you need to return to your searching; if you can answer them, then you're off to a good start on your introduction and literature review. On that positive note, we'll move on to the next topic.

The next topic is another potential minefield, namely the role of research in society. All research is conducted in a social context. Most students get through their projects without ever having to think about this, like civilians walking along a path cleared long ago by the mine clearance team, but (a) from an ethical viewpoint, more students should think about this context and (b) from the cockroach viewpoint, some topics can throw you into the middle of the minefield, far from the path.

Research in society – agendas, context and the like: things we take for granted, and things that can cause you trouble

In the end I must rely on the judgement and standing of the few scientific leaders who have ... enough independence of thought to weigh my data on its own hideously convincing merits or in the light of certain primordial and highly baffling myth cycles.

(*At the Mountains of Madness*, p.11)

This section is something of a miscellany, and the fact that it's a miscellany says something about the nature of research in society. If you look up statistics in a dozen different textbooks, you'll find the topic structured in very similar ways in all of them, reflecting the degree of consensus about the topic in the discipline; if you try looking up research in society in the same textbooks, you'll probably find very little consensus. This is partly because there is little consensus in the field, and partly because reflection about the nature of research in general with relation to society isn't high on most people's agendas. Research into specific topics such as stem cell research is high on some agendas, but that's a different animal.

There are several reasons for treating this general topic as important. One very practical one is the concept that as a researcher you have a duty of care in various directions. You have a duty of care to your subjects; you are legally obliged to treat them with due care and respect. You also have a duty of care to people you're working with: for instance, if you have research assistants, you need to treat them with due care and respect. In addition, you have a responsibility to other members of society. How does this translate into specifics? For your research subjects, if you did something to them which caused them needless distress, then you would be failing your duty of care – for instance, if you tricked them into believing that they had a fatal disease, to see their reaction to it. Research ethics in this sense is reasonably well codified, though more so in some fields than in others. Similarly, if you required your research assistant to do something which needlessly distressed them, you would be failing in your duty of care there – for instance, sending them out into a dangerous neighbourhood alone late at night to study criminal behaviour. For duty of care to other parties, the situation becomes more complex. The extreme cases are pretty straightforward: for instance, if you were trying to find a cure for leukaemia, and were following all the ethical guidelines, then that's a pretty clear example of a worthy topic and best practice. Conversely, Mengele's experiments in concentration camps were clearly right off the scale in terms of unethical behaviour. In between, though, the situation is often a lot more unclear or grey.

Some of the choices you have to make involve the balance between the small picture and the big picture. So, for instance, you might study some compulsive gamblers so that you can understand what causes compulsive gambling. Every minute you spend studying them is a minute you could have spent trying to make them give up the compulsion. Does this make you unethical? No, since it's pretty clear that simple persuasion doesn't work, which is why research into the topic is needed in the first place; once someone has found a solution, possibly based on your research, then you can apply that solution to your group. That's pretty much in the white end of the greys. At the other end of the scale, if you're studying burglars, then it would not be a wise idea to help them burgle someone's house, since it's unlikely that this would give you any new insights that couldn't have been gained via other routes. In the middle, there are famous cases such as Milgram's experiments on obedience to authority, which caused distress to his subjects, but which produced findings that gave profound new insights into human behaviour; weighing the balance on such cases is not easy, and there's no easy answer about whether the end justified the means in such cases.

There are also questions of a different sort which affect research. There's the whole question of what you're researching, and why you're researching that rather than something else. There's also a related set of questions about the presuppositions built into your research. A classic example is research into cults in the 1970s; this reflected a societal concern about cults in the west, with an explicit assumption that these were a bad thing. An interesting thing about this research was the way in which it faded into the background. It did this because one key issue was defining a cult, as opposed to a respectable religion. Rather embarrassingly for the underlying assumptions, researchers encountered serious problems when they tried to find a clear-cut criterion for distinguishing cults from religions – for pretty much any odd feature of a given cult, there was at least one branch of a respectable religion which also exhibited that feature. This led to a general acceptance within that research community that a cult was simply a low-status religious group with strong group controls. This conclusion meant that there wasn't much point in studying cults per se, as opposed to studying low-status religious groups, and/or groups with strong group controls.

Such cases have interesting implications. It's quite common for researchers in a given field to have reached a consensus which is at odds with society's beliefs about the topic. An example of this is the long-running battle between biblical creationists and biologists over the teaching of evolution in the American Bible belt. If you get caught up in such cases, it can get pretty ugly. Another is that societal preferences influence which topics get researched. Governments, charities and private funders decide which areas of research merit funding, which provides a positive incentive for researchers to work in those areas, and a negative incentive steering researchers away from other topics. It's possible to do research without funding, but it's more hassle, and doesn't help your career much, so the funding issue tends to move research in particular directions. There's also the implicit social threat of being pilloried in the media, or even imprisoned, if your research breaks social taboos, as researchers into human sexual behaviour are well aware. It's an interesting but depressing exercise to list the top ten causes of human death around the world and then to see how this correlates with the amount of research funding and the number of research publications dealing with each.

So, where does this leave us? It leaves us in a world which includes many moral uncertainties. Even if you have a clear, well-informed social conscience, you'll be aware that by working on one area, you're not working on another which may be more important; you may also be unwittingly working on a problem which simply can't be solved yet, like a sixteenth-century doctor wrestling with a problem which could only be solved once X-rays were discovered. You may be working on something which your society believes to be a problem, but where the wider world community believes that it's your society which is out of step with reality – there are numerous examples of this in relation to the internet, where beliefs about the relative boundaries of free speech and of inciting political unrest vary widely across societies, as well as in relation to anything involving 'national security'. There aren't easy answers. One rule of thumb which might help you is to imagine looking back at your research from your deathbed, and asking yourself whether you would feel that you asked the right moral questions before starting it. What matters is whether you asked, rather than whether you always got the answer right. We all make mistakes, often with the best of intentions, but we're a lot less likely to make them if we ask the right questions in the first place. If you do get it wrong, then another thought which might help is that one measure of a person is what they do after making a mistake. If you did everything reasonably possible to avoid making the mistake in the first place, and you then learn from the mistake, and do what you can to set right the damage you caused, then that's about as much as can be asked from a fallible human being.

That concludes this overview of the nature of research. The next chunk of the book is about research design. There are various types of design, such as case studies, field experiments and controlled experiments. We describe each of these, discuss how to select the appropriate one for your needs, and describe how to use each type. Each type tends to fit better with some data collection techniques than others, and to fit better with some analysis techniques than others, and there are chunks of this book which deal with those. After reading those chunks, you might decide that your original choice of research type wasn't the best, and might go for a different one. This is not just normal, but is actively a Good Thing, since it shows that you're making an informed choice rather than rushing headlong into something just because it's familiar. The key thing is to make sure that you know before you start how you will analyse your data, and why you'll do it that way: this can save you a lot of hassle, and can let you achieve much more for no extra effort.

2

Research design

> *There he followed the secret paths along which his dark genius led him.*
> (*Night Winds*, p.22)

Types of design: which to use and how to use them

At the level of sordid practicalia, good research design is a Good Thing because it lets you achieve more and better things for the same effort (or for even less effort, if you know what you're doing). For some people, that alone is reason enough to go through the motions of adherence to good research design. To others, that statement raises a batch of further questions, such as what constitutes 'good' design anyway, as opposed to 'bad' design, or why one thing is considered 'good' while another is considered 'bad'. We'll say a bit about those questions here, since they'll help make sense of research design, and since we're quite keen on this area (yes, we've said quite a bit about the same topic elsewhere in this book too, but it's an important concept, and bears restating from different perspectives).

Research is about finding things out, and the term covers a multitude of sins and virtues. The sixteenth-century explorer setting out to find Eldorado was doing a kind of research, and it usually ended in tears. Research design (as opposed to just research) is about finding things out systematically – map making as opposed to treasure hunting. If you plan your research design properly, then whatever you find should be a useful contribution to knowledge. It may only be a small contribution to knowledge, but that's fine: nobody's expecting you to revolutionise your field at this point of your career.

Research design is closely allied to statistical analysis of data, for sound reasons. These reasons may appear less than obvious to readers from some disciplines, so we'll say a bit about them here. The main reason that they're allied relates to kibbles and bits. This is a term which we're told has biblical origins, but it's most memorably expressed by Faith in an episode of *Buffy the Vampire Slayer*, where Faith is explaining how after the Mayor's apotheosis and the resultant carnage, she will end up sitting at his right hand, and everyone else will be kibbles and bits. Whatever the precise etymology of the term (there's another plausible explanation involving pet food), the underlying concept is a useful one, namely insignificant small detritus. If you're investigating something, then most likely a few factors will be really important, and the rest will be kibbles and bits. For instance, if you're studying what appears to influence whether or not the local birds will decide to visit your bird table, you could imagine enormous numbers of possible influences – perhaps, for instance, they're less likely to turn up on the day the bin lorry comes, because they can scavenge food that falls from the bins, or they might be more likely to turn up when the sun is shining because the food looks fresher. What you'll probably find is that a handful of things make a big difference (for example, whether they can see anyone moving at a nearby window, or whether a cat is in the garden) and that all the other possible influences that you've thought of have no discernible effect and are effectively kibbles and bits.

All well and good, but how do you decide what size of effect is worth bothering with, and what isn't? This is where statistics come in. They don't claim to give you The Truth, but they do give you an agreed set of conventions within which you can discuss your findings with others in a more constructive way. In case you're wondering why that should motivate you, the answer is that if you've got some solid stats behind you, then you've also got a century's worth of heavy maths behind you, and would-be critics will need to treat you more carefully. It's possible for them to claim that they don't believe in stats, but that's a stance similar to Custer's alleged last words at the Little Big Horn (according to one film version, his last words to his troops were 'Take no prisoners!'). Strong on fighting spirit, perhaps, but not closely matched to reality. (Yes, we know that the reality was a bit different from Hollywood, and could quote all sorts of obscure facts about that unfortunate episode of history, such as that he was wearing his hair short that day, but it was too good a quote to ignore, even if it was almost certainly apocryphal.)

Anyway, back to the main plot, and to you, sitting there wondering where you start designing a study. The place to start, as usual, is at the end. What sort of outcome do you want from this study? Do you want to demonstrate that you have a particular skill, or do you want to find the answer to a particular question, or what? Once you know that, then you can focus on the relevant aspects, and keep the others as simple as possible. For instance, suppose that you want to come out of your research having demonstrated that you have excellent skills in applying critical incident technique. It's a useful technique, and one which not many people have, so that's a reasonable aim. The next question is: what are you going to apply critical incident technique to in your study? You'll have to apply it to something, so you might as well apply it to something that moves you towards what you want in life. If you want a career in consumer behaviour, you might apply critical incident technique to consumers' online shopping behaviour; if you're more interested in theology, then you might apply it to people's accounts of life-changing spiritual experiences. At this point you've already nailed down two of the three main things you need to sort out regardless of the research design you want to use. The last one is the research question that you're asking: what is it that you want to find out using your chosen technique in your chosen area? For instance, you might want to find out whether critical incidents have more effect on people if those incidents are unpleasant rather than pleasant ones.

The relative importance of these three factors (method, area of application, and research question) is different for different people. Some are primarily concerned with the research question (for example, what causes cancer?) and will use whatever method looks most likely to answer that question. Others are more interested in the area of application (for instance, they want a career in mental health work). Others are mainly interested in methods (for instance, demonstrating that they are proficient in a skill which will make them highly employable). Because there are so many methods out there, and because asking the right research question is a delicate, tricky skill, you'd be wise to take advice about those. There are usually several right answers, and many more wrong answers. With area of application, there usually aren't any right answers if the area of application is an end in itself for you (for instance, wanting to work in rural development), but if you're viewing it as a means to an end (for instance, wanting to work in rural development because you think that will bring you a more fulfilling life), then taking advice would be wise.

You may by now be wondering whether we've forgotten about research design. If so, you'll be reassured to know that we haven't; research design is something you use to answer a research question, rather than something that exists in splendid isolation. For different research questions, different research designs are needed, and you need to understand where you're trying to go before you get into the details of the research design. A good research question is the crucial factor in good research, which is why we discuss this topic at great length elsewhere in this book. It's a skill that takes time, which is (a) why you are issued with a supervisor to help you in your research and (b) why your supervisor will probably advise you to conduct a pilot study before doing the main study: this is a good way of finding any flaws in your research question that you and your supervisor might have overlooked.

So, there you are with a shiny new research question, a supervisor, an area of application, and possibly a method too. Now what? The answer is that now you try to figure out what sort of research design will give you the most solid answer you can get to your research question.

Research designs

As with data collection methods and statistical methods, you won't be short of choices for research designs. There are various ways of summarising them. We'll start with the most apparently informal approach, and work through increasingly formal approaches after that. This subsection is a swift overview; we'll then return to each research design in more detail in subsequent subsections.

A non-intervention case study

The most apparently informal project that we've supervised involved the excellent Farah. She was an undergraduate who had unusually good access to a group of companies which had pooled resources to tackle the Millennium Bug – the risk of major software problems at the start of the year 2000. She also had excellent social skills, and a lot of good sense. When she described the way that the companies had pooled resources, it was clear that they had built a team using a very unusual approach, and that the outcomes could be very interesting. She and Gordon (who was her supervisor) decided that the best research design for this situation was for her to study what the team did, without trying to change their behaviour in any way, and to see what happened. Nobody had studied this situation before (since the Millennium Bug was a new, unique problem), so whatever she found would be interesting. What she found was that the team worked very well, and achieved objectives without significant problems. When we examined her data afterwards, it all made sense in hindsight, but in a way that we hadn't anticipated. For instance, the unique features of the Millennium Bug meant that some factors normally affecting successful team structure did not apply in this case, allowing the companies to be very successful with a team-building approach that would normally have been highly unwise.

There are several aspects of this study which are worth considering. One is that Farah only looked at one team. The advantage of this was that Farah could focus in detail on this team, and get a richer understanding of the detail than would have been possible with a sample of several teams. However, the disadvantage was that we were only able to say: 'here's what this team did'. For all we knew, it may have been the only team in the world which used that particular approach, or it may have been pretty much like all the other teams. With a sample size of one team, we couldn't tell. That's one limitation of case studies like this one.

A second feature of this study is that it was non-interventionist: we didn't try to change the team's behaviour (for instance, by giving them helpful advice). This was, with hindsight, probably just as well, since the factors leading them to a happy ending were not obvious in advance, and if we had tried to give them advice it might have led to an unhappy ending. It's clearly more or less impossible to do a study of this sort without changing the team's behaviour in some way or other (just having a student show up and ask questions will probably change a team's behaviour in some way), but there's a clear difference between a case study where you just try to observe, and a case study where you try to get the team to use your new improved method for doing something. Because there's no way of being sure in advance whether your effect on the group's behaviour will be positive or negative, the issue of your effect on the group's achievements or failures is an interesting one from an ethical viewpoint; if you're considering a study of this sort, you may need to get ethical clearance from the relevant part of your department or The System.

This study found quite a few interesting things, and raised a lot of interesting questions. For example, there's the issue of whether this team was unusual, or whether there were lots more like it. The only way to answer that question would be to look at more teams, which leads us out of case studies and into surveys. There's also the issue of whether the team might have performed better (or worse) if we had given them some helpful advice; that would lead us into an interventionist case study. If we gave helpful advice and it appeared to have an effect (either for better or for worse), that would raise the issue of whether the same advice would have the same effect on other groups, which takes us out of case studies and into field experiments.

Surveys

In a survey, you try to find out how widespread things are. For instance, Farah could have tried to find out how many teams tackled the Millennium Bug in the same way as the team that she studied. For most problems, life's too short to ask all the relevant people, teams, organisations, or whatever it is that you're studying, so the usual approach is to ask some of them, and then scale up their responses to give you an estimate of the total numbers. For example, if Farah knew that there were 10,000 teams in the UK tackling the Millennium Bug, she might decide to survey 100 of them, and see how many used the same approach as the team that she studied. If a fifth of the teams in her survey used the same approach, then she could estimate that a fifth of the teams in the country also used that approach, giving her an estimate of 2,000 teams in the UK using that approach.

This raises various questions, such as the age-old favourite, namely how big a sample you need in your survey. Students have a touching belief that the bigger the sample, the better the survey. The reality is a bit different. If your survey is badly designed and therefore producing only garbage, then a bigger sample size will only lead to a bigger pile of garbage. Even if your survey is beautifully designed, then bigger is not always better; there's a point of diminishing returns where you won't be learning anything very new from gathering any more data, and where you're starting to waste everyone's time if you continue to gather data. How do you know if you've reached that point? This is where statistics loom into view, and this is why it's a good idea to take advice about stats before getting started on your study. We'll return to that later. Another issue is that sometimes you'll want to leave some people unsampled, so that you can use them for a further piece of research, without affecting their behaviour by surveying them in your first study.

Another question is what method to use for your survey. Some observant readers will have noticed that we haven't used the word 'questionnaire' so far. One good reason for this is that surveys are not synonymous with questionnaires: there are plenty of other (and often more appropriate) methods that can be used for surveys. Another good reason is that questionnaires are easy to do badly, and difficult to do well. From a cabinetmaking point of view, if you want to impress people with your use of a questionnaire, you'll need to be very, very good. There's a large literature on how to design and use questionnaires properly. Most students don't read it. The results are pretty predictable.

Setting aside our standard 16-minute rant about questionnaires, surveys can produce some interesting findings, but as usual, these will just produce more questions, such as 'why do they do that?' or 'could we educate them so they don't do that any more?' This leads us out of surveys, and into other designs.

Field experiments

'What-if' questions are often interesting, but are often difficult to answer. You can ask people what they would do if something happened, but there's no guarantee that what they tell you will bear much relation to the truth. A better way of finding out is to make that 'what-if' happen, and then see how people respond. If you do it in the outside world, then it's a field experiment. A master of field experiments was the late Stanley Milgram (yes, the same Milgram who did the experiments on obedience to authority). Some of his field experiments wouldn't get past ethics committees today, but most of them were beautifully simple and effective. For instance, if you want to check whether there are differences in honesty between inhabitants of two towns, you can simply walk up behind a randomly chosen inhabitant in the street, and ask them politely whether they have just dropped a pound coin/five dollar bill/other relevant currency, while holding out the money. You know that they didn't drop it, because you have just taken it out of your own pocket. What proportion of people will honestly say that they didn't drop it, and what proportion will say, whether through honest mistake or through more base motivation, that they did drop it? This field experiment will give you an answer. (An expensive one, perhaps, but an answer.) It's different from an interventionist case study because you're using a larger sample size: large enough to give you some idea how your results would scale up to the population at large. (As with surveys, the precise size will depend on the statistics you're using.)

Field experiments give you answers to a lot of questions that you can't answer through case studies and surveys. They still don't give you all the answers. For instance, they can't tell you what might produce changes for the better in the behaviour of the people you're studying. If you're working in an area such as public health, then you might be very interested in finding out which of two approaches is most likely to persuade people to eat more healthily (for example, a scare campaign about the dire effects of bad diet, or a positive campaign about the benefits of a healthy diet). You can speculate as much as you like, but ultimately you'll only know if you try out both approaches and see what the results look like. This takes us into the most formal research design, the controlled experiment.

The controlled experiment

In a field experiment, you're doing something to people, and seeing the results. However, one major limitation of the field experiment is that you're doing it out in the field, to any apparently suitable people that you can find. You have no control over what sort of people are happening along. For instance, with the field experiment investigating honesty, it's possible that you just happened to run one set of data collection in a street near the Episcopalian Church, and the other in a street near the meeting house of the Expatriate Elbonian Liars' Society. In that case, it's conceivable that any differences in your results between the two towns were due to the type of person who happened to frequent that street, and were unrepresentative of the towns as a whole. This sort of stray variable can cause havoc with the less formal research designs, which is why the controlled experiment (also known as the formal experiment, or planned experiment, or various other names) is generally viewed as the best way of getting a definitive answer to a research question.

In a controlled experiment, you design things so that all the stray variables are kept out of the way when you do something to your experimental subjects. Any changes can then only be due either to chance or to the thing that you're doing to your subjects. If there are changes, you can then use statistics to say how likely it is that they are the result of chance; the less likely this is, the greater the likelihood that you're dealing with something that really does make a difference. Suppose, for instance, that you want to investigate whether your new Accelerated Teaching Method (ATM) really does teach numeracy faster than traditional methods. If you take a hundred pairs of identical twins, randomly assign one twin of each pair to be taught using the ATM method and the other to be taught using the traditional method, and then find that all the ATM twins perform much better than the traditional method twins, you have a pretty strong initial case for arguing that ATM is responsible for the difference. There's no obvious reason to suspect that there's anything else that's different between the two groups, apart from the teaching method. If it's the only thing that's different, and the two groups perform differently, then the apparent conclusion is that ATM is responsible for the differences. The statistical analysis might then show that there's only one chance in ten thousand that the two groups would produce such different results because of random chance (for instance, that all of the traditional method group happened to be having a bad day). That's a pretty strong initial case.

There's obviously more to formal experimental design than we've described in this example, but that's the basic principle. We'll elaborate on it in the relevant later section.

Summary

There are numerous research designs, which fall into a limited number of main types. Each has advantages and corresponding disadvantages. The most common trade-off is between precision and reality. Usually the more precisely controlled your design is, the more unrealistic the experimental task and setting are. If you're a professional researcher (including PhD students, for this purpose) then you can often handle this problem to at least some extent by doing a set of increasingly controlled studies, and building in some sort of cross-calibration between them. You might, for instance, check whether the error rates from the subjects doing the experimental task in your lab experiment are consistent with those from subjects in a more naturalistic setting (for example, if you're studying programming errors, you could see whether the number of bugs per thousand lines of code was significantly different in the lab from the number in their normal output). If you're a student on a taught course doing one single study, then you can't do that sort of cross-checking. You can, however, write up your single study in a way that makes it clear that you're perfectly well aware of the strengths and weaknesses of relevant approaches, so that you can get the brownie points for that knowledge.

On that positive note, we'll bring this chunk to a close, and proceed to a more detailed description of the various research designs described above.

Surveys and sampling

> . . . it was just for surveying the Horn, the Straits and the Chile coast – little chance of any prize, unless we happened to run into a pirate.
>
> (Blue at the Mizzen, p.72)

Proper survey methodology is a bit like driving safely: agreed by pretty much everyone to be a good thing, but with most people falling short of the standards on which the experts agree. Fortunately, the basic principles are fairly straightforward, and there's fairly good agreement about them, so you can savour that experience while it lasts.

With research involving human subjects, you have to decide what type of people to use, and how many of them to use. Firstly, the easy question, namely how many to use.

There's a widespread but erroneous belief that the answer to 'how many?' should be 'as many as possible'. The right answer is 'as many as necessary'. Beyond that point, you're just wasting resources, including other people's time as well as your own. How do you know how many that is? There are various ways. One is to work out the number in advance, via statistics – if you know the statistical power of the hypothetical effect that you're testing for, then you can work backwards from that to calculate the sample size. The best way of doing this is to ask a friendly statistician for help; the concept is simple, but the maths gets fiddly. This is a good approach if you know what you're testing for, but if you're just doing a fishing expedition, to see what you can catch, then you can't know in advance what you'll be dealing with, and this approach won't work.

If you're doing a fishing expedition, then (mixing metaphors somewhat) you may need to decide your sample size by the seat of your pants while on the fly. An important factor is diminishing returns – when you stop finding anything much that you haven't found already. You can measure this statistically via various methods. One is the split-group method, where you randomly allocate your subjects' data to two different groups. At first the mean scores will probably be different, because of randomness, but the differences will diminish as you add more data to each group, until eventually the two means converge, at which point you've probably hit the point of diminishing returns. You can also do something similar via a statistical test for diminishing returns; again, it's best to ask a friendly statistician for help. The disadvantage of these approaches is that they require you to analyse your data, and we're not keen on analysing data while you're still doing data collection, because of the risk of interference effects – you notice something interesting in the analysis, and are then subconsciously biased towards looking harder for that in the rest of your data collection.

There are also some quicker and dirtier approaches to sample size, but departments and disciplines vary in their reactions to these. One simple one is to see what sample sizes were used in papers in the literature on your topic, and then to use a sample size which is comfortably within that range. A related one is to see what sample sizes were used in previous recent projects in your department on similar topics, and use a sample size comfortably within that range (though arguing that other students used that sample size is not as strong a case as arguing that three Nobel Prize winners used it). Another, which can be used as a first pass and then combined with one of the others described above, is gut feel. When you're collecting data in a live session (as opposed to having questionnaires come through the post), it's highly likely that you'll soon reach a point of utter boredom, where you're hearing the same tired old responses that you've heard over and over before, and where it strains your professionalism to the limit to simulate interest in what the respondents are telling you. That's a pretty good hint that you've reached diminishing returns.

If that point also happens to be within the range of sample sizes in the published literature, then you might as well stop. You can then analyse the data and, if you have the time and the inclination, throw in an analysis for diminishing returns as icing on the cake (though this could backfire if the analysis concludes that you hadn't actually reached that point). More rarely, you might be running your twentieth respondent, and starting to panic because there doesn't seem to be any rhyme or reason in any of your data, and because all of your respondents seem to be completely different. This probably means that you've hit a different type of diminishing return, where the key finding is the fact that the population is highly variable. For instance, if you found that no two of your thirty respondents used the same criteria for assessing ethical choices, then that's a very interesting finding. You could probably find some weak regularities if you kept going through a huge sample, but these would probably be less important than the sheer degree of variability.

Right, back to what type of people to use. At one level, this is pretty simple – you will specify this in your research design, either by saying explicitly that you're looking at an identified group, or by saying implicitly that you're looking at the world in general. At another level, it's trickier. Sometimes you can gather data from everyone in the group that interests you, but more often you can't, and in that case you need to find a sample from that group which you can use, which gets you into all sorts of interesting questions about the representativeness of your sample.

In an ideal world, you would be able to use some sort of random process which would produce a completely representative sample. As you may have guessed by now, this is not an ideal world. For a start, there's the issue that 'random' is not necessarily the same as 'representative'. What you normally want to do with your research is to scale up the results from your sample and extrapolate them to the entire population, but you can't do this if your sample isn't representative. A random selection process will tend towards representativeness, becoming more representative as it becomes larger, until you hit the point of diminishing returns. That's usually not the main problem; the main problems are usually simpler ones, such as how to set about selecting a random sample in the first place, and then how to recruit subjects from that selected shortlist. Suppose, for instance, that you want to investigate people's attitudes to homelessness. It would be fairly easy to choose, say, every hundredth name from the electoral list for your town, or randomly select 1 per cent of the names on the list. However, that already raises questions about how representative of the country your home town is. There's also the issue that some people won't be on the electoral register (for instance, many homeless people). Even if you manage to sort out this problem perfectly, there's then the issue of persuading people to be respondents. Usually quite a few will refuse, so your resulting sample will only be a self-selecting subset of your original list, and will probably be unrepresentative of the population at large – the self-selecters will by definition be volunteers, who are demonstrably different from the population at large, and may in addition be self-selecting on the basis of whether or not they have strong views about the topic of your research. For example, if potential respondents knew that you were researching attitudes towards transubstantiation, you might get the impression from your resulting sample that most people were remarkably well informed about Christian theology.

One point worth mentioning is the distinction between a truly random sample, where you're using an identifiable randomising device such as random number tables, and a haphazard sample, where you're grabbing anyone vaguely suitable looking who happens along. With haphazard sampling, there's the risk that the people who are happening along are not random, and that there's some underlying factor predisposing them to be where you find them. A lot of students talk about using a random sample when they've actually used a haphazard sample, such as 'whichever of my friends happened to be free'. Two related concepts are convenience samples ('whoever happened to be conveniently available') and snowball sampling (asking each respondent whether they could give you the names of some other potential victims). Both of these are widely used in student projects.

Students and professionals alike tend to agonise about the problems of sampling for surveys. The topic is well covered in the standard literature, so we won't say much more about it – there aren't many brilliant solutions to report. One thing worth mentioning, though, is that the problem is less acute if you're not aiming to generalise to the population at large. One strategy that we often use is to compare haphazard samples of clearly defined groups, in a way which specifically avoids classic problems. For example, one group could be 'people in my workplace' and another group could be 'final year undergraduate mathematics students'. This type of sampling makes no claims about being generalisable to other groups such as elderly people who don't have phones, or itinerant labourers, which are notoriously hard to include properly in large-scale surveys. As a student, there are limits to what people can reasonably expect you to tackle on a project, so using manageable-sized groups in this way has obvious advantages. If you can manage to recruit a group which is normally difficult to recruit, then so much the better – if, for instance, you're on good terms with the local bikers, you have a chance of getting wonderful data of a sort that most researchers can only dream about. On that edifying note, we'll return to research design.

Field experiments: doing research in the world

Twice he was absent from the city on week-long trips, whose destinations have not yet been discovered.

(*The Case of Charles Dexter Ward*, p.233)

Field experiments are not usually carried out in fields, though they can be, nor are all experiments which are carried out in fields actually field experiments

(Gordon once conducted some of the data collection for a formal experiment in a field, next to a circus, but that's another story). A field experiment is one you carry out in The Field, i.e. anywhere outside your office or lab. How does it differ from a field study? A good question, though probably not one that would occur to most novices. The borderline is fuzzy. In a field experiment, you're doing something to something and seeing what that intervention does to something else. In a field study, you're studying something, but that study doesn't necessarily mean you're intervening in any way. This distinction (and the reason it's fuzzy) should become clearer as we proceed through this section.

Doing things out in The Field has various methodological attractions. The main one is that this is likely to be a more realistic setting than your dingy office, shared with taste-challenged and impoverished colleagues; you have a better chance of seeing how things really are in the outside world. Let's take a fictitious example, inspired by the master of field research, the late Stanley Milgram. Suppose you believe that nice music inspires people to behave in a nobler way. How can you test this hypothesis? One way would be to play some nice music to people, and see if they behave more nobly than would otherwise be the case. With a bit of ingenuity, there are ways that you can do this fairly realistically. For instance, you could sweet-talk the manager of a local store into letting you run the experiment in the store. You then play either nice music by a clean-living band, or some nasty music by immoral youths, over the store's Muzak system. That gives you the 'nice music' bit (though we'll set aside for the moment the question of how you'd define 'nice music'). How do you assess noble behaviour? One way would be to set up a situation where people had the options of being noble or of being all too human. For instance, you could have a confederate drop a coin underneath a display stand next to a grimy and horrid bit of floor. You could then count how many people offered to help when the nice music was playing, compared to when the nasty music was playing; you could also measure how long they hesitated before offering, if you were game for some more sophisticated analysis. At the end of a day or two, you'd have a batch of data which would probably be unique, and rightly so.

The advantage of this design (assuming that you got it past the ethics committee) is that you would have data from a realistic setting – a real store, a real music system, and a plausible task that the subjects would be undertaking. The disadvantage is that when it came to who those subjects were, you wouldn't have any control – you'd be at the mercy of whatever selection of individuals Fate happened to send in through the door. Suppose, for instance, that you had the more specific hypothesis that nice music had more effect on teenagers than on older people (who were already set in their ways). What happens if you camp out in the store for a month and there's no sign of a teenager in all that time? The answer, for readers who listen to the wrong sort of music, would be that you were screwed. (We've resisted the temptation to phrase it in a variety of musical lyric styles, but it was a struggle.) You wouldn't have any teenage subjects, and that would be the end of it. If you went out and bribed some young people to come into the store, then you would no longer be doing a field experiment, and you'd lose the validity which was the main attraction of this design.

What makes this a field experiment, rather than a field study? In the design above, you were changing something in the experimental setting. Some of the subjects were hearing nice music; others were hearing nasty music. You could control which subjects heard which music, if you wished – for example, to randomise it so that there were no complicating extra factors about which music you played at which points in the day, and what sort of people might be naturally predisposed to come in at those times. Now let's suppose that you have a different hypothesis. Suppose you believe that people who buy rap music are less kindly than people who buy Goth music. You could repeat the design above in a music store, with the difference that sometimes the confederate drops the coin in front of the rap music section, and sometimes in front of the Goth section. In this design, you're no longer controlling anything in the environment; you're just watching what happens when your confederate drops the coin. Strictly speaking, this lack of control makes this a study, rather than an experiment. It might be that any differences are due to the rap/Goth divide; however, they might be due to different grot and nastiness factors in the stains on the two sections of floor involved, or any of a herd of other factors that a fertile mind might dream up as explanations. Unless you can alter a factor and see what happens, you'll never know for sure. That's why experiments carry more credibility than studies among those who know about such things.

As should be clear from the hypothetical example above, field experiments and field studies have some obvious attractions, ranging from higher validity to better anecdotes to tell envious colleagues. They also have obvious problems, ranging from ethical approval through to downright risk of physical injury or litigation if something goes wrong. A problem which should not be underestimated is the sheer logistical difficulty of setting up something like the experiment described above. It can take a lot of time to get the relevant agreements from the relevant people (in writing, just in case anything goes wrong), and a lot of time to set up the physical infrastructure. In this experiment, for instance, one of the first things we'd check was what format the music needed to be in, just in case the store was using some bizarre format such as 3.97 mm seven-track tapes that the proprietor had bought from a guy in a pub ten years ago. Even if the store used CDs, there would still be a fair chance that your beloved unique copy of Perry Como's greatest hits played live at Lollapalooza when he supported Siouxsie and the Banshees would be accidentally thrown away by a shop assistant at the end of the first day, leaving you unable to continue the experiment afterwards. (Moral: always have back-ups.) There would also be issues such as where you would stand or sit for the data collection, and what would happen if your confederate gave up halfway through the data collection, driven over the brink by one boy-band track too many, thereby introducing a second confederate as a complicating factor in your experimental design, and so forth.

We'd planned to go on about this at much greater length, since it's a lot more fun than some of the things we have to do in the day job, but that seems to cover the main points, so we'll draw a close there, and move on to controlled experiments.

Controlled experiments: changing things systematically and seeing what happens

You may as well know that I have a way of learning old matters from things surer than books.

(*The Case of Charles Dexter Ward*, p.243)

Readers of a facetious turn of mind and short memory might be tempted to ask what an uncontrolled experiment would be like; such individuals would do well to read the section on field experiments. This section deals with controlled experiments, also known by various other names such as laboratory experiments or formal experiments. The advantage of these is that, as the name suggests, they involve controlling the things that interest you, and seeing what happens; the disadvantage is that there's usually a trade-off between how much control you have and how realistic your experiment is. (From now on, for brevity, we'll use the word 'experiment' to mean 'controlled experiment' unless otherwise stated.)

Most experiments involving human subjects follow a fairly standard sequence, which goes roughly as follows:

- *Step 1*: Design experiment, prepare materials and prepare instructions.
- *Step 2*: Recruit a couple of people as pilot subjects (i.e. guinea pigs to try your experiment out on). Try the experiment on them, including analysis of data from their session, using steps 4 onwards below. Redesign experiment, materials, instructions and/or analysis method. Repeat this step until the pilot session works (usually one repetition is enough).
- *Step 3*: Recruit subjects for main study. Allocate subjects to experimental groups.
- *Step 4*: Run each subject in turn (unless you're running them all at once, as described later). Give subject briefing materials, check that they've understood what they're doing, give them the materials (if appropriate) and get them to do the task. Gather data. Thank them politely. If appropriate, debrief them (i.e. explain what the experiment was about).
- *Step 5*: After you've run all the subjects, analyse the data.

- *Step 6*: Do final write-up.
- *Step 7*: If necessary, do a small follow-up study to clear up any questions which emerge in the data analysis.

That's the overall process, and the overall process is pretty obvious once you know it. The underlying principles are also pretty obvious with hindsight, and once you understand them, then you can do research efficiently and well (if you really know what you're doing, you can do a project good enough to publish in a journal). If you don't understand these principles, then you'll probably be able to muddle through and do fairly harmless research by copying the outward appearance of good research like an amateur cook following a recipe that they don't really understand, but there's more to life than that. The following sections unpack these underlying principles, so that you should understand how to plan formal experiments properly.

The core concept in formal experiments is keeping everything the same apart from one specific thing, and then seeing what happens when you poke that thing around. The classic example of this is Lind's pioneering work to find out the causes of scurvy. In essence, he took a batch of sailors with scurvy, making sure that all the sailors in the batch were as similar to each other as possible. He divided the batch of sailors into groups, then gave each group a different diet and watched what happened. As every neophyte researcher knows, the group who received citrus fruits recovered from scurvy. Since the only substantial difference between the groups was their diet, the obvious inference was that there was a causal connection between the sailors' diet and whether or not they contracted scurvy. (More experienced researchers with a knowledge of the dark underbelly of scholarship will be aware that there are different versions of this story floating around – for instance, in one humane version, the recovered sailors help feed citrus fruits to their shipmates and nurse them back to health; in another version, the recovered sailors help bury their less fortunate shipmates when Lind pursues his experiment to its remorseless conclusion – but the underlying main points about the experimental design and the outcomes are sound.)

The key thing which distinguishes this design from a field experiment is that Lind was able to keep everything the same in the experiment apart from the thing that he systematically varied. In a field experiment, there will by definition be things which are outside your control. Suppose, for instance, that Lind's captain had insisted that Lind try the citrus fruits on all the scurvy victims. They would presumably all have recovered, but Lind would not have been able to tell whether their recovery was due to the citrus diet or to something else which was also happening to all of them – for instance, a more conservative contemporary doctor might have argued that their recovery was due to the ship's sailing into a region away from foetid vapours, and had nothing to do with the citrus fruits.

Keeping everything the same apart from the thing that you are systematically varying is a simple concept, and is at the heart of formal experimental design. The concept really is that simple; there's no catch. Cynical readers may, however, wonder if there is a catch somewhere further down the line. How, they might ask, do you make sure that everything else really is the same? That's a good question, and is what this section is about. Most of it is, as usual, obvious with hindsight.

A handy way of tackling experimental design is to imagine that some nit-picking pedant will be asking whether you allowed for various devious sources of potential error. You get a brownie point for each one that you've thought of in advance. (You also make sure that you claim your brownie points in your write-up, by mentioning them tersely but clearly in the appropriate section on your experimental design.) If this metaphor doesn't appeal to your better nature, then you can try working with a friend, and doing helpful critiques of each other's designs (it's a good idea to lay in a stock of comfort food if you do this, to help you make up if the exercise turns more adversarial than you'd expected). This is one of the reasons that you have a supervisor for your project: your supervisor should be well aware of sneaky sources of trouble in experimental design, and should be able to steer you clear of them. Most people make at least one error in their experimental design, sometimes large, sometimes small; professional researchers develop an aesthetic taste for elegant experimental designs, and tell each other about particularly elegant designs that they have encountered. At one level, you might wonder whether they should get out more; at another level, good research is a way of answering questions that make the world a better place (and yes, we've read enough history to be aware of the debates about what constitutes 'better', and enough about the sociology of science not to get into that debate here).

Anyway, returning to the plot, there are various classic causes of trouble which lurk around when you're planning a formal experimental design. The following paragraphs deal with some of these. We've deliberately not tried to rate them for seriousness, since seriousness depends on context – something which is serious in one design may be relatively minor in another.

An initial problem is simply finding your subjects in the first place, particularly if you want to sample representatively from a particular population. That's a real problem, and an important one, but it's a problem which belongs upstream of this stage, in the 'survey and sampling' section.

A classic source of numerous problems is allocating subjects to groups. Most designs involve two or more groups, like Lind's sailors on different diets. Suppose that Lind had systematically put all the non-smoker sailors into one group, and all the smokers into another, what would have happened? What would have happened is that the group which recovered would be different from the others in two ways, namely diet and smoking. There would be no way for Lind to know which of those things was responsible for the recovery – it might be, for instance, that something in the tobacco was the key factor. So, what can you do about this?

One thing that you can do is to allocate subjects evenly to groups, so that each group contains the same proportions of smokers and non-smokers, for instance. This is fine in principle, but how do you know which are the relevant factors to take into account when doing this allocation? The more you do research, the more you discover about unlikely-sounding factors which really do make a difference – for instance, the relative lengths of index fingers and ring fingers are correlated with foetal testosterone levels and sexual preferences, via a chain of embryonic events too lengthy to be described here. Even if you do know what factors to take into account, you can end up needing some pretty rare individuals to balance the groups. One of Gordon's experiments, for instance, required left-handed expert female flint-knappers, who are not exactly thick on the ground.

One common response is to allocate subjects to groups randomly, instead of evenly. This is usually more convenient, and the larger the groups, the more likely it is that the subjects will be evenly allocated by chance. However, it raises all sorts of obvious and less obvious questions. For instance, what happens if the random allocation happens by pure chance to give you a group A consisting only of females and a group B consisting only of males, when gender is one of the factors in your experiment and you need to have balanced numbers of males and females in each group? You can get out your dice and start again, but it leaves you with a guilty feeling of having done some namelessly bad thing. That's an extreme example, but with small sample sizes you'll hit less extreme examples quite often – for instance, group A having 60 per cent males and 40 per cent females, instead of the 50:50 ratio you wanted. Where do you draw the line between accepting what you've got and getting the dice out again? Good question, and there's been a lot of debate about it, without a unanimous answer emerging yet.

Novices often fail to distinguish between genuinely random allocations and haphazard allocations. The latter often takes the form of the novice mentally deciding which group to put each person into, with no underlying principle, in the fond belief that this is the same as randomness. In practice, human beings are notoriously bad at producing random sequences of things – professional gamblers make and lose money via their awareness of this. Some researchers use random number tables to allocate subjects to groups; others toss coins; we have a well-used collection of dice. (In some fields, such as psychology, respondents often suspect deep meaning beneath the way in which they are allocated to a group in an apparently random manner, and sometimes rightly so; if you use transparent dice, and allow them to throw the dice, then this usually reassures them. Alternatively, you can simply omit to tell them that there is any other group to which they might have been assigned, if it's ethically appropriate for you to do so.) Yet another method which is widely used is to allocate the first volunteer to group A, the second to group B, the third to group A, and so on.

Once you've allocated respondents to groups, there's the question of what to do to them and when. Sometimes you're only doing one thing, like feeding them a particular diet. Other times, you're doing more than one thing – for instance, showing them photos of phytoplankton and asking them to rate each one for attractiveness. (Yes, we've had students do that, and very interest-ing results they got, too.) In the latter case, the obvious and wrong way to do it is to show each subject the same photos in the same order, 'to be systematic'. Why is this wrong? It's wrong because it would be systematic in the wrong way. The first photo would be systematically novel to the respondents; by the time they had got to the fifteenth photo, the novelty would have worn off, and the respondents would be systematically fed up with phytoplankton. The rat-ings for attractiveness for the first and last photos would probably be system-atically skewed just as a result of their being the first and last photos, regardless of how attractive they were. So what can you do about it? Again, you can randomise, so that there's no systematic order effect, or you can systematically permute the order in which each photo is shown, so that each photo is shown first the same number of times as each other photo. As usual, there's a lot of debate among purists about this, and there isn't a single correct answer, but there are answers which are definitely wrong (such as always showing photo one first), so you get a brownie point for choosing one of the reasonable answers.

Sometimes the things you do to the respondents will be more substantial. For instance, you might collect data from them once via card sorts and once via think-aloud technique, to see whether there are any systematic differences between the two techniques. If so, the sensible thing to do is to use card sorts first with one group, and think-aloud first with the other group, so you sort out the order effects for the two techniques.

That's fine for some procedures, but there are others where you can't do the two procedures on the same group, and have to use more than one group. Why should you want to do this? A classic instance is when the two procedures interact with each other. Suppose, for instance, that you want to compare two methods of teaching reading. You teach a group of 6-year-olds via method A, and then after three months you teach them via method B; you teach a second group with method B first, and then method A. What will happen? What will almost certainly happen is that the poor little things will get hideously con-fused, and it will all end in tears. If you want to compare method A and method B, then you'll need to test each on a separate group, to avoid inter-action effects. How do you make sure the two groups are truly comparable? That takes us back to our starting point, about identifying the relevant factors and controlling for them.

Sometimes, things are less drastic; one common device to reduce or elimin-ate interaction between two parts of an experiment is to use a distractor task in the middle, to wipe clean the respondent's memory of the first session. If the tasks are pretty simple and short, then distractor tasks are well worth consider-ing. Suppose, for instance, that you've been getting respondents to rate the attractiveness of brochures for tourist attractions in Australia and you also want them separately to rate the attractiveness of similar brochures for tourist attractions in Brazil, then you might give respondents a distractor task which is completely unrelated to tourist brochures, but which is heavily visual, to clear their visual memories of the first set of images as far as possible – for instance, playing solitaire.

Right, that's the basic picture. Time to recap.

Summary and technical terms

The account above deliberately used non-technical language, in the hope that this would encourage non-technical readers to keep reading. However, using non-technical language in a dissertation is inadvisable, partly because the non-technical language is imprecise, and partly because it sends a signal of cluelessness. How can you phrase all this so you can claim your richly deserved brownie points?

Lind allocated his experimental subjects to groups using *balanced* factors rather than *randomisation*. He *manipulated the independent variable* (diet) and observed the *dependent variable* which was affected by it (whether or not the sailors recovered). Readers of an etymological bent might remember these terms by imagining the dependent variable hanging down from the independent one like a pendant.

In the experiment investigating perceived attractiveness of images of phyto-plankton, the images were shown in different orders, to prevent *order effects* (such as the first or the last in a sequence being perceived systematically differ-ently). A classic example of an order effect is the *primacy effect*, where people tend to remember the first thing in a list better than things in the middle; the opposite of this is the *recency effect*, where people tend to remember the most recent thing in a list better than the ones in the middle.

Where we did different things to the same respondents, such as using both technique A and technique B, we used a *within-subject* design. When we used two different groups of respondents because of interference effects, and used technique A on one group and technique B on the other, then we used a *between-subject* design. When we systematically used technique A first with half the respondents in our within-subject design, and technique B first with the other half, we used a design *counterbalanced for order*.

Is this all there is to it? Not quite. There's a whole rich world of research design out there, but the description above at least covers the core concepts. You may be wondering about things like whether or not you need to have the same number of respondents in each group; if so, you're wondering about the right things. There is a literature on such topics. If you like your literature neat and structured, then you'll like the classic literature on experimental design; if you don't, you may be gratified to hear that there's a growing number of chatty and informal guides intended for normal mortals.

An important point about design of a formal experiment is that it inter-acts with statistical analysis. So, for instance, if you use equal numbers of respondents in your groups, then you can use some statistical tests that you couldn't use with unequal numbers. Similarly, if you use within-subject designs, then you can normally use more powerful stats on the same sample size and draw more powerful conclusions. To do this properly is a skill, and the wisest strategy at this point in your career is to do a bit of background reading, then ask a specialist for advice while you're still at the planning stage. Not many students do this; quite a lot of students instead plough ahead, collect a large pile of grot masquerading as data, and then drag it to the office of someone knowledgeable and ask for help, with predictable results. Wiser, then, to ask for help in advance.

On that edifying and generally applicable principle, we'll draw this section to a close, and move on to the chapter on generic advice. There are some issues which crop up with most types of research, so rather than duplicate them ad nauseam, we've gathered them together. This includes things like how to recruit subjects, how to plan sessions, practical points to remember, and things to beware.

3

Generic advice

Arranging a study: subjects, equipment, procedures, things to remember,
things to beware • Location and kit • Handling subjects • Recording

> *We were marvelously well equipped for our various purposes.*
> *(At the Mountains of Madness, p.14)*

Arranging a study: subjects, equipment, procedures, things to remember, things to beware

Recruiting subjects

One of the first things to think about when planning a piece of research is whether you will be able to get suitable subjects. If you're doing a survey, then you'll need to work out what sort of people you want, and work out how to find a suitable sample, and so forth, as discussed in the section on surveys and sampling. It's a lot of work. For most student projects, it's more sensible to study a defined small subset of the population, rather than trying to find a sample representative of the entire population of the country. The small subset may be bikers from Frome, or members of the St Luke's in the Wold church congregation, or second-year undergraduate maths students, for instance.

For most researchers, the most conveniently accessible subjects are under-graduate student volunteers. Finding subjects who don't fit into that category is considerably more hassle. The more responsible the position which someone holds, the less time they will have, and the less likely it is that they will be willing or able to help you. A touchingly high proportion of computer science students each year express an interest in doing a project involving a survey of the security strategies used by the main financial institutions; we then have to break the news to them that major banks may be reluctant to tell a final year undergraduate the innermost secrets of their defences against hackers and other sinners, even though that information would result in a project which would be really cool.

One way of recruiting subjects which is normally effective is to use your social and/or professional networks: if you know people in a relevant area, then you can ask them to be subjects, and/or ask them to recruit subjects for you. Your chances of success are affected by assorted variables, such as how charming you are, how much fun your research method is, how long the session will take, and so forth. Good quality coffee or tea, plus upmarket chocolate biscuits, are surprisingly effective inducements. Another effective inducement in some types of research is to offer participants a copy of your report (if that's permitted under your institution's rules; if in doubt, ask your supervisor). Some research has directly relevant implications for the subjects, and may in effect be giving them results for free which they would otherwise have to pay for: for instance, if you are comparing people's perceptions of the quality of major car manufacturers' websites. This is particularly likely to work if you are using advanced, sophisticated methods which give the impression that you might find something particularly interesting and useful, though a surprising number of people have faith in large questionnaire surveys. Another method which works well if you have good social skills is to phrase your recruiting in a flattering way – most people are all too ready to dispense advice to students who are good listeners, so they're likely to respond well to a carefully phrased request for advice to help your study. If they agree to give you ten minutes of their time, then at the end of ten minutes, make it clear that you're very grateful, and that you're prepared to leave now. Surprisingly often, if you've been a good listener, they will find that they can spare you another half hour, and perhaps more help than you'd initially asked for.

This issue interacts with your research design. For example, there's a solid literature on expertise, and on the basis of that literature it's a pretty safe bet that if you compare experts in your chosen domain with novices, then there will be marked differences between them, with all sorts of implications for training and so forth. You could therefore compare your smallish group of hard-to-get experts with a larger sample of easy-to-get novices (who usually happen to be undergraduate volunteers) and see what you find. This raises various issues of appropriate statistical tests for comparing different group sizes etc., so you need to think that through, but once you do, it's a pretty safe bet as a topic. What happens if you don't find differences between the novices and the experts? The answer is that this would be so unusual that it would be an interesting significant absence in its own right, so you win either way.

Most of the preceding paragraph assumes implicitly that you're dealing with volunteers. This is the case for most studies, for numerous reasons, most of them practical and/or ethical. There is, however, evidence that volunteers are different from non-volunteers; they're typically more intelligent and more outgoing, for instance. In other words, the volunteers doing your study are likely to be different from the rest of the population. This raises awkward questions about what proportion of the population are similar to your volunteers, and about the extent to which this limits the applicability of your findings to the population at large. It's normally considered bad manners to ask questions of this sort too loudly in research communities which depend heavily on volunteer subjects (and, similarly, which depend on undergraduate students as subjects, whether volunteers or conscripts in a lab class). We will therefore tactfully change the subject by reminding you to think carefully about sample sizes, allocation to groups, and the like. One favourite bad habit of beginners is to gather every bit of demographic data about the subjects – age, gender, occupation, etc. – that they can think of, on the grounds that this is what researchers do, and then fail to analyse the data in relation to these variables. It's wiser and more efficient to think very carefully about what your research questions will be, and then gather information efficiently. It's wiser still to pilot your study carefully, including piloting the data analysis, which will give you a much sounder idea of how much data you actually need, and what the best way is to collect and analyse it. You can then get a much more interesting, solid result from a much smaller amount of effort.

A closing thought is that it's easy to find yourself thinking that your subjects are awkward, unreliable agents of chaos. There are various reasons for this; the more interesting ones (i.e. the ones more likely to lead to fortune and glory for you) go beyond your subjects actually being awkward, unreliable agents of chaos. For instance, there's a literature on the experiment as a social situation, with its own rules of behaviour, which are known to 'good subjects' who are familiar with research (e.g. undergraduate volunteers) but which are not known to normal people. This leads into assorted questions about the validity of the research design: the subjects' apparent awkwardness and tendency to chaos might be an indicator that they're being asked to do an experimental task which is meaningless to them. It might also be an indicator that your lovingly crafted page of information for subjects has omitted crucial information for some reason (probably because you are so familiar with something that you've assumed that everyone else knows it as well). Another thing worth remembering is that your subjects are people; people have other things to do with their lives apart from being subjects for your research. It's wise to budget in an assumption that a proportion of subjects will turn up late to data collection sessions, or miss the session completely, for reasons such as being stuck in traffic, or having heard that your experimental task is boring and that you're short tempered and unpleasant. Try looking at it from their point of view, and where possible tailor what you're doing so that you're giving them a reason to want to help you; it makes life better for everyone.

Booking sessions

In an ideal world, this would be a straightforward task, too trivial to merit mentioning in a book such as this. In reality, there are issues both of practicalia and of research design which make this a task to take seriously.

You might think that the first thing you need to do, if you're doing lab-based work, is to recruit some subjects. Not quite. You'll need to recruit them, and this will involve some careful crafting of letters, notices, or whatever is appropriate, but first you need to think about research design.

If you just run the subjects in the order in which they turn up, then your results are likely to be systematically skewed. One source of distortion is that the first subjects will probably be different from the later subjects (usually keener, able to do things at short notice, so groups such as mature students with children will be under-represented in the early stages). Another source of distortion is yourself. For the first few subjects you'll probably be getting into your stride, possibly mastering a data collection technique which is new to you. For the last few, you'll probably be at home with the data collection technique, but starting to get bored with the study, and wishing you could get on with the data analysis. If you run all of one group of subjects first, and then all of the second group of subjects next, then your expertise, motivation, etc. will be systematically different between the groups, and this may well affect your results. A lot of research designs therefore include counterbalancing or randomisation of order – in other words, you systematically run your subjects in an order which removes any systematic order effects. If you're comparing experts and novices, for instance, you might run them in a sequence of 'expert – novice – expert – novice' and so forth (counterbalancing them), or you might flip a coin to determine whether each session in your schedule will involve an expert or a novice (randomising).

Either way, you'll need to draw up a schedule, listing subject number, subject group (for instance, expert or novice), name of the subject who will be put in that slot, and date and time of session. Figure 3.1 shows a typical schedule, with invented names, etc. This shows a fairly typical pattern, where the novices were easy to recruit, whereas the experts were harder to recruit, and the second expert has still not been recruited. For this reason, if you expect trouble getting access to subjects, and you need to control the order in which you run them, you need to book the sessions early. Note also that the expert was available at 8: for some groups of subjects, you'll need to fit in around their hours, which may be pretty antisocial.

There are various ways of organising session dates and times. It's often useful to use both a schedule like the one in Figure 3.1, which is structured around the subject numbers and groups, and also a weekplanner schedule, listing all the slots in which you can run subjects during the week. The reason for using two is that with the first type of schedule it's easy to check that you've allocated subject numbers and groups correctly, but it can be hard to keep track of the session times and dates, since they'll often have to be rescheduled because of

Subject number	Group	Name	Date	Time
1	Expert	Chris Green	22.3.2001	8–9
2	Novice	Robin Brown	15.3.2001	10–11
3	Expert			
4	Novice	Lesley Grey	17.3.2001	2–3

Figure 3.1 A partially completed schedule

things like subjects being ill and having to cancel the original session. With the second type, it's easier to keep track of time, so you don't end up booking two people into the same slot, but it's harder to keep track of who has been allocated which subject number.

Once you've sorted all this out, then you're about ready to start recruiting subjects. There's a section elsewhere in this book on the underlying theory behind this – convenience sampling, quota sampling, and so forth. That's important, and you need to get it right. Once you've worked out the type of sampling you're using, then you're ready to start the grind of recruiting. Gordon was once helped on an informal basis by the wonderful Karen, who had awesome social networks and social skills to match. Once she knew the type of person needed as a subject for a study, she would vanish discreetly into the distance, and a steady stream of suitable subjects would then turn up, with the opening line that Karen had sent them. If you know someone like that, make it very clear that you value them highly; they're wonderful. If you don't, then you need to start legwork. One route is to put up posters and/or circulate letters and emails, describing the sort of person you're looking for, and saying just enough about your research to entice them to sign up. If you go down this route, then make sure that you don't spam (i.e. send out illegal quantities and types of unsolicited email) or flypost (i.e. put up posters where you shouldn't – if you make that mistake, it doesn't require a Sherlock Holmes to work out who's responsible for the poster, since it will have your name somewhere prominent on it). If you do this and you're lucky, you might actually get some subjects. You might not. It's a wise idea to use your social skills, and chat with someone relevant over a cup of coffee. For instance, if you want to study risk perception among extreme sports enthusiasts, then a cup of coffee with the secretary of the local extreme sports society would be a good place to start. They'll want to know what you're doing, how long it will take, why you're doing it, and so forth. They'll also wonder (usually politely) what's in it for the long-suffering subjects, which is a fair question. If you're doing good research, then it should make sense of something previously obscure, and that should in turn be useful to people in the field you're studying. With extreme sports, for instance, practitioners might be very interested in a finding which will help them understand their sport better and might help their performance. If all goes well, then the relevant person might agree to have a word with potential subjects and do some recruiting for you. If so, be appreciative, and remember to thank them properly at the end of your study. Remember to be honest and realistic about how long the task will take, and to tell them what you can about what the task involves (often you can't tell them everything because of the nature of the design, but people are usually understanding about this).

In case you're wondering, it's usual to run subjects separately, rather than trying to run more than one at once, and it's also usual to ask them not to talk to potential subjects about the experiment after they've finished (if, for instance, they happen to have housemates who have also decided to volunteer as subjects). Some will talk to their friends anyway; others won't, particularly if they decide that you're a decent sort. Life's like that sometimes; there isn't a brilliant way round this one, so it's usually a good idea to avoid experiments which depend entirely on the subjects not having prior knowledge of what you're going to do. In practice, this isn't usually too much of a problem; if in doubt, ask advice from someone who's played this game a few times, such as your supervisor.

Important note

Unless there's good reason to do otherwise, you should work on the assumption that all subjects are genuinely anonymous, and should not show to anyone the list saying which people have been allocated to which subject number. In some cases, there may even be ethical issues about letting your supervisor see the list – for instance, if you've been studying cheating among students in your department. If in any doubt, then sort this out with your supervisor at the earliest stages of planning your project. Remember that subjects need to be genuinely anonymous, particularly if you're investigating something sensitive: a statement in your report such as: 'Subject 5 was a 43-year-old working in the campus bookshop, who used to be a heroin addict and prostitute' is unlikely to protect that individual's identity for long, and is likely to lead to character-forming encounters either with the British justice system or someone large in a dark alley.

Location and kit

We landed all our drilling apparatus, dogs, sledges, tents, provisions, gasoline tanks, experimental ice-melting outfit, cameras . . . aeroplane parts, and other accessories.

(*At the Mountains of Madnesss*, p.17)

Before you encounter your first subject, you need to sort out the location for your study. Forethought, piloting and attention to detail will all make your life much better at this point. If you're doing an observational study in the field (for instance, watching shoppers' behaviour in a town centre) then you need to find a good pitch in which to lurk, and this can be non-trivial – other people also lurk in town centres such as *Big Issue* vendors, buskers, drunks and market researchers, for example, and all of these will be experienced in finding places with good visibility, out of the draughts and the rain. You might need legal clearance for some types of data collection – if in doubt, ask your supervisor or the long-suffering projects co-ordinator. If you're running subjects in a shared office, then you need to reach an agreement with your office mates about getting some privacy: it's not much fun trying to calm down subjects who have just been on the receiving end of sarcastic comments about their clothing from a tactless office mate. If you're running them in your own space, then you need to think about security – what happens if someone who has signed up as a subject starts behaving in an intimidating manner and you're all alone in your student house?

A lot of research involves kit of some sort, ranging from recording equipment to clipboards to laptop computers. Kit usually doesn't like being in the rain, being knocked on to the floor, or having coffee spilled on it. It also has an interesting habit of malfunctioning at the worst possible time. You need to practise with the kit until you're completely familiar with it and can fix the commonest problems fluently. Most research also requires space to spread things out, so it's a good idea to try permutations until you find one that works well. With card sorts, for instance, you need a good-sized flat surface such as a desktop on which to spread the cards: simple enough in principle, but you need to make sure that there aren't any sticky patches on the desktop from an injudiciously dropped chocolate biscuit, and that the cards can't slip into any awkward crevices, such as underneath a desktop computer.

For some reason, subjects seem a lot more happy about being audio recorded than video recorded. If you're using either method, you'll need the subject's agreement; if they don't agree, then don't argue, just accept it and cancel that session while maintaining a friendly, professional attitude. Video data can take a lot of time, skill and effort to analyse, so think carefully before going down this route. With audio recording, there's plenty of high quality kit available to choose from, with more appearing every month. The newer computer-compatible technologies have a lot of advantages over the old audio tapes, but also a few disadvantages. One thing you need to watch for is whether the allegedly computer-compatible kit is actually compatible with your particular computer. One positive advantage of the old technology for some purposes is that you may get interesting information from subjects when they see you take the tape out of the machine – they quite often relax and tell you the real version, as opposed to the version they've given you on tape. With a physical tape, they can see you take it out of the machine, and they know they're not being recorded; with the newer technologies, they're not so sure. We've tended to use language like 'analysing straight off the tape' partly out of habit and partly for brevity.

Handling subjects

On one side of the door stood a rack of savage whips.
(*The Case of Charles Dexter Ward*, p.277)

Once all the preliminaries have been sorted out, the subject arrives (assuming that you're not doing an observational field study – we'll discuss those later). If it's your very first subject, you're likely to be nervous and forget things. This is where piloting comes in handy: piloting with someone familiar and friendly is a nice, gentle way to get some practice. It's also a good idea to have a list to remind you what to do. You may find it useful to prepare a subject pack in advance, and to work through that sheet by sheet. The first thing to do with the subject is to make them feel welcome, even if they've turned up late and dripped water all over your floor. Without subjects helping you, you won't get any research done, so be genuinely grateful. We usually offer coffee and biscuits, but this needs to be thought through – with some research designs, they can do the task while sipping and crunching in a companionable manner, but usually they need to have the coffee either before the data collection or after it, rather than during. Around this point, you should check whether they need to leave early, or there's any other complication, and you should check that they know how long the session is expected to last. You should also note the current time on your own record sheet, so you know what time to stop.

You now need to describe the task to the respondents, and explain what viewpoint you want them to adopt for it (for instance, whether you want them to comment on a web page design from an aesthetic or a consumer viewpoint, or whether you want them to answer questions in their role as office worker or their role as a father). It's a good idea to include a demonstration of what you want, using an example which won't cue them in a particular direction. For example, if you want the respondents to comment on the factors affecting their choice of car, you might demonstrate how you would comment on the factors affecting your choice of house, such as whether it's semi-detached or detached: these factors are clearly irrelevant to choice of car, but this demonstration can show to the respondent the degree of detail that you'd like, etc. Some students worry about whether even this is too much intervention. The trouble is that if you don't give enough explanation, the respondents will either keep asking for more detail, or will invent their own rationales, which can lead into some very strange territory, so on balance it's usually wiser to do a demonstration. If in doubt, you can always pilot to see what effect, if any, the demonstration has.

Procedure

This is where the subjects actually do something. Quite what they will do is another question; it doesn't always bear much relation to what you're expecting. Most students have great faith in their inadvertent ability to influence subjects' behaviour, and agonise at length about 'bias' if they're of one ideological persuasion, or dismiss 'bias' as having been eliminated by their brilliant experimental design or their brilliant professionalism, if they're of a different persuasion. It doesn't work quite like that. In practice, subjects' responses can be radically different depending on the viewpoint from which they are doing the experimental task for you: in that sense, it can be horribly easy to produce unintended effects. That's why it's so important to think carefully about the wording in your instructions to subjects when it comes to the viewpoint from which you are asking them to answer, and the nature of the task itself. However, once subjects have opted for a particular viewpoint and understanding of the experimental task, they can be remarkably resistant to even blatant attempts to influence their responses. There's an interesting literature about this, with concepts such as the 'good subject' prominent in the debate. The debate looks likely to continue for some time. The main points of relative agreement which have emerged are that (a) sometimes subjects' answers are artificial products of the experimental task, but sometimes they're not; and (b) one ubiquitous source of problems is the subconscious tendency for researchers to steer the data analysis in the direction that they want, for instance via minor errors in tabulation. This latter problem appears to be genuinely subconscious – it's rare for researchers to engage in outright fraud, but quite common for them to make minor errors in adding numbers while tabulating data, and these errors tend to be in the direction that suits their hunches and prejudices. This is one reason that it's best practice to use independent judges who don't particularly care what you've found.

During the data collection, your task is to appear pleasant, professional and interested, while not being obtrusive. It is incredibly inadvisable to be judgemental, to correct them, to suggest answers to them, to ask them leading questions, to start conversations with passers-by about where to have lunch today, or to make jokes about their profession (yes, we've seen all of these, and more). It can be challenging to maintain this façade of professionalism while listening to long-winded and factually inaccurate ramblings, but it's a useful skill for later life, such as when you're in committee meetings with your line manager and various other individuals higher in the food chain than you are, and when the outward semblance of being a loyal party member will improve your chances of a better life in this world. There's more detail on this in the section on face-to-face interactions with respondents.

It's advisable to watch for the types of skills that the respondent is using – for instance, whether they're using pattern matching or compiled skills (these are described in the section on choosing data collection technique; the key point is that neither of them involves conscious deliberation). The presence of either of these would be grounds for caution about taking the respondent's comments on the relevant topic at face value. For instance, if they see something and immediately identify it, then they're probably using pattern matching; if they then spend ten minutes explaining how they knew what it was, that may be true, but it's derived from a different type of mental processing from the type they were using to make the identification. If they do something so fast that there's clearly no conscious deliberation involved (for instance, clicking on a series of options in some software so fast that they're clearly not needing to read the screen), then they're probably using a compiled skill, i.e. one so habitualised that they no longer need to think about it. The presence of either of these is not a bad thing in itself, but to investigate the relevant skill you'll need to use other techniques (probably experimentation and/or observation).

Recording

So my method has been, while keeping as closely as possible to the general sense of the words that were actually used, to make the speakers say what, in my opinion, was called for in each situation.

(*Thucydides*, I, 22)

With some techniques, such as card sorts and repertory grids, it's easy to keep accurate records during the session. With others, especially if you're gathering data in natural language, it isn't. Even if you're good at shorthand, you won't be able to keep an accurate verbatim record of what your subjects are saying. (You might be able to keep a fairly accurate record of what you think they mean, but that's not the same thing, and isn't good enough for this purpose.) Typically you get longish periods of silence, interspersed with short periods of fast talking; what the respondents say often appears incoherent when you listen to it in detail. We normally use a tape recorder to do an audio recording. That seems to be less intrusive to most respondents than a video recording, for various reasons. For some purposes, you'll not have much option and will have to video record, in which case you'll need to do some careful piloting to find the least intrusive set-up. It's inadvisable to use hidden cameras unless that's well established in the particular field where you're working – hidden cameras can lead you into all sorts of ethical issues.

Before starting the data collection, you should check that the subject has no objection to being recorded. If they have any objections, then don't argue, just stop the session immediately, and tell them with genuine politeness that there's no problem, and you won't take any more of their time. You might want to offer them coffee and biscuits to show there are no hard feelings. The reason for this is that if you persuade them to be recorded, and they subsequently complain that you pressured them into it in an unethical way, then you're facing deep trouble. At an ethical level, pressuring them is wrong; at a practical level, it's asking for problems. Wiser to be pleasant, and to view it as a chance to catch up on some paperwork in the rest of the slot.

Respondents vary widely in how much they say and in how comprehensible they are. Some talk continuously; others say hardly anything unless prompted. The usual convention is that if the respondent is silent for more than a specified time, such as five seconds, then you use a standard prompt, such as: 'Could you tell me what you're thinking about now?' to get them to say what they're thinking. (Preparing the list of standard prompts is one of the things that you do when planning your procedure; the list might well be modified in light of what you encounter during the piloting.)

If you're audio recording, then a classic mistake is to let respondents use terms like 'this one' and 'that one' which make perfect sense when you can see where they're pointing, but which will be completely meaningless when you're listening to the audio tape six weeks later. If they start doing this, then it's a good idea to interject some tactful remark along the lines of 'the one in the top left corner' to clarify what they mean.

End of session

At the end of the session, you should check that they have actually finished, especially if they haven't finished the experimental task (sometimes they're just having a think, and other times they don't realise there's more to do). If they've run out of things to say, then don't pressure them or embarrass them. It's helpful to all parties if you keep an eye on the time and stop the session when it's due to stop – the subject may have another appointment immediately after the session. Most researchers have to fit data collection into one-hour slots or less, and the one-hour slots normally end a few minutes before the hour, to give everyone time to sort themselves out before whatever they're doing next.

Having stopped the session, it's a good idea to take the tape out of the recorder and start writing the subject's number, etc. on it. This makes it clear to the subject that they're no longer being recorded, and they often make interesting off-the-record remarks at this point. Often you won't ethically be able to use these remarks (sometimes you will), but they can be invaluable as a reality check. For instance, subjects may remark that you'd be horrified to know how things are actually done in their organisation. That's depressing at one level – it suggests that they've just spent an hour telling you a front version divorced from reality – but at another level, it's telling you that there's a juicy back version just waiting to be explored. Quite how to explore the back version is another question, but the fact that your subject has mentioned it is a useful start, and you might get some helpful leads from using your social skills while there's no tape in the recorder. (This is one advantage of using older techno-logy, rather than digital recorders, where the subjects may not be sure whether you're still recording or not.) If you reply with something along the lines of 'Really? How interesting. Do tell me more' then there's a fair chance that you'll be given some useful insights.

Analysis

With natural language data, the method of analysis is usually determined by the overall context and purpose of your study (unlike, say, card sorts, where there's a fairly standard recipe for analysis). For some purposes, you can do analysis straight off the tape. For others, you need to transcribe the tapes, which is a pretty soul-destroying exercise. You need to transcribe your own tapes, rather than hiring someone else: the tapes will make some sense to you, but even a skilled audio typist will have trouble making sense of them. Also, other people do odd things when transcribing. The transcription needs to be as utterly accurate as you can make it – ungrammatical bits, swearwords, pauses, ums and ers, the whole works. All those bits tell you important things. For instance, if you're assessing a piece of software using reports, and a mild-mannered respondent suddenly starts swearing at the software, then that's extremely important information; the last thing you want is for some well-meaning audio typist to leave out the rude words. Unlikely? That's hap-pened to us and to people we know; you too could end up paying someone for a transcript, then throwing it away because it's useless, and doing the transcription yourself.

Transcribing is usually boring, often demanding (because you may need to listen to the same bit several times before you're sure what the respondent is saying), time-consuming (an hour of tape can take up to ten hours to tran-scribe, depending on how loquacious the respondent is, and whether or not you can touch type), and physically gruelling (since you're engaged in a very repetitive physical activity, with a risk of backache and repetitive strain injury).

Usually the analysis consists of content analysis or discourse analysis; these are described in their own sections. If you've phrased your research question elegantly, then you may be able to do content analysis directly off the tapes, without having to transcribe the sessions. For instance, if you're simply noting whether or not each respondent mentioned a particular topic, then you can do that straight off the tapes. If you're counting how often each respondent mentions a particular topic, then you may be able to do that straight off the tapes, but it's horribly easy to lose count if some well-meaning colleague or friend drops by to ask if you fancy a quick coffee. If they do it when you're 39 minutes into a 45-minute tape, and you have to start again, then you might not be too well disposed towards them.

That's about it on generic advice. As you may have guessed by now, it's a world in its own right, and we've only given a notebook sketch of it, not a millimetrically accurate map, but it should help you avoid the worst of the swamps that students tend to encounter. The next chunk of the book deals with the methods that you can use to collect data. Most students are unaware that any techniques exist other than interviews and questionnaires; a lot of students don't realise that using the correct technique can get you better data for less effort, and can answer a whole batch of questions that you can't get at with interviews and questionnaires.

4

Data collection

Data collection methods: the methods, and choosing and using the appropriate method • Reports: getting respondents to talk about how things happen • Observation: watching what happens • Card sorts: getting respondents to categorise things • Laddering: unpacking the respondents' concepts systematically • Repertory grids: a systematic representation for respondents' knowledge • Interviews: asking people questions • Face-to-face interactions with respondents: the nuts and bolts of asking questions • Questionnaires: when to use, when not to use, which questions to ask, what format to use

> *The gaps of information which the alienists noticed [were] brought out by adroit questioning.*
>
> (*The Case of Charles Dexter Ward*, p.146)

Data collection methods: the methods, and choosing and using the appropriate method

One thing from which you are unlikely to suffer when it comes to data collection methods is lack of choice. There are many methods, ranging from undisclosed participant observation to repertory grid technique, and from illuminative incident technique to laddering, not to mention the usual suspects of interviews and questionnaires. Which do you choose, and why? What methods are there anyway? Why are there so many of them? Does it make any difference which you choose? This section tackles these questions and a few more.

The first thing to remember, as often in research, is the three more or less noble principles: cockroach, cabinetmaking and cartography. These can be very useful for reducing the size of the problem.

From the cockroach point of view, if you mention to your supervisor that you are toying with the idea of using implication grids, and are treated to a 16-minute tirade about the methodological heresies on which implication grids are based, then it is time to scuttle back into your nice safe crevice and find a method which will not lead to the equivalent of an encounter with a very large boot. Within any given discipline, some methods will be anathemised, and others will be grimly tolerated. If you set yourself up as an evangelist for one of these methods, either deliberately or out of ignorance, then you are looking for trouble, and you need to ask yourself whether this is a bit of trouble that is worth it. Often the reasons for the anathema are perfectly sensible ones, and you may be able to learn a great deal from uncovering this background. On other occasions, the reasons are more questionable, but that is another story.

The second step in reducing the problem space is the cabinetmaking metaphor. Does the method you're thinking of using demonstrate a required or desirable skill for someone doing research in your chosen area? If you're a sociologist, for instance, then knowing about participant observation (if you can get through the ethical hurdles associated with it) is a useful skill, whereas cognitive causal maps are more peripheral. You obviously need to get the essential skills on to your CV; it's also highly advisable to get a range of desirable but not essential skills on to it as well. Among other things, you never know when they might come in handy. As usual, a combination of intelligent reading of the literature and having coffee with a well-informed colleague can give you a pretty good idea of what's desirable and what's essential.

The third step involves the cartography metaphor. If a method gets past the cockroach test and the cabinetmaking test, does it offer the chance to add to the map of your chosen area? Using methods which have not been used before in a given area can lead to important new insights. For instance, sociologists using undisclosed participant observation gained a lot of new understanding of psychiatric wards and of urban gangs, which would probably not have been gained using other techniques.

These three principles are useful for eliminating some options and for shortlisting others, but they still leave quite a lot of room for choice. There are various other criteria for choosing techniques. One is practicality: what resources are needed for each technique? Another is the output: what sort of data do you get out of each technique, and what can you do with that data? A third involves the types of data to which you can obtain access via each technique: what types of knowledge, memory or skill are you trying to reach, and which techniques can give you that access?

Those readers who have a taste for biographical snippets may be interested to know that there is a paper discussing these issues in considerable detail, co-authored by one of the authors of this book (Maiden, N.A.M. & Rugg, G. 1996. ACRE: a framework for acquisition of requirements. *Software Engineering Journal* 11(3), 248–257). It would be pleasant to report that the paper is a masterpiece of lucidity, suitable for persons of the meanest understanding, but unfortunately that would not be utterly accurate – it's a brute of a paper, written to a deadline, and with software engineers as the intended audience. It does, however, do a fair job of tersely summarising the key issues in method selection, with pointers to key literatures. The following pages build on the concepts covered in that paper.

Memory and methods

In a simple world, virtue would always be rewarded, bad people would be easily identifiable because they wore black hats, and memory would be memory. In practice, however, things are more complex. Psychological research has uncovered enough different types of memory to keep a swarm of psychologists out of mischief for decades: episodic memory and semantic memory, long-term memory and short-term memory, active memory and passive memory, to name a few. If you add to this the number of different skill and knowledge types which have been discovered, then the list becomes a fair size. If these had no relevance to data collection methods, then this topic would be of only passing significance for anyone other than psychologists. Fortunately for anyone who appreciates a new challenge, this topic has far-reaching implications for data collection methods.

A classic example is short-term memory. This is quite different from long-term memory; the usual analogy is with computers storing information in RAM and on disk respectively. Short-term memory, like RAM, is ephemeral and of limited capacity; a glitch such as a distraction or a power failure (for humans and computers respectively) will normally lead to the information stored there being lost for ever, whereas information stored to long-term memory or to disk will remain there for years. Human short-term memory can hold about seven chunks of information (enough for a phone number or a car registration number) for a few seconds; you can retain these contents in short-term memory by repeating them continuously, but once you stop doing that, they will be lost from short-term memory for ever.

So what? you might wonder. Well, if you want to know what people are thinking about when they're making decisions (such as deciding what product to buy from a website) or doing complex tasks (such as flying an aircraft), then those people will almost certainly be using the relevant information via short-term memory. Since short-term memory is ephemeral, once they complete the task, they will almost certainly not remember the details of the information they were using, unless something has caused it to be transferred to long-term memory. No amount of detailed interviewing can recover the memory, because it just isn't there to recover. They might well have a vivid idea of what information they were using, and it will quite probably be incorrect. The only way of getting at the information directly is to have them think aloud while they are doing the task. This is fine if they are doing something straightforward such as choosing products from a website, but can lead into obvious problems if they're doing something more demanding, such as avoiding a mid-air collision. There are ways round this problem, and there is the longstanding question of how short-term memory interacts with long-term memory, but those are part of another story; the main point is that some types of memory simply can't be reached via interviews or questionnaires, so you need to use a variety of methods depending on the type of memory, skill, or whatever it is that you're trying to get at. That's what this section is about.

Maiden and Rugg, developing work by Rugg and McGeorge, put together a framework of four main types of memory (and skill, communication type, etc; memory for short), with various subdivisions. This brought together a wide range of concepts which were well established in other disciplines, so we can't claim much credit for originality in that bit, but the way we put them together was new, and we claim modest credit for that. We use a modified version of that framework in this book. The four main types are:

- predictive knowledge
- explicit knowledge
- semi-tacit knowledge
- tacit knowledge.

Please note that some of these terms are used in different senses in other literatures (particularly 'tacit knowledge').

Predictive knowledge is what you use when asked about how you would react to some future situation (for instance, how you would feel about working with a person from a particular group, or whether you would pay more for energy from a sustainable source). We have used this term to make the point that answers to questions of this sort involve people predicting their own attitudes, behaviours, etc. We have made that point because there is a lot of literature showing that people are surprisingly bad at this – for instance, the literature on attitude theory, which investigates the (usually poor) fit between people's stated attitudes and their actual behaviour, or the literature on judgement and decision making, which investigates things such as people's ability to predict their own future behaviour. The obvious way to tackle this is via scenarios, though other methods are possible with a little thought.

Explicit knowledge is knowledge to which we have valid, conscious, introspective access under all normal circumstances. Most of this is episodic memory (about episodes in the past, such as the lecture where Dr West told us about his work in France) or semantic memory (about facts not linked to a specific episode, such as knowing that Paris is the capital of France). Semantic memory may be codified to varying degrees – for instance, experienced teachers will have organised their knowledge of their topic so that it can be presented to learners in a more structured fashion. Explicit memory can be handled via any elicitation technique, though you need to remember that it is dependent on memory, which is liable to various biases and distortions, both systematic and random.

Semi-tacit knowledge is knowledge to which we have valid, conscious, introspective access under some conditions. This may take various forms. Some forms of semi-tacit knowledge involve the way that the human brain is set up – short-term memory is a good example. Others involve the way that humans communicate – for instance, most professions have one version of reality which is shown to outsiders (the 'front' version) and a different one which is only shown to group members (the 'back') version. We return to this topic below in more detail. For semi-tacit knowledge, it's important to choose an elicitation technique, or a combination of techniques, best suited to the relevant form of semi-tacit knowledge.

Tacit knowledge, in the strict sense in which we use it, involves knowledge or skills to which we have no valid introspective access – in other words, we can use the skills, but we do not know exactly what they are or how we use them. A classic example is an expert car driver, who can change gear perfectly, but who would typically not be able to say in which order they did which actions for the gear change. A high proportion of expert behaviour involves tacit knowledge in one form or another, raising difficulties for anyone trying to study it. We also return to this topic below in more detail.

Because by definition people don't have valid access to their own tacit skills, they can't articulate their knowledge about these skills, so the only way to get access to the skills is indirectly, via observation and/or experimentation.

Semi-tacit knowledge and tacit knowledge can each be subdivided into various categories which have serious implications for choice of data collection method. The main categories are listed below.

Semi-tacit knowledge

Short-term memory is the mental 'scratchpad' that we use for storing information for a few seconds. It has very limited capacity (about seven chunks of information), and its contents are gone for ever after a few seconds. If you're trying to find out about the contents of short-term memory, then you have to collect data during the few seconds that those contents are in memory. You can usually do this using think-aloud technique, but in some cases this interferes with the task being performed; in such cases, you may be able to use experimentation by systematically manipulating variables during a simulation of the task, and seeing what this does to performance.

Recognition and recall are passive and active memory respectively; recognition is typically much stronger than recall. If you ask someone what they want from a good web page, for instance, they will typically recall a lot of features, but if you then show them a web page and ask them which features are good, they will then typically recognise a lot of other features that they forgot the first time round. Similarly, if you ask them how to perform a task, they will typically remember most of the necessary steps but not all of them. Simply showing the respondent the relevant item, or getting them to perform the relevant task, will usually elicit the information that was missed during recall.

Front and back versions are the versions of reality which groups present to the outside world and to group members respectively. The front version is usually sanitised, to give a good impression, but doesn't necessarily involve intention to deceive. Most researchers are outsiders to the group they're studying, so they're usually given the front version. This is a particularly important issue if you're investigating sensitive topics. You can get at back versions in various ways, such as using projective techniques, or participant observation or indirect observation.

Preverbal construing is when someone is making distinctions consistently, but can't put their finger on how they're doing it. This overlaps with the various forms of tacit knowledge described below, but differs from them in that it typically involves categorisation rather than physical tasks. What sometimes happens during data collection is that the respondent suddenly realises how they were making the distinctions, and can describe it clearly and consistently, which is another thing differentiating it from tacit knowledge, where there isn't the same feeling that the difference is on the tip of their tongue. For instance, during one of our data collection sessions, an archaeologist respondent suddenly realised that they had been able to discriminate between two pottery types because one type had an angular base, and the other had a slightly rounded base.

Taken-for-granted knowledge involves one of Grice's principles of communication. To keep communication down to manageable lengths, we don't state explicitly anything which we can assume the other person to know. For example, we don't say: 'My aunt, who is a woman' because we can take it for granted that other people know that aunts are women. This is fine while it works, but it often goes wrong because we are wrong in our assumptions about what the other person knows. This is a particularly nasty problem because we typically take something for granted precisely because it is important and/or routine. The outcome is that important and/or routine things, which are often the most important, are also the most likely to be missed. Taken for granted knowledge can usually be caught by using observation or think-aloud technique, where the respondent works through the relevant task; it can also often be caught using laddering, because of the remorselessly systematic way in which laddering unpacks each concept mentioned into its constituent parts.

Not-worth-mentioning knowledge is similar to taken-for-granted knowledge in that a filtering process is involved. The difference is that if you detect some taken-for-granted knowledge which had been missed, the respondent will typically look incredulous and/or pitying and say something to the effect of: 'Yes, of course that's important; doesn't everyone know that?' With not-worth-mentioning knowledge, the difference is what you'd expect: respondents will typically tell you that something wasn't worth mentioning. This is a problem because often the knowledge involved is a low-level skill on which lots of other higher level skills are built – the craft skills which are viewed as too lowly to merit mention in the textbooks. Much of this book is about craft skills of this sort. Again, think-aloud technique, observation and laddering will usually pick this up. It's particularly important for training, though it's also important for education, and has been seriously neglected until recently.

Tacit knowledge

Compiled skills are skills which were once explicit, but which have become so practised that the respondent can now perform them without needing to think about them. Because they're habitualised, they can be performed much faster and more efficiently than the explicit version – the classic example is the expert car driver compared to the novice driver. The problem is that the respondent will usually have forgotten the explicit version years ago, and will therefore be unable to tell you much about how they now perform the task. Professionals in competitive sport use a lot of compiled skills, but are usually unaware of the literature relating to this, and use language such as 'going with the flow'. By definition, the respondent doesn't have access to what they're doing in compiled skills, so anything they tell you has to be taken with a large pinch of salt. The best way to get at it is via observation and experimentation. The best way to disrupt it is to ask the respondent to think about what they're doing: this will usually cause huge interference effects, and do things like make expert skiers fall over on a downhill run. A useful rule of thumb is that if the person can perform the task while maintaining a non-trivial conversation, then a compiled skill is involved. Compiled skills need a lot of continual practice to acquire, so the presence of a compiled skill tells you some useful things about what the respondent has been spending time on.

Implicit learning differs from compiled skills in that the respondent learns something without ever being consciously aware of how they are performing the task. There is considerable debate about its nature, but the key features appear to be that it involves seeing lots (typically thousands) of examples, with very rapid feedback after each example saying which category the example belongs to, or whether the learner's guess is correct (depending on the task). A lot of the things referred to as 'gut feel' involve implicit learning.

Pattern matching is a mechanism which cuts across many of the categories mentioned above, but its essence is tacit. It's what we use when we do something like recognising someone's face: we recognise the face as a whole, i.e. as a pattern, rather than identifying it feature by feature. Experts typically use a lot of pattern matching, regardless of domain; for instance, a good doctor will have a good idea of what is wrong with a patient before hearing a word from the patient, simply by pattern matching the patient's gait, posture, etc. against examples that they have seen previously. Some forms of pattern matching only require seeing one example (for instance, once you've seen one computer mouse, that's enough to identify any future examples you see). Other forms require large numbers of examples, and overlap with implicit learning (for instance, learning to identify conchoidal ripples on a struck flint as opposed to a potlid fracture in archaeology). The thing to watch for is when someone is actually performing a task via pattern matching, and then explains it to you using the explicit knowledge version, which may be equally true but utterly different. If we have a tame geologist in the audience, one elegant demonstration of this is to ask them to identify a rock sample: they usually identify it before it's even been put on the table, via pattern matching, and they can then talk for ages (at least half an hour in some cases – we timed them) about how to identify it using explicit knowledge. As a rough rule of thumb, if the respondent can reach a decision within a second or two, they're probably using pattern matching.

The following sections describe a variety of techniques for data collection. These include reports (when the respondent reports on something), observation (when you watch someone doing something), card sorts (when you get respondents to group things), laddering (where you use a small set of questions to unpack the respondents' knowledge systematically), repertory grids (where you get respondents to represent their knowledge in a matrix-like format that lets you do powerful statistical analysis), and the familiar interview and questionnaires. Interviews and questionnaires are widely used by students, usually badly – because they're so familiar, it's easy to overlook the issues involved in using them properly.

Reports: getting respondents to talk about how things happen

It's one of B.J.'s little eccentricities, burying people by the garage.
(People of Darkness, p.6)

Overview

Reports are, in one sense, what you'd expect from the name. They involve someone reporting what they did (self-report) or reporting someone else's activities (report of others). People of a tidy-minded disposition can further divide them into reports of what's happening now, reports of what happened in the past, and reports of what is expected to happen in the future. Such persons will doubtless be glad to hear that each of these categories is already recognised, and will probably be less glad to hear that the names for these categories are somewhat unsystematic. Figure 4.1 shows the various permutations, and various named techniques that fit into each slot.

Person involved	Past activities	Present activities	Future activities
Oneself	Critical incident technique or offline self-report	online self-report (aka think-aloud technique; aka concurrent verbalisation)	Scenario
Someone else	Critical incident technique	online report of others	Scenario

Figure 4.1 Types of report

Note that critical incident technique is not the same as offline self-report; more on that later. There are various techniques which are variants on these six main themes; the main variables, however, are the tense, and who is involved.

Reports are useful in various obvious ways, and various less obvious ways. One obvious use is in giving people the chance to explain how something happens in their own words. This gives you an insight into how they perceive it, and how they mentally organise their own perceptions of it. Experts typically have richer and more highly structured categorisation than novices. Getting an expert to report on how they do something, and comparing that with results from a novice tackling the same task, can give you all sorts of information that can be used for training, task design, and so forth. It can also give you useful insights into something – for instance, the reasons for people doing what they do, which can be very useful even if the reasons turn out to be based on serious misunderstandings (in fact, this can be particularly useful when the reasons are based on misunderstandings, in contexts such as public health education or safety training). The results can be surprisingly different from what you expected.

Less obviously, but at least as importantly, reports give you access to types of memory, skill and knowledge which you can't get at with interviews and questionnaires (or with most other techniques, come to that). One important type is short-term memory (also known as working memory, though there are debates about whether the two terms are completely synonymous). This is a completely different type of memory from long-term memory, which is the sort we use to remember things like what our names are, or what the capital of France is. Long-term memory has enormous capacity and lasts for decades; short-term memory is more like a scratchpad, with a capacity of about seven pieces of information and a duration of a few seconds; it's what you use in situations such as when someone gives you a piece of information over the phone, and you need to remember it until you find a pen and paper to write it down. It's no accident that phone numbers and car registration numbers are typically about seven digits long: they were designed with this sort of memory in mind.

When we're doing tasks which involve processing lots of information (such as driving a car, or handling queries), we use short-term memory a lot as a temporary store. It's swift and efficient; the disadvantage is that it's ephemeral. Unless we happen to have shunted something from short-term memory into long-term memory, then once it's gone from short-term memory, it's gone for ever. The usual analogy is losing data when your computer crashes – anything that was saved to disk (analogous to long-term memory) is safe, but anything that wasn't is lost and gone. This means that after we've finished a task, we won't remember everything that we did, or everything that we used.

This is a serious problem for anyone trying to gain an accurate understanding of how someone tackles a complex task. For instance, if you're trying to design a flight control system for an aircraft, then you need to strike a balance between giving the pilots the information that they need on the one hand, and overloading them with detail on the other. On a more humble level, if you're trying to design a website to tell the world how wonderful you and your work are, then you're in some ways the worst person in the world to tackle this job, because you're so familiar with yourself and your work that you'll have real problems envisaging things from the site visitor's viewpoint. What's the balance between detail and clarity? How will they interpret what they see? Interviewing them afterwards will only give you a part of the answer, the part which happens to have made it into long-term memory. Asking them to make mental notes so they can tell you afterwards isn't a good idea, since it will interfere with their normal way of doing things. Observing what they do can tell you some interesting things about what they're doing, but not everything, and it won't tell you why they're doing it. To get a better insight, you need some form of report.

There are obvious risks with reports. One is that you'll get a sanitised version of events, the 'front' version intended for public consumption rather than the 'back' version that's normally only shared with other members of the same in-group. Another is that you'll cause interference effects because the reporting gets in the way of the task. There are ways round (or at least partially round) both of these risks, which is why there's a matrix of types of report.

One elegant way of getting beyond the sanitised front version is to ask people to report not their own behaviour but the behaviour of other people. For instance, you can show the respondents a video of someone else doing a task, and ask them to report on what that person is doing. Careful choice of experimental instructions can then give you some very interesting insights. For example, you can tell the respondents (assuming ethical clearance if needed) that the person in the video is a tired employee who is trying to process some work last thing on a Friday afternoon. People are usually quite happy to explain the ways in which incompetent, slothful or otherwise sinful individuals behave, and in this example, you'd probably be told quite a lot about unofficial shortcuts that people use.

Interference effects pose a different type of problem. The interference isn't always obvious. It's fairly obvious that if you ask someone to think aloud while doing simultaneous interpreting, it's physically impossible for them to talk to you about what they're doing while at the same time talking to the people for whom they're interpreting. It's also fairly obvious if you ask someone to think aloud while doing a task such as driving: some of the time they will happily think aloud, but at other times, when they need to concentrate, they'll go silent while they do the tricky bit, and start talking again afterwards. It's less obvious if the task involves some sort of problem solving, particularly one involving pattern matching: there's evidence that reporting while tackling such problems leads to decreased performance in the problem solving. If you have the time and resources, and/or if it's essential to make sure that the report isn't interfering with the task (as in the design of safety-critical systems) then you can simply compare the performance of the people doing the reports with the performance of people not doing reports, and see whether there's a significant difference.

So far, we've focused on reports involving the present, since these demonstrate most clearly the advantages and problems associated with reports. There are obviously times when you can't do reports of what's currently happening, and this can take you into some grim territory, such as trying to make sense of what happened in a lethal accident. This is territory where critical incident technique is often used, with survivors explaining what happened, who did what, and why they did it. The term 'critical incident' is important: this approach looks at incidents which were important in some way, such as near misses, not just at cases where a disaster actually happened. Critical incidents can give important insights into the boundaries of an area – for instance, the critical incident might be how someone handled a customer complaint, with the incident throwing light on the unspoken assumptions within the organisation about how customers should be treated.

Used with care, critical incident technique and related methods can give important insights into what actually happened in real cases. Used without care, they can encounter the 'Napoleon at the gates of Moscow' problem. This refers to an apocryphal story about how in 1912 a French historian found the last survivor of Napoleon's Grande Armée, a man who a century before had been an eight-year-old drummer boy and who had actually seen Napoleon standing at the gates of Moscow. This discovery, on the centenary of the great event, attracted enormous attention, and the interview was lovingly recorded for posterity on a gramophone record. The veteran began by telling the assembled media and historians: 'I remember seeing him as if it were yesterday. He was a tall skinny man, with a long white beard . . .'

The third main group of reports involve future events. These are usually lumped together under the name 'scenarios'. The advantage of scenarios is that they allow you to explore possibilities which have not happened yet. If you use them systematically, you can do some very interesting things. Neil

Maiden, for instance, took a list of the steps involved in using an ATM (a 'hole in the wall' bank machine), then used a standard list of human errors, and combined the two to generate a set of scenarios which systematically investigated what would happen in the event of a given error at a specified point when using the ATM. You can also use them to explore extreme cases, for events which have not happened yet – useful for emergency planning, for instance.

A problem with scenarios is that they involve people making predictions about future behaviour. There's an extensive literature in psychology showing that people are not very good at this, particularly in relation to their own behaviour. There's a big difference between someone predicting their own behaviour when they've been in a similar situation before, and when they've never been in a similar situation. Likewise, there are regularities in human behaviour which are predictable once you've seen enough cases, but which you wouldn't expect in advance: a classic example is that the more people there are in a room, the longer it will be before anyone does something if smoke starts coming from under the door.

Whichever variant you use, the underlying principles are the same. The output is also much the same: human beings expressing themselves in their own words. They're also invaluable for catching 'taken for granted' knowledge, which the respondents would normally not think of mentioning in an interview, because they took it for granted that everyone knew that. It's surprising what people take for granted. A related issue is 'not worth mentioning' knowledge, which often involves useful tricks of the trade that would be very useful to other people, but which the respondents just don't bother to mention in interviews. On balance, then, reports require care, like any other technique, but can give you insights that you wouldn't get with any other technique.

Materials

You'll need the materials and facilities required for the task: piloting is invaluable here, because you normally discover that the task needs something which you would have no way of expecting. As usual, you need to test the materials and facilities, plus your recording equipment, before starting the data collection. You need a contingency plan for what to do if something gets broken, damaged or lost, especially if it's something rare or expensive which has been loaned to you.

Given a quarter of a chance, experts will usually ask for more detail, more information, more equipment, and more of everything else. The ideal would be to do the report in their natural setting. This can lead to some interesting situations: in one study that Gordon did, the natural setting would have been volcanoes in Iceland. Usually this is not feasible, so you end up doing a less realistic version in the lab, and have to strike a balance between the information that experts want and the information that they need. If you're not dealing with experts, then this is less of an issue: you can scope the task to fit what's feasible.

We sometimes use laminated screen shots of websites and suchlike, so that we can use the same materials with all the respondents without the materials getting dog-eared and tatty. We also sometimes use unlaminated screenshots or photos, and encourage respondents to write notes and scribble on them, in conjunction with a report. This can be very useful for getting round the problem of your audio tape telling you that 'this bit is far more interesting than that bit'.

Briefing and demonstrations

These are pretty much as for any other sort of briefing and demonstration. You need to make it clear to the respondents what the task is, and what the viewpoint is from which you want them to report.

One thing specific to reports, particularly reports of present activities, is that you need to give clear instructions about how much to say. The usual rule of thumb is that if the respondent goes quiet for more than a specified time (for instance, three seconds), then you will use one of a list of pre-chosen prompts, such as: 'Could you tell me what you're thinking now?' You may need to vary this: in some cases, you might want to let them do the relevant chunk of the task in silence if they need to be silent, and then ask them to explain afterwards what they have done. If they're doing a report on someone else's behaviour in a video, and the activity is something fast moving such as driving a car in hazardous conditions, then the respondent might want to see an entire chunk of activity in one go, rewind the tape, and report on that chunk in a series of smaller chunks, pausing the tape between each of them.

As usual it's a good idea to give a demonstration of what you'd like them to do, and as usual it's a good idea to use an example which is unlikely to steer the respondents in a particular direction. For example, if you want the respondents to comment on a video of someone driving, you might give a demonstration of how you would set about identifying a rare coin. The features, attributes and processes used in coin identification would be irrelevant to driving, but the underlying procedure of thinking aloud, explaining what you're doing and why you're doing it, would be the same. In some situations, if you're concerned about the risk of interference effects from too much explanation, you might choose not to give a demonstration and to let the respondents give whatever extent and type of report they want. In practice, though, respondents tend to ask you what you want them to do, and you end up having to give them either more detailed instructions or a demonstration anyway, so it's wise to have one prepared.

Procedure

The basic procedure for present event reports and scenarios is simple. You give them the briefing and the demonstration; you sit them down with the materials; you turn your recording equipment on (usually an audio recorder, as discussed below); you let them get on with it; if they're silent for more than the predetermined time, you use one of your predetermined prompts.

The prompts are chosen by working backwards from what you want to find out. If you want to know what they're thinking about, you can ask them: 'Could you tell me what you're thinking about now?' If you're trying to find out whether or not they like something, or why they're thinking about whatever it is that they're thinking about now, then things can become trickier, since the explanation may take some time, which may interfere with the task. In such cases, you'll need to have a policy about what to do, whether to get the explanation and delay the task, or to store up a list of questions and ask them all at the end of the report.

It should be needless to say that the prompts should not be leading questions (such as 'Have you thought about doing it this way?' or 'I suppose you do X, don't you?'). Unfortunately, a surprising number of students do just this. The point of gathering data from respondents is to gather data, not to tell the respondents what you want or expect them to say.

For critical incident technique and related techniques such as illuminative incident technique, there are well-established procedures, and you would be well advised to follow those unless you have very good reasons to depart from them. You would also be well advised to work directly from the primary sources. These methods are more standardised than present event reports and scenarios, which is why we've concentrated on the latter, to spare you the hassle of trying to make sense of a widely scattered literature.

It's advisable to watch for the types of skills that the respondent is using – for instance, whether they're using pattern matching or compiled skills. The presence of either of these would be grounds for caution about taking the respondent's comments on the relevant topic at face value. For instance, if they see something and immediately identify it, then they're probably using pattern matching; if they then spend ten minutes explaining how they knew what it was, that may be true, but it's derived from a different type of mental processing than the type they were using to make the identification. If they do something so fast that there's clearly no conscious deliberation involved (for instance, clicking on a series of options in some software so fast that they're clearly not needing to read the screen), then they're probably using a compiled skill, i.e. one so habitualised that they no longer need to think about it. The presence of either of these is not a bad thing in itself, but to investigate the relevant skill, you'll need to use other techniques (probably experimentation and/or observation).

Recording

It's not usually possible to keep accurate written records in real time when using reports, since respondents tend to talk fast when they do talk, so you'll almost certainly need to record the session.

The amount that respondents say will vary depending on factors such as how much thinking they are having to do, how familiar they are with the task, and how talkative they are. You should decide before the main data collection how long to allow them to be silent before using a standard probe on them. The usual convention is to prompt them if they've been silent for more than five seconds (which you count silently, rather than looking at your watch). For some tasks, though, they might need to be focusing on the task for several seconds at a time, so you may need to use your judgement: for instance, if they're thinking aloud while landing a light aircraft, and go quiet when they're nearly on the runway, it would not be advisable to prompt them to speak.

If you're audio recording while the respondent is doing a visual task, then a classic mistake is to let respondents use terms like 'this one' and 'that one' which make perfect sense when you can see where they're pointing, but which will be completely meaningless when you're listening to the audio tape six weeks later. If they start doing this, then it's a good idea to interject some tactful remark along the lines of 'the one in the top left corner' to clarify what they mean.

Analysis

With reports, you may be able to do analysis straight off the tape if you're asking some types of research question. For instance, if you want to know which factors people mention, then you can work straight off the tape. If you want to know how often they mention these factors, then you may find it simpler to transcribe the sessions, and use word search on the soft copy. You'll probably also want to do a couple of pages of transcription of a session for your appendices in the final write-up.

As we mentioned in the generic advice section, transcribing is time consuming and soul destroying in large quantities. You'll need to transcribe your own tapes, since other people will misunderstand what they hear, through not having the detailed knowledge of the topic that you have painfully acquired. The transcript needs to be utterly faithful: swear words, ungrammatical bits, pauses (one dot per second of pause) and so forth. When we're marking a piece of work involving transcripts, one of the things we look for is whether the transcripts include these things. It may just be that your subjects speak clear, grammatical English without a single grunt or swear word, but frankly we doubt that you'll experience this. As a rough rule of thumb, one hour of session takes up to ten hours to transcribe; this figure drops considerably if the respondents are silent a lot, which is often the case with reports.

Usually the analysis of the tapes and/or transcripts consists of content analysis or discourse analysis; these are described in their own sections. You can also do a lot of analysis from techniques such as timelines, described elsewhere in this section.

Writing up

For reports on present events and for scenarios, there isn't a standard format for writing up. For critical incident technique, there's an established framework, and it would be advisable to follow that if you're writing up for a readership familiar with critical incident technique. If you're writing up for a readership which is not familiar with reports, then you'll need to explain clearly why you've used reports, and to include references to the literature, so that critical readers can follow things up if they wish. (Using this book as your only citation is not a wise idea.) In that situation, you'd also be well advised to give clear, practical instances of what reports can offer to the discipline in which you're working.

Hints, tips and thoughts

Reports are easy in one sense: you just sit there listening to the respondent, and occasionally asking them to say a bit more. They are also good (often excellent) for juicy anecdotes and significant insights. They're less than wonderful when you come to analyse them. The respondents usually appear to be giving you every third link in their chain of thought, and to be incapable of saying anything clearly. Transcribing sessions can be extremely laborious and boring, so there are advantages in designing your research so that you can work straight off the tape.

A risk when analysing reports is that you may be accused of partiality in your coding of the responses. It's therefore best practice to get at least one independent judge (usually a fellow student or a long-suffering partner) to do the coding for you. A great bonus of this is that someone else ends up doing the analysis for you, so you are not just spared that effort, but are actually given brownie points for doing so. Best practice is to compare the results from these independent coders to see how well they agree.

It's worth remembering that you can analyse the same tape repeatedly for different purposes. This is probably the last thing you feel like doing when you're halfway through your initial analysis, but if you're doing a PhD or professional research then it's possible to get another batch of analysis out of the same tapes (perhaps via a funded research project).

We use reports quite a lot: in conjunction with other techniques such as laddering, they can give you a lot of useful information in a fairly realistic setting.

Relevant literatures and further reading

There are various relevant literatures, most of which don't cross-refer to each other. For methodological underpinnings, there's a significant literature in psychology on short-term memory and working memory. There's also a fair amount of work in psychology and related fields using this approach, under various names.

For reports dealing with past events, it's advisable to read the literature on shortcomings of human memory (for instance, Loftus' work). There are various methods and literatures relating to reports of past events. A prominent example is the literature on critical incident technique. There are also related approaches such as illuminative incident technique. The literature on disasters and on safety-critical systems draws heavily on reports of past events, and contains numerous well-documented examples.

For reports of current activities, the best starting place is the psychology literature, as described above.

For reports of future activities, the literature on scenarios is a good starting place. Some of this literature is based in psychology, some in computer science, some in the area of overlap between these disciplines. It's also worth looking at the literature on judgement and decision making (J/DM), which has some pertinent findings about people's inability to predict their own future behaviour with much accuracy.

Reports involve getting someone to talk about how things happen, often while demonstrating the thing in question. This leads on to the issue of what you can learn from watching those demonstrations, and that's the topic of the next section, on observation.

Observation: watching what happens

But his eyes had spent more than forty years looking at drunks, at knife fighters, at victims, at what happens when pickup trucks hit culverts at eighty. They were old eyes.

(*People of Darkness*, p.30)

Overview

Observation can be subdivided in several ways. One useful distinction is between direct observation and indirect observation. With direct observation, you observe something directly, such as watching how people behave in supermarkets. With indirect observation, you don't observe the activity itself, but instead you observe something else which indirectly tells you about the thing that you really want to observe. For instance, if you wanted to find out about premarital sexual behaviour among the Pilgrim Fathers in the sixteenth century, it wouldn't be possible to observe this directly, for various and fairly obvious reasons, but it would be possible to observe it indirectly by looking at registers of marriages and births. Another useful distinction is between participant observation, where you join the group that you are studying (for example, in an ethnographic study where you live with a South American tribe or in a psychiatric ward), and non-participant observation, where you remain on the outside of the group. Within participant observation, there is a further distinction between disclosed and undisclosed participant observation. With disclosed participant observation, you tell the group that you are studying them; with undisclosed participant observation, you don't tell them that you're studying them (which raises obvious ethical issues, as well as a whole swarm of non-obvious ones).

Why might you consider using observation? As the categories above suggest, there are various ways in which it can be useful. One strong point of observation is that it shows you something, without the filtering effect of language. Other things being equal, you see how something actually happens, warts and all, including all sorts of things that are so familiar to the respondents that they would never think of mentioning them in an interview. For instance, the inimitable Aisha found via observation that the IT managers she was studying frequently didn't stop for lunch, and simply worked through the day because of pressure of work; they hadn't thought this was worth mentioning during her previous interviews with them. You can also infer a lot from observation: for instance, if the respondent does a task swiftly and without apparent thought, while continuing a conversation with you, then it's a pretty fair bet that they do that task pretty often; if they do another task slowly and with assorted pauses, episodes of trial and error, swear words and eventual recourse to the manual, then it's a pretty fair bet that they don't do that task very often. This can be useful for working out what they really do often or rarely, as opposed to what they claim they do. (This makes the distinction between direct and indirect observation a bit fuzzy, but it's still a useful one, which is why we've retained it.)

Observation is used widely, and in widely different fields. The fields vary in terms of which varieties of observation they favour, and how many varieties they use. For instance, social anthropology and sociology have a long and honourable tradition of participant observation, both disclosed and undisclosed, with groups ranging from Samoan villagers to vagrants in Wales. Occupational and organisational psychology have a similar tradition of using very focused varieties of observation, often under names which make no reference to observation, such as 'task analysis'. Computer science also has a respectable tradition of using observation, ranging from ethnographic studies to clarify the users' requirements, through to forms of task analysis for designing software interfaces.

If things go well, observation can give you large amounts of rich, interesting, valid data. If things go badly, observation can give you large amounts of rich, interesting and dubious or downright misleading data; in extreme cases, if you're silly or reckless enough, you can get yourself arrested, beaten up or killed. It's unlikely that your supervisor and department will let you get into a dangerous project, but it's quite possible that you'll collect data of very dubious validity if you're not careful. For instance, suppose that you're living in a rural village using disclosed participant observation, and you decide to interview the local teenagers about their sexual experiences. Do you really think that teenage males are going to tell you the truth about this, especially if they know that you're going to publish an account of your findings? Pushing the question a bit further, if you'd originally gone into the village to study local boatbuilding traditions, and if you had no previous experience of researching sexual behaviour, would you reckon that your interviews would provide good enough data to stand up to scrutiny by experts around the world?

Once you have the data, you also face the interesting challenge of analysing it. Depending on the variety of observation you're using, your data may consist of anything from notes scribbled on napkins, through to video footage and possibly, if you're in psychology or computer science, data from eye-tracking equipment. As usual, it's essential to think about analysis before committing yourself to a study which depends on observation; it's also essential to include analysis in your piloting.

Since the varieties of observation are so diverse, we've included subsections on each of the main varieties before discussing the usual topics of materials, procedures, etc. so that you can see the big picture before we get into the detail and practicalia.

Disclosed participant observation

One main variety of disclosed participant observation is the ethnographic study, where you study a group of people in much the same way as an ethnographer or social anthropologist would. This is worth considering if you're already part of a group that someone is likely to find interesting – being an established member means that you don't need to spend ages gaining admittance to a group, and means that you'll have a pretty good idea of what normal life in the group is like. What is an interesting group? In practice, pretty much everything is fair game, particularly since the group can often be an elegant example of a widespread feature, such as group pressures to conform. Another variety of disclosed participant observation, namely shadowing, is widely used in studies of organisations and of individuals' work; in shadowing, you simply follow someone round in a 'fly on the wall' manner. For instance, you might follow a manager round, and observe how much time is spent on which tasks.

An advantage of disclosed participant observation is that you can gather data openly. This may not sound like a huge plus until you imagine some of the alternatives, such as trying to record data surreptitiously while posing as a Glasgow gang member using undisclosed participant observation, to use one genuine example. An obvious disadvantage is that if you're not already a member of the group, then you're likely to be shown the front version of how the group behaves (i.e. the sanitised version for public consumption, as opposed to the behind-the-scenes reality). A less obvious disadvantage may occur if you do manage to get at the realities. What would you do when it came to writing up your results, and those results included unpleasant truths about a group that you had come to like? It's possible to end up feeling strong social bonds with the most unlikely sounding individuals after getting to know them well, and this can lead to deep emotional and moral dilemmas, when you're torn between telling the full story on the one hand, and being tactful to people that you like on the other.

A second main strand of disclosed participant observation is task analysis. Its focus is usually a specific task (as opposed to the day-to-day behaviour of one or more people, which is the usual focus of ethnographic studies). Usually the task analysis involves getting several people to do the same task separately from each other, and then looking for regularities and/or errors, or efficiencies and/or inefficiencies in how they perform the task. If you're designing a new piece of software, for instance, you might want to use task analysis to investigate how people do the task that you're trying to automate. If you're studying management, then you might want to do a task analysis to identify inefficient workflow patterns. If you're a psychologist, you might use it to investigate how people try to solve a particular problem, as a way of gaining insight into cognitive processes.

Undisclosed participant observation

In this variety of participant observation, you don't tell the group that you're actually studying them. A couple of classic examples of this have involved people joining gangs; another involved becoming an inmate in a psychiatric ward. This approach hits obvious problems with ethics and risks. It also hits less obvious ones, such as becoming emotionally attached to the group, and being unwilling to write up their behaviour in a way which might appear critical of them. There are also risks of becoming involved in criminal behaviour during the study; claiming that you committed the acts as part of your research gets you into some dodgy legal ground. As usual, there are a lot of grey areas: murdering a rival gang member would clearly not be something where you would be let off if you claimed that it was part of your research, but if you were doing participant observation of graffiti artists, and were sponsored by the local council as part of a drive to reduce graffiti, then you could probably get away with spray painting your tag on to a few walls (though it would be wise to get written clearance for this from the council in advance). In between these extremes, it can be a judgement call, and if you're an undergraduate or Master's student, then you'd be wiser staying clear of this approach unless you clearly have appropriate approval and backup from your department.

Data collection

There are numerous forms of data collection which you can use within observation. If you're doing a task analysis of someone purchasing something on the internet, for instance, then you could gather data via eye-tracking equipment, keystroke monitoring software in the computer, and via video recording from two angles (one camera on the screen and keyboard close up, one showing the respondent and the computer/keyboard in longer shot). At the other extreme, you might gather data by watching and listening to the other members of the motorbike gang that you have joined.

It's a good idea to use different levels of data collection at different stages. For example, observation can be useful for getting a general understanding of the domain as part of your initial familiarisation. This can be particularly useful for working out what types of knowledge you are going to be dealing with. If you're looking at how archaeologists do initial identification of artefacts, for instance, then some initial observation will soon show that they surprisingly often lick artefacts, or lick a finger and then rub it against an artefact, sometimes to clean off surface dirt and sometimes to assess the porosity of pottery. At this stage, it's advisable to keep an eye open for compiled skills and implicit learning; if these are predominant in the area that particularly interests you, then there could be problems finding out precisely what's going on within that tacit knowledge. After you've done some initial reconnaissance of this informal sort, in as naturalistic a context as you can manage, you can then decide what will be viable for more systematic data collection.

For more systematic data collection, you can do things like activity logs. These take varying forms, including diaries kept by the respondents, and time-line sheets. These are tables which list activities on one axis, and times along the other axis; you observe what the respondent is doing, and tick the appropriate box in the relevant time column. This can be handy for field observation. For example, the diligent Lucy used this approach to study interpersonal interactions between serving staff and customers in a fast food outlet; she was able to sit at a table drinking coffee without raising suspicion and gather data inconspicuously. This sort of data allows you to identify recurrent patterns of behaviour, to quantify time spent on each activity, and so on – in this case, quantifying the opportunities for human contact with the current system, to assess whether a shift to an automated system would lead to serious loss of interpersonal contact. An example of a fictitious timeline sheet is shown in Figure 4.2.

In this example, the numbers for the columns are sequence numbers, so you can refer to action number 6, for instance. It's also possible to use the columns to show times, but this can involve trying to watch activity and a stopwatch simultaneously, which can be problematic in fast-moving activities. In this case, for simplicity, we've shown only the interpersonal actions, not the actions involving food handling or money exchange. This example shows the employee smiling before making eye contact with the customer, and then

Activity	1	2	3	4	5	6	7	8	9	10	11	12	13	14	15
Smile	•														
Eye contact		•													
Break eye contact							•								
Ask question				•											
Answer question															
Laugh					•										
Frown															
Turn away								•							
Make comment			•			•									

Figure 4.2 A fictitious timeline sheet

making a comment before asking the customer a question. Once you're observing at this level of detail, you can start spotting all sorts of regularities that you might otherwise have missed, such as how many employees use unscripted remarks to customers as a way of humanising their work. It's worth remembering, before getting too keen on this approach, that in some environments this is perceived as being horribly similar to the time and motion studies which traditionally were precursors to staff redundancies, so you need to use appropriate caution if you're using timeline sheets in public (you can, of course, use them to code recorded video data, etc. which spares you this issue).

We use observation quite a lot, often for an initial reconnaissance, and often in parallel with other activities. You can tell a lot about an organisation by discreet observation while waiting in the reception area to meet your contact there, for instance; you can also learn a lot about the realities of something by keeping your eyes and ears open, and knowing what to be on the lookout for. What should you be on the lookout for? That's where your literature review comes in, by helping you to identify classic things to watch out for, and also identifying things which haven't been adequately addressed in previous work.

Reports and observation give you a lot of rich data, but making sense of it can be a challenge, and might leave you with a frustrating feeling that you haven't been able to capture the respondents' knowledge in a form that really gets beneath the surface. Card sorts, laddering and repertory grids are three related techniques which allow you to elicit the respondents' knowledge systematically using the respondents' own categorisation, and to get beneath the surface.

Card sorts: getting respondents to categorise things

The earliest reference to cards of any kind is in 1332, when Alfonse XI, King of Leon and Castile, banned them.

(*The Definitive Tarot*, p.3)

Overview

After spending ages collecting natural language data in the respondents' own words, and then spending even longer on analysing, coding and tabulating those words into what are in effect someone else's words, you might find yourself wondering whether it wouldn't be simpler just to ask the respondents to tabulate the data themselves in the first place. By a fascinating coincidence, it is possible to do just that, by using card sorts. Card sorts have been around for years, and have tended in the past to be used pretty informally, usually as an initial way of scouting out a new area. More recently though, they have started to be used in a much more systematic way as a main method of data collection, rather than as an ancillary one. There are numerous varieties of card sorts; we'll start by describing our preferred version.

The underlying concept is simple. You prepare a set of cards relating to the topic you're investigating: the set will either contain words or pictures. (It's also possible to sort objects, if they're small enough, such as mobile phones.) For instance, each card might have the name of a person, or a description of a situation such as 'driving in rush hour through an unfamiliar large town', or a picture of an outfit that women might wear to work in an office. Each card is numbered. You give the cards to the respondent and ask them to sort them into groups using a criterion of their choice; you make it clear to the respondent that they will be able to sort the same pack as often as they want, and that they should use one criterion at a time. Once they've sorted the cards into groups, you record the name of each group, the numbers of the cards in each group, and the criterion for that sort. You then give them back the cards to sort again using a different criterion. At the end of an agreed time, or when they run out of criteria, they stop sorting (they usually run out in under an hour).

At the end of the session, you should have a neatly organised set of data, all arranged into the respondent's own categorisation, all named using their own words (and usually named pretty concisely, with a short phrase). You can then analyse the data in various ways. For instance, you can count the number of criteria used for sorting (for instance, do experts use more sorting criteria than novices in this area?). You can count the number of categories into which they sort the cards each time (for instance, do experts tend to sort into more groups than novices?). You can also look at which criteria and groups were used, and what that suggests (for instance, which are the most commonly used criteria for sorting, and are there any significant absences?).

As usual, this method doesn't give you absolutely everything you could ask for, but it's neat, simple and powerful, with the considerable advantage that you're getting neat data out in the respondents' own format and words. The main disadvantage of this method is that it can raise tantalising questions which require further work – for instance, Sue Gerrard's finding that half of her male respondents spontaneously sorted images of women's working dress into 'married' and 'unmarried' groups. Most people who use card sorts also use laddering, which lends itself well to answering further questions of this sort, and which fits neatly with card sorts.

Materials

Most people use between ten and twenty cards; with much below ten, the sorting can feel a bit silly, and with much over twenty, the sorting can be hard going. If you're using words or descriptions, then index cards are a convenient size; if you're using pictures, then use whatever size works well when you try it out. We often do card sorts with full-sized, full colour screen shots of web pages, using A4 laminated images. The cards should be numbered clearly and in a consistent place (we use the upper right corner). If you're using verbal descriptions, then you can be quite creative, and use an entire paragraph per card if you want to. This can be helpful for getting at people's conceptualisation of complex situations or difficult choices.

Briefing and demonstrations

We use a standard briefing sheet (there's a 'copyleft' one in the Rugg & McGeorge papers that you can use if you want), and also give respondents a demonstration of sorting so that they can see how it works. It's a good idea to do the demonstration using cards and criteria which are unlikely to cue the respondent towards a particular set of criteria. For instance, if your main cards contain verbal descriptions of road hazards, then you could use demonstration cards with pictures of houses on them, and use the criterion 'building material' with the groups 'stone', 'brick' and 'wood'. None of these could be meaningfully applied to driving hazards, so the risk of cueing is minimal. We usually then tell the respondent that we could sort the cards again using criteria such as 'number of floors' or 'roof material', to make it clear that the respondents should do the sorting using one criterion at a time.

As usual, you can get very different responses depending on the framing of the initial instructions, and on the viewpoint from which the respondent answers, so it's advisable to check these carefully during piloting.

Procedure

The procedure is just the same as in the demonstration, except that the respondent does the sorting, and provides the names of the groups and the criterion for sorting. It's also possible to ask respondents to sort cards into groups using criteria that you provide, so you can see how much agreement there is between respondents about which cards belong in which groups, but in practice we usually find the respondents' own categorisation more useful.

If the respondent is choosing the groups and criteria, then you should resist the temptation to offer advice or help, even if they ask for it. If the respondent appears to be genuinely stuck, then you can take two cards at random and ask the respondent to tell you the main single difference between them; this usually provides the necessary inspiration. It's worth knowing that there is often a 'drying up' point where the respondent can't bring any more criteria to mind. If you use the two random cards, the respondent will usually generate a few more criteria and then tell you that there aren't any more worth mentioning. There doesn't seem to be any pattern regarding which criteria come before the drying up point versus those which come after it.

Respondents usually enjoy card sorts; the method is a fairly restful one both for the investigator and the respondent (unlike, say, interviewing, where you need to think fast about what the respondent is saying), and respondents often say that they find it gives them new insights into their own knowledge. Typically sessions last between thirty minutes and an hour, and produce between three and seven criteria, though you can get twenty criteria or more from an articulate expert dealing with their own area of expertise.

The only place where problems often occur is on the first sort, where respondents may try to use two different criteria at once (e.g. 'big and expensive'). If you politely check whether this could be better handled using one criterion of 'big' followed by a separate sort using the criterion 'expensive' they will normally get the idea and follow the standard procedure from then on. If they're insistent that they really do mean 'big and expensive' as a single concept, then just let them use it – it may well lead to interesting and unexpected findings.

Recording

We normally record directly on to paper; it's possible to audio tape the session as well, but usually that doesn't provide much extra information. Our preferred method uses a pen and a blank sheet of A4 paper, but you can prepare recording sheets if you want. At the head of the sheet, you record any 'housekeeping' details such as date, time, respondent's identification number, and the group to which the respondent belongs. You then leave some empty space.

When the respondent sorts the cards, you ask them what the name of each group is, and then ask them to read out the number of each card in each group. You write down the name of the group, followed by the numbers of the cards in that group, then start a new line, and write the name of the next group, followed by the numbers of the cards in it, and so on. After you've done that for all the groups, you then ask what the criterion was for the sort, and write that down above the names of the groups. (Why this way round? If you ask for the criterion first, and then the group names after that, respondents quite often change their minds halfway through the recording, whereas if you ask for the group names first and then the criterion, they normally don't change their minds. Nobody knows why.)

You then ask the respondent to sort the cards again, and record the next sort in the same way, remembering to leave plenty of blank space so that your records are clear. The result might look something like this. (Note the use of commas, distinguishing e.g. 12 from 1, 2.)

Respondent 1, February 29, 10.00

Sort 1: under my control or not
not under my control: 1, 3, 4, 5, 7, 9, 10, 11
under my control: 2, 8, 12
not applicable: 6

Sort 2: seriousness
very serious: 1, 3, 4, 8, 9
moderately serious: 6, 7, 11
not so serious: 2, 5, 10, 12

Analysis

There is a well-established standard set of procedures for analysis of card sorts, which can be a great comfort to a novice researcher. First, you analyse the number of sorts performed – for instance, does one group of respondents typically perform more than others? Novices will typically perform fewer sorts than experts, and you can use this as an indirect measure of people's expertise in an area.

Next, you analyse the number of groups into which people sort the cards. One typical finding is that one batch of respondents will perform noticeably more sorts into two groups (dichotomous sorts) than the others. The reasons for this are obscure. Sue Gerrard found this among her male respondents, and speculated whether it might reflect a social tendency for males to simplify issues into binary choices, but subsequent work has found that the situation is more complex.

After this, you can start analysing the criteria. One way of doing this is to compare them against criteria from the literature. For instance, the literature might claim that one group of people tend to use more concrete terms than another. You could test this by getting an independent judge to assess which of the criteria were concrete and which were abstract, after which you could look at the number of instances of each in your groups.

Another way is to work from the raw data towards higher level categorisation. The usual way of doing this is to start with a table of the exact words used as criterion names by respondents, counting how many respondents used each name. This is known as verbatim agreement. So, for instance, the criterion names 'colourful' and 'lots of colour' would be treated as different names at this stage. The reason for this is that in many domains experts use terms which look very similar (e.g. 'wheel made' and 'wheel thrown') but which have quite different meanings. Verbatim analysis reduces the risk of being caught out in this way.

The next step is to group together any terms which can reasonably be treated as synonyms (so 'colourful' and 'lots of colour' would now be grouped together, and their numbers pooled). Usually an independent judge is used for this stage, which is known as gist agreement.

The next stage is to group together terms which are related but which are not synonyms (so 'colourful' and 'monochrome' are related because they are to do with the amount of colour, even though they mean opposite things). This is known as superordinacy – the lower level terms are grouped together into the superordinate term. Again, an independent judge is normally used for this. You can repeat the superordinate grouping to bring together these superordinate terms into higher level terms (and repeat the process as often as you want, though usually two or three levels are enough for anyone).

The end product of this is that you have full traceability of your coding – anyone looking at your tables of results can see how you reached the numbers that you did, and could in principle recalculate using their own coding if they felt that they really had to do so.

It's also possible to do some interesting multidimensional analysis of the data, by counting how often each card occurs in the same group as each other card. Although the underlying concept is very simple, it's very powerful, and allows you to look for clusters of cards which tend to occur together. You can also do things like measuring the perceptual distance between two cards, and identifying where two cards differ (very useful for things such as product differentiation in market research). The full details of this go beyond the scope of this section, but it's well worth exploring.

Writing up

Since there's a standard method for analysing this form of card sorts, that part of writing up is fairly straightforward. You may have trouble in some domains if you try to write up with your focus on what you found rather than the method you used to find it – most journals and conferences prefer to have either new data or a new method, but not both simultaneously. If this is the case for you, you could try writing a method-driven paper to start with, and using that to pave the way for data-driven papers using card sorts.

Rugg and McGeorge explicitly link this version of card sorts to Personal Construct Theory, giving it a useful metalanguage. This doesn't mean that you need to buy into Personal Construct Theory yourself; you can use card sorts independently of that framework. It's worth remembering that there are other versions of card sorts, in particular Q sorts, so you may need to distinguish explicitly between those versions and the version that you're using, to reduce the risk of misunderstandings among readers familiar with other versions.

Hints, tips and thoughts

There's a small but growing community of researchers using this version of card sorts. If you're planning to use it, then you might find it useful to make contact with that community (an online search for people publishing using card sorts, and who are citing the Rugg & McGeorge paper should find some names).

Card sorts are a pleasant method to use, and combine data in the respondents' own words with a well-standardised procedure. They can also be used quite creatively – for instance, you can use the criteria from a sorting session as the cards to be sorted in a different session, to explore higher level categorisation. You can also ask people to role play, and to sort as if they belonged to a different specified group, to see to what extent they can see things from that group's point of view (for instance, women sorting pictures of women's working dress, as if they were men doing the same task).

Despite this flexibility, there are some things which card sorts do not handle well, such as explanations of terms that the respondents use, or clarification of the higher level goals associated with a particular concept. For both these purposes, laddering fits neatly together with card sorts, and most people who use card sorts also have laddering in their repertoire.

Relevant literatures and further reading

In this section, we have focused on a version of card sorts which fits neatly with Kelly's Personal Construct Theory. A quite different version of card sorts is part of Stephenson's Q Methodology. As with Personal Construct Theory, this provides a substantial theoretical framework within which a version of card sorts is located. We have described Personal Construct Theory elsewhere, since it is closely linked to repertory grids and to laddering; for reasons of space, we will not do the same with Q Methodology. The version of card sorts usually associated with Q Methodology involves a fairly large pack of cards containing statements which have been derived from extensive piloting using other techniques. Respondents are then asked to fit these cards into a specified distribution close to a normal (Gaussian style) distribution – for instance, three cards in a 'strongly agree' pile, three in a 'strongly disagree' pile, and then increasing specified numbers in the intermediate piles between these extremes. Sophisticated statistical analysis can then be used on the results.

It is also possible to use card sorts in other ways. One popular method is to ask respondents to sort a large number of cards into a matrix (so, for instance, cards bearing specified driving hazards might be sorted into a matrix of low to high likelihood versus low to high severity of outcome). It is also possible to ask respondents to sort cards into hierarchies, with the layout of the cards on the table mirroring a branching hierarchy or some other specified distribution. Again, there are sophisticated statistical techniques available for this.

Overall, we prefer the version we have described above, since it elicits respondents' own categories directly (rather than inferring them via statistics), but also allows us to do sophisticated statistics if we want to, which looks to us like an all too rare case of being able to have the best of both worlds. As usual though, the method you should choose is the one best suited to your individual needs, which may well be one of the other versions we have just described.

Card sorts can provide fascinating information, but they can also raise as many questions as they answer. In particular, they often elicit categorisation that looks intriguing, but which they do not unpack. A convenient way of unpacking concepts turned up by card sorts is laddering, which is described in the next section.

Laddering: unpacking the respondents' concepts systematically

Officer Dodge's voice was incredulous. 'What kind of a Navajo would use a mole for an amulet?' Officer Dodge left for Gallup without waiting for an answer.
(*People of Darkness*, p.26)

Getting the respondents' thoughts on record in their own words is one of those things which gives people a warm glow of contentment, often accompanied by a benevolent feeling of mild pity for those poor benighted souls whose data consists only of ticks in boxes, constraining their victims into a Procrustean dilemma of either choosing box A (that their idea of a brilliant evening is dinner with the British national darts champion) or box B (that they would instead much prefer to stay home and learn to play the bagpipes). That glow feels good while it lasts, and it normally lasts until the glowing researcher tries to make sense of the said data. This usually leads to a swift mood change, as the previously glowing researcher realises that their respondents appear unable to find any better pastime than making a string of inscrutable comments with no visible logic to connect them. There is something very depressing to the soul in statements like 'and you know what Vietnamese ex-nuns are like' or 'he had painted his Purdeys green, sir': what are Vietnamese ex-nuns like, and what are Purdeys, and is painting them a good or bad thing, and is the colour significant, and how are you going to make sense of 30 hours of tapes of stuff like that? One possible source of salvation is laddering, a technique designed to elicit explanations for statements of this sort in a systematic, methodical way.

Laddering was invented by Hinkle in the 1960s, within the context of clinical psychology. (If you're planning to cite him in your PhD, then you should be aware that the seminal text is his unpublished PhD thesis, stored on the shelves of an American university library, and that if you cite it as a primary reference, the external examiner may well decide to ask questions about how you obtained a copy, and what you thought of it.) Laddering was quite widely adopted by the Personal Construct Theory community, where it was publicised by people like Don Bannister and Faye Fransella. It is also used in other areas ranging from market research to requirements engineering, and has been extended and formalised by these other communities. This section describes the version used in requirements engineering, unless otherwise specified, since this is probably the most formalised version.

Laddering deals with hierarchically arranged knowledge. One classic example of this is explanations, where an explanation might require subexplanations for technical terms used in the original explanation, and then each of these might in turn require yet further explanation. Another is classification, where a person might identify categories, each of which might contain subcategories, and so forth. Another is goals and values, where a high-level goal may consist of subgoals, each of which may in turn consist of lower level goals (and likewise for values). Yet another example is activities, which may consist of subactivities, and so on. Not all knowledge is organised hierarchically. If you try using laddering when the respondent's knowledge is not arranged hierarchically, then you know about it pretty soon, via indicators such as the respondent staring blankly at you, or telling you that they don't think that way.

As you may guess from your memories of knowledge representation, this approach assumes directed graphs, and more specifically trees (this is discussed in more detail in the section on knowledge representation). So what? So the responses don't spread out forever, and you can use laddering to unpack an explanation without having to worry about whether you will spend the next seven years following leads to every concept in the respondent's field of knowledge.

Another thing that is worth knowing about knowledge representation and laddering is that if you're dealing with hierarchies you need to be thinking about facet theory and polyhierarchies. What this means, in non-mathematical language, is that you can slice the same cake in various directions, each of which is true, and all of which are different. So, for instance, if you're using laddering to unpack someone's categorisation of animals, they might have one way of categorising animals using a hierarchy based on zoological classification into genera, species, etc. and they might also have a quite different way of categorising those same animals using a hierarchy based on habitat, and yet another way of categorising them based on what the animals eat. As long as you know which hierarchy is which, there are no problems, and you can gain a lot of valuable insights about the ways that people organise their knowledge. If, however, you confuse two or more hierarchies with each other, then you end up with an inconsistent heap of grot, as a result of your mistake rather than the respondent's inscrutable construing. This is why you need to be careful about the phrasing you use in your questions, so that you don't accidentally skip from one hierarchy to another. This is something which is widely recognised in the form of laddering used in knowledge acquisition and requirements engineering, but it doesn't seem to have received so much attention in the forms used elsewhere.

Anyway, on to some specific examples and concepts. We'll start with laddering on explanations, and then work through some of the underlying concepts in more detail before going on to laddering on categories and laddering on goals and values. There doesn't seem to have been a lot of work on laddering on activities, so we won't cover that, but it looks like an area that would repay further work, if any readers feel like a challenge.

With laddering on explanations, there is one verbal probe that you use: 'How can you tell that . . .?' So, for instance, you can ask a student: 'How can you tell that a dissertation is well written?' and you might get responses such as: 'It would be clear, interesting, and have lots of web references.' You then tackle each chunk in turn, asking 'How can you tell that it is clear?' and 'How can you tell that it is interesting?' and 'How can you tell that it has lots of web references?'. These may look like silly questions, but in fact they're the place where you'll start finding really useful, interesting things. So, for instance, 'clear' may unpack into something like 'not too many technical terms' and 'not too many references cluttering the flow'; 'interesting' may unpack into 'new to me' and 'written as an eyecatching story' and 'lots of web references' may unpack into 'ten to twenty'. So what? So, if you posed the same question to one of the academics who would one day be marking that student's dissertation, you might get a response such as 'clear, interesting, and lots of good references', which looks identical, but these might unpack into utterly different concepts. 'Clear' is likely to unpack into something like 'well structured, with good narrative spine', 'interesting' might unpack into 'novel application of concept not frequently used in this area' and 'lots of good references' might unpack into 'thirty to sixty references from a range of sources including journals and conference proceedings, rather than just web pages'. The academic would also be likely to mention the need for plenty of references and technical terms. In other words, the two respondents would be viewing the same topic in diametrically opposite ways. An extreme example? No, we found precisely this sort of response when we used laddering to investigate students' understanding of academic skills. You get similarly divergent responses in all sorts of other areas too, and laddering is good at bringing these out clearly into the open, so you can see where misunderstandings arise between individuals and between groups. (A classic example is different groups' interpretations of 'professionalism'.)

One of the key things that differentiates laddering from interviews is that you use a very small set of standard verbal probes (so you don't get your hierarchies muddled). An advantage of this is that since you're using the same probes all the time, you can use a brief notation for each probe. So, for instance, instead of writing in your notes 'How can you tell that something is X?' you can simply write the 'X' with a symbol next to it which indicates that you're using the 'How can you tell?' probe. In fact, because laddering is so structured, you can take written notes during the session which are detailed enough to act as your main data. We'll rework the example above with the standard notations used in the requirements engineering version to demonstrate this.

Laddering on explanations

In the requirements engineering version, 'How can you tell that something is X?' is indicated by writing the X with a downwards-pointing arrow beneath it. Under the arrow, you write each separate chunk of explanation, starting each chunk on a new line and ending each chunk with a semi-colon. (The semi-colon is in case you get a very long chunk that goes on to a second line, so that you can distinguish a two-line chunk easily from two single-line chunks.) The notations for: 'How can you tell that a dissertation is well written?' and the responses above are as follows:

> dissertation is well written
> ↓
> clear;
> interesting;
> lots of web references;

You then leave some clear space, so that the probe and responses form a clear block, and repeat the process for each response in turn:

> clear
> ↓
> not too many technical terms;
> not too many references cluttering the flow;
>
> interesting
> ↓
> new to me;
> written as an eyecatching story;

lots of web references
↓
<u>ten to twenty:</u>

What's the underlining for beneath the 'ten to twenty'? It's there to show that this particular bit has bottomed out, i.e. reached a point where any further questions would be meaningless. The answers at the bottoming-out level are usually the really interesting ones, where you hit specific, tangible answers that are often very different from what you might expect. What often happens with laddering is that you hit answers quite early on which appear to be so unambiguous that there's no point in unpacking them to the next layer down. However, if you do unpack them, you find something quite unexpected and usually important. How can you tell whether you're stopping too early, or whether you've bottomed out? Bottoming out takes you to a small number of types of response. One type is numeric, as in the 'ten to twenty' response. Another type is simple pattern matching on colours or shapes – for instance, 'brown' or 'oval'. A third type is the sort of pattern matching where you just need to see one example – for instance, if you see one computer mouse, then that's all you need in order to recognise computer mice in the future. A fourth type of response tells you that you've hit a tacit skill, via phrasing such as 'You'd need to see lots of examples' or 'You just know through experience' combined with the respondent's being unable to tell you any of the relevant factors. If you've hit one of these, then you've bottomed out.

A considerable advantage of taking written notes this way is that it encourages respondents to give their answers in clear, short chunks, rather than long rambling monologues. If you demonstrate laddering using an example from another domain, with short, clear chunks in the response, then this cues respondents towards this pattern of response. If they also see you writing down their responses, then most respondents will have the heart to slow down and not ramble, so you can keep up. In case you're worried about whether this leads to oversimplified responses, then be reassured: when a respondent hits an area where the answer doesn't fit neatly into this format, they'll normally tell you so and explain the problem in great detail.

This form of laddering is very useful for unpacking what people mean by things, which is particularly handy if you're dealing with subjective terms or with identifying gaps in skills and understandings, and also if you're dealing with misunderstandings between individuals and groups. By unpacking subjective terms like 'good' or 'professionalism' you can identify where the gaps and differences occur, which is a good start towards fixing them.

Laddering on categories

Laddering on categories is pretty similar to laddering on explanations. You start with a seed question such as 'Can you tell me some types of X?' and then unpack the successive layers of response. So, for instance, the seed question:

'Can you tell me some types of academic publication?' might generate the following set of responses:

<u>academic publication</u>
book;
periodical;
emphemera;

<u>book</u>
reference book;
textbook;
monograph;

And so forth, through subcategories of each of these and through the successive layers of further subcategorisation. The notation for 'categorisation' laddering is the underlining beneath the item being subdivided; as with laddering on explanations, each chunk of response starts on a new line and ends with a semicolon; as with laddering on explanations, when a branch bottoms out, you draw an underline beneath it to indicate this (okay, so you end up with two underlines, but the world goes on despite this inelegant notation).

Laddering on goals and values

We've lumped the two things together because they overlap a lot, even if they are conceptually not identical. There's been a lot of good work on this type of laddering in clinical psychology and in market research. One thing to be careful about when using laddering on goals and values is that you can soon get into a respondent's core personal beliefs and values, which can be an ethically difficult place to be. Respondents can be uncomfortable about having their core beliefs and values explored by someone else, and might not realise the full extent of their unease until after the session has ended. Unless you have appropriate professional training and ethical clearance, our advice is to err on the side of caution; a useful rule of thumb is that once the response takes you out of the workplace, then it's time to stop going upwards through their higher level values. Different disciplines have different takes on this issue, so it's also wise to check how your own discipline feels about this.

There are various ways of doing this form of laddering. One neat one is to start with two options, and ask the respondent which one they would prefer and why. Once you know what the reason is for preferring the chosen option, then you ask why they prefer that reason, and so on until you either 'top out' with a highest level belief, or you decide that you've moved into excessively sensitive territory. Topping out tends to happen pretty quickly – a handful of levels. So, for instance, you might ask someone whether they would prefer to have a china teapot or a silver one, and why. They reply that they would prefer the china one because it's more homely. You ask why they would prefer something more homely, and they reply that homely things are more comfortable. When you probe about this, they tell you that more comfortable things make it easier for the family to have shared pleasant experiences such as afternoon tea together without having to worry about damaging expensive belongings, and that belief in turn might lead to a top level belief that families simply should have shared pleasant experiences.

With upward laddering like this, you're going from the bottom of the hierarchy up towards the top, and what you'll typically find is that as you go up the number of branches decreases, so you'll keep hitting the same responses and the same high level goals and values eventually, more or less regardless of where you started from. One striking feature of upwards laddering is how quickly the most mundane starting points lead into very different responses from different respondents – the example of the china and silver teapots is one that we often use when teaching laddering in workshops, and participants are normally very surprised at the range and the types of response which emerge.

There are numerous different conventions for notations in upwards laddering on goals and values, depending on the version of laddering you're using. Our advice is that if you're doing upwards laddering choose the appropriate form of laddering for your discipline, and then use the notation that is conventional in that form.

General points

One thing to watch for with laddering is the risk of slipping from one facet to another without realising it. The wording of the probe is important here. For instance, you can subcategorise cars into types of cars; you can also subcategorise cars into constituent components of cars. In this instance, it would be pretty obvious if you switched from one of these ways of subcategorising into the other; in other instances, it would not be so obvious (for instance, switching between 'contains materials' and 'contains components'). You'll often need to add some wording around the core verbal probe to put your question into context, but you need to keep the core verbal probe identical, otherwise there's the risk of problems. So, for instance, you might say something along the following lines: 'You mentioned "lots of good web references". I'd like to unpack the "lots of" first, and then the "good web references". How can you tell that something has "lots of" good web references?' That's a bit of a verbose example, but it gives the general idea.

We tend to use laddering a lot in conjunction with other techniques, particularly to unpack subjective terms and technical terms. So, for instance, a think-aloud session or a card sorts session might produce a term such as 'made by indirect percussion' or 'threatening looking', which is just too tempting to ignore; with laddering, you can unpack just what they mean by these terms. You don't need to tell the respondent that you're using laddering, since there's no element of deception involved; you simply ladder downwards and unpack the terms. Similarly, you can ladder upwards when they mention an ethical dilemma, or you can ladder downwards to unpack their categorisation of (for instance) types of shoplifters.

It's also possible to use the different forms of laddering within a single laddering session. You might, for instance, use laddering on people's categorisation to find out, say, how experts on corrosion categorise different types of corrosion, and you might then follow this up by laddering on explanations to unpack how they can identify each of the categories they have identified.

Students often feel the temptation to invent their own notations for laddering, usually by drawing a diagram that looks like a mind map. This is an extremely bad idea, for various reasons. One is purely practical: the resulting trees rapidly become unmanageably cluttered. Another is technical: you need to be able to show to which facet each block of responses belongs, and tree diagrams normally fail completely to show this. As a rule of thumb, unless you can explain clearly and accurately to someone else what is meant by 'polyhierarchy' and 'tangled graph' you should not be inventing your own notation – the existing notations are based on a lot of thought and a lot of technical factors about graph theory and the like, so your chances of improving on them via general knowledge and good intentions are slight.

We've mentioned facets and viewpoints repeatedly, but for clarity have left discussion of them till now. A respondent can usually conceptualise something from several different angles, quite explicitly. For instance, if you ask them about how they could tell if something was a good car, they might be able to answer from the viewpoint of someone driving that car, from the viewpoint of other road users, from the viewpoint of how well that car meets its intended function and from an ecological viewpoint; each of these might be wildly different from the others. A good example is four-wheel drive vehicles such as Range Rovers, which provide a lot of protection to the driver and are therefore good vehicles from that viewpoint, but which cause considerable damage to other road users in a collision compared to, say, a Mini, and are therefore bad vehicles from that point of view. You can usually specify viewpoint at the start of the session, but often the respondent will ask you quite explicitly what viewpoint you want them to use when a new viewpoint becomes relevant. A simple way of recording this is to note the viewpoint in brackets after the seed item, as shown below:

good car [driver of that car]
↓
gives me good visibility;
gives me lots of protection in an accident;

Analysis

There are various ways of analysing laddering data. One is to use standard content analysis, as described elsewhere in this book, on the responses. An issue specific to laddering in this context is that you have a choice of levels at which to do the content analysis. You can, for instance, do content analysis on everything that was elicited from the respondent. The trouble with this is that you're then lumping together results from several different levels, so you're not truly comparing like with like. A more useful approach is to choose a level, such as the second level down, or the bottoming-out level, and analyse the results from that level. A practical tip if you do this is to photocopy your notes, and then use highlighter to show the blocks at the chosen level (this is another reason why using the standard notation, with plenty of white space, is a good idea).

Another thing you can do with laddering is to look at similarities and differences in responses at chosen points. This can be particularly useful when you are trying to identify where novices have skill gaps compared to experts. If you compare experts' and novices' categorisations of academic publications, for instance, then you'll usually find that the novices have little or no categorisation of journals, whereas the experts have rich, well-developed categorisation of journals. Similarly, you'll find that students' explanations of 'well written' or 'professional looking' are very different from lecturers' explanations and prospective employers' perceptions of those same concepts.

A third thing you can do is to carry out a quantitative analysis of the numbers of branches at each point, to see how broad, deep and richly differentiated the graphs are for each respondent's knowledge. A typical pattern is for novices to have graphs which are broad (often as broad as an expert's) at the first level, but which then rapidly peter out, whereas the experts have deep graphs which are fairly even in their richness at each level – along the lines of half a dozen initial branches, each of which has about half a dozen subbranches, compared to a novice with seven initial branches, most of which don't have any subbranches.

Endnote

Just in case you're wondering, the Purdeys and the nuns are both real incidents. Purdeys are extremely high quality, and correspondingly expensive, shotguns; owning a brace of Purdeys is the equivalent of owning a Rolls-Royce (and indeed, people who own Purdeys often own a Rolls as well). Painting them any colour is the height of barbarity. We were told that one chap did so to camouflage them, having read a downmarket American shooting magazine for background research after being invited to an aristocratic pheasant shoot, and was blackballed when the fellow guests saw what he had done. We never did find out what Vietnamese ex-nuns are like, and we're not sure that we want to know.

The next section describes a technique related to card sorts and laddering, namely repertory grids. Most of the literature from which card sorts and laddering sprang was originally produced by the repertory grid research community. Repertory grids involve representing the respondents' knowledge in a matrix format, which has some similarities to card sorts, but which makes it possible to use various other forms of analysis.

Repertory grids: a systematic representation for respondents' knowledge

Hippodameus of Miletus . . . employed a nuanced grid.
(*Geology and Settlement: Greco-Roman Patterns,* p.202)

If you're fed up with trying to make sense from respondents' ramblings in natural language, then you might be interested in repertory grid technique. Developed by Kelly and his students in the 1950s, the technique offers an interesting combination of on the one hand allowing respondents to respond using the concepts that they want, and on the other representing their responses in a systematic fashion that allows both qualitative and quantitative analysis.

The core concept is that the grid shows entities relevant to the respondent, and attributes which the respondent considers relevant to those entities, combined with the appropriate values for each combination of entities and attributes. Suppose, for instance, that you're interested in how children perceive authority figures. What you could do is to choose some authority figure roles such as 'favourite teacher', 'least favourite teacher' and 'head teacher' and ask the respondent to think of the people who fit those roles for them. You then ask the respondent what two of these have in common that the third doesn't. So, for instance, the respondent might say that the least favourite teacher and the head teacher didn't smile very often, whereas the favourite teacher smiled a lot. The respondent then describes all the people on the list in terms of how much they smile. You then choose another three from the list and repeat the process; this time, the respondent might decide that two of them were successful in life, whereas the third wasn't. You keep going until the respondent runs out of relevant descriptors, or until you reach the end of the allotted time. The resulting grid looks something like Figure 4.3.

The grid is partly completed: it has nine elements, identified by number in italics, and one construct line ('didn't smile/smiled a lot') partly completed with numbers on a scale of 1 to 7. The first three elements have been given scores of 3, 7 and 4 respectively. When that line is completed, the next line will be done, using a different construct.

At this point, you can start doing some interesting things with the analysis. For example, you can look at which attributes the respondent mentions, compared to attributes that other respondents mention or attributes mentioned in the literature. You can also look at which attributes the respondent doesn't mention, which can tell you a lot. In addition, you can look at the distributions of the values. What if, for instance, the respondent has described all the 'didn't smile very often' people as 'successful' in the two relevant lines of the grid? It might be coincidence, but it might be that the respondent has drawn the conclusion from those school experiences that successful people don't

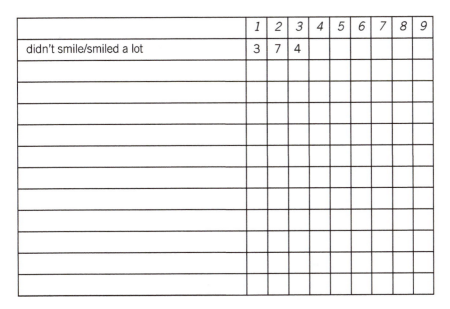

	1	2	3	4	5	6	7	8	9
didn't smile/smiled a lot	3	7	4						

Figure 4.3 A partially completed repertory grid

smile very often. Improbable? Clinical psychology is full of case studies of just that sort of conclusion, which have gone on to damage lives. Repertory grids offer a way of picking up such reasoning, which is one reason that they're well established in clinical psychology. They're also widely used in various other fields where it's important to get insights into how people actually construe the world, as opposed to how you think that they ought to construe it. The rest of this section examines the technique in more detail.

One important issue is how you choose your elements. They need to be at the same level of granularity, so respondents will be comparing like with like. So, for instance, elements such as 'bicycle' and 'car' are at the same level of granularity, but 'aircraft' and 'Y registration hatchback Mondeo' are at different levels. If the elements are people, then these are usually specified by roles, such as 'someone you would like to know better' or 'your line manager', with the respondent choosing specific individuals who fit these roles as the elements. This takes you into the question of how to choose the roles so that you cover a reasonable number and spread of them. For example, if you're looking at how people handle interpersonal stress, and you don't include any elements along the lines of 'someone who makes you stressed', then you're likely to get results whose relationship with reality is minimal. The usual convention is to use a minimum of about eight elements, which is the lowest number that one of the statistical tests for rep grid data can handle, but you can go below this if you're not using that test. Once you get much above a dozen elements, then respondents slow down noticeably. Something to remember is that respondents shouldn't use the same person as an element for two different roles. This can be trickier than it looks, since some roles will be strongly linked, such as 'someone who causes me stress' and 'my line manager' for many respondents.

Once you've sorted out your elements, you have various choices about how to handle the constructs (i.e. the attributes used to describe them). Usually rep grids are used to elicit the respondents' constructs, with these constructs being the focus of the research. This isn't invariable, though. It's methodologically difficult to compare results directly between rep grids which use different constructs, so there can be advantages in getting respondents to use the same constructs as each other. One way of doing this is to do a preliminary study to gather constructs from people comparable to your intended respondents, and then select constructs from that set as the ones to impose on the respondents in your next study. Another way is to get a few constructs from somewhere (e.g. a preliminary study or the literature) and then conduct the data collection on each respondent in two phases, with the first phase eliciting the respondent's own constructs in the usual way, and the second phase imposing your selected constructs on the respondent once the first phase is finished. In this case, if the respondent has already spontaneously generated one of your intended constructs, you don't need to repeat the process for that particular construct.

The usual process for eliciting constructs is via triadic elicitation as described above – choosing three elements and asking what two of them have in common that the third doesn't. For each line of the grid, and each corresponding construct, you use a different set of three elements. How do you decide which three to use? There are various methods, all with strengths and weaknesses, and not mutually exclusive – you can use combinations of methods. One is to choose sets of three at random. Another is to choose sets of three (triads) based on theoretical questions that you want to test, such as how well the respondents differentiate between authority figures and disliked figures. Yet another is to choose triads systematically, so that (for instance) you compare elements 1, 2 and 3 in the first row, 2, 3 and 4 in the next, and 3, 4 and 5 in the third. Respondents often suspect deep psychological ploys in your choice of triads, so the systematic approach has some advantages in steering them away from second-guessing about this. If you use some creative thought in your ordering of the elements, you can make sure that the triads will cover the comparisons of elements that you want to make (for instance, by having the authority figure as element 1 and the disliked figure as element 2).

There are various issues involving the nature of the constructs. Most grids ask respondents to say what it is that two elements of the triad have in common; handling the third one is trickier. One thing to watch for is when respondents conflate two different constructs (for instance, elements 2 and 4 are nice people, whereas element 5 is enthusiastic: this may be because the respondent believes that 'nice person' is the opposite of 'enthusiastic' but is more likely to be because the respondent has conflated the two separate constructs of 'niceness' and 'enthusiasm' on to one line of the grid). A more complex problem involves the nature of the construct. Do you treat the construct as a bipolar scale, with opposites at each end, or as a scale going from zero at one end to a maximum value at the other end? It can make a difference. For instance, if you treat 'niceness' in the first way, then you get a scale from 'nice' to something like 'nasty'; if you treat it in the second way, then you get a scale from 'not nice' to 'completely nice'. Why does this matter? It matters because the second way would allow a respondent to handle cases such as people who were neither particularly nice nor particularly nasty (i.e. near the zero end of the scale for both 'nice' and 'nasty') and also people who were capable of being both nice and nasty. Why not impose the second way on all the respondents? Because you might be trying to elicit the respondent's own preferred representation, precisely because you want to see whether they're treating such constructs as a single bipolar scale between two opposites, or as a pair of scales ranging between zero and 'completely', or as something else again. There's no brilliant single correct answer; you have to use judgement on this.

The next thing to think about is what values to use for the cells. In the earliest forms of rep grid, the values were just 'yes' and 'no'. These days, the tendency is to use scales, usually with values ranging from one to seven. There are arguments for and against each form of scale; for instance, there are questions such as whether a scale should start with zero rather than one (if you want to indicate that an element shows none at all of a particular construct), or with a minus value, if the respondent wants to use a scale ranging from 'very bad' to 'very good'. You can allow respondents to rate (so that they can give several elements the same value), or allow them to rank (so that the elements' values are ordered from lowest to highest); if you use ranking, then you need to decide whether to allow tied values such as 'equal third'. In addition, you need to decide whether to impose a single type of value on all the constructs, or to allow respondents to use different value types for different constructs, such as ranking for one construct and rating for another.

As if that wasn't enough choice, you also need to think about how to handle values such as 'don't know' or 'not appropriate' or 'usually this but sometimes that'. You can use a code to represent that value, such as 'DK' for 'don't know', but this will have implications for your statistical analysis – the stats test will probably require you to treat such cases as if they were missing values, or may simply refuse to work if you have missing values. This can get problematic because the distribution of such values can tell you a lot – for instance, which elements are thoroughly familiar to the respondent and which are less known. The cases where a value simply doesn't fit into your chosen framework are also important, because if there are a lot of them, this implies that you're using the wrong framework and need to change to a more appropriate one.

Some types of construct are very difficult to represent on a repertory grid, such as nominal categories. With the construct 'colour' for instance, you would only be able to represent values such as 'red' or 'yellow' by using one line of the grid to handle 'red', a second to handle 'yellow', and so forth, rather than being able to fit them all on to a single line where you enter the name of the relevant colour in each cell. (Yes, you can physically do that, but if you do, you're no longer using a rep grid in the proper sense, but rather a matrix, which is perfectly respectable, but which loses you the advantages of a method located within the sophisticated setting of Personal Construct Theory, in the form of rep grids proper.) This is one reason why we tend to use card sorts more than rep grids, since card sorts are good at handling nominal categories, and other categories such as 'either/or' which are difficult to handle via rep grids, and which are common in the domains where we do most of our work.

There are numerous variants on repertory grids. One useful variant is exchange grids, where you get respondents to fill in a grid as if they were someone from a specified group, and then compare the results with those you obtained from that other group; this allows you to measure the extent to which one group can see things from another group's viewpoint. Another is implication grids, where you ask respondents to say how strongly each construct in their grid implies each of the others (for instance, how strongly does 'nasty' imply 'professionally successful'?), which can be useful for identifying which correlations in the analysis are meaningful ones, and which may be purely accidental.

Rep grids are useful for extracting information from respondents systematically, but in a way which also allows them to use their own words. Another advantage of rep grids is that the statistical analysis allows you to do various things that would be different with most other techniques. A classic example in clinical psychology is using grids which include the elements 'myself as I am now' and 'myself as I would like to be'. This allows you to measure the statistical distance between these two elements at the start of the clinical intervention and then at intervals along the way, to see whether the intervention is reducing the distance between the respondent's perceptions of their actual self and their goal. (Yes, you could do something similar with questionnaires, but the questionnaires would almost certainly involve constructs pre-chosen by someone else, rather than being based on the constructs which the respondent chose as being particularly relevant to them.)

As with card sorts, rep grids can raise interesting questions which they can't answer, such as what someone means by a particular construct, or how the constructs fit together into a bigger framework of values and beliefs. Laddering provides a good complement to rep grids for this purpose, being well suited to representing explanations and frameworks of beliefs and values. It is also derived from Personal Construct Theory, so it integrates neatly with rep grids, as well as with card sorts.

There is an extended and sophisticated literature on repertory grid technique, much of it accessible via the internet, as well as various software supporting the technique both for data collection and for data analysis.

The techniques described in this and the previous sections are well-established techniques, and ones that we use a lot. They are not as widely known as they should be. The next sections describe methods which appear to be all too well known, if only at a superficial level. Most students use interviews or questionnaires for data collection. Both techniques are considerably more difficult to use properly than they might appear. We're not saying that you shouldn't use them, but we are saying that you should think carefully about whether they're the most appropriate method for your purposes – do they have advantages for data collection, and will they demonstrate better cabinetmaking skills?

Interviews: asking people questions

> THE ESCAPED WOLF
> PERILOUS ADVENTURE OF OUR INTERVIEWER
> (Dracula, p.125)

The late Stephen Jay Gould was fond of a journal article entitled 'What, if anything, is a jackrabbit?' The article discussed how the term 'jackrabbit' was applied to several different types of animal; for everyday purposes, this was not a problem, but from the viewpoint of a zoologist, those animals were so different from each other that the term was worse than useless. There's a plausible argument that the same principle could be applied to the term 'interview': it's applied to so many different things that it has become almost meaningless. It also suffers from the same problem as questionnaires: everyone thinks that they know how to do an interview, without needing to do any background reading or undergo any training, and most people make a sad botch of it when they try their hand at it. From a cabinetmaking point of view, you need to think long and hard about whether an interview actually is the correct method of data collection for your purposes, and if you decide that it is, you need to be very careful about ensuring that your write-up demonstrates loudly and clearly that you have done the requisite background reading, training and piloting.

So, what are the various beasts lumped together under this name? The standard introductions make pretty much the same distinctions between types of thing labelled as 'interviews' and give similar definitions of what 'interview' means, such as 'a conversation with a purpose'. The core concepts are that the process is:

- *interactive* – two or more people are interacting with each other (unlike, say, direct observation, which may not involve any interaction at all)
- *real time* – the interaction happens 'live', unlike, say, using a retrospective think-aloud, where the respondent carries out a task, and then reports on it afterwards
- *in natural language*, unlike, say, repertory grids, which use a constrained subset of language.

Apart from that, pretty much anything is up for grabs. The term 'interview' is applied to one-to-one interactions, to one-to-many interactions and to many-to-many interactions; it's applied to interactions where the researcher has a prepared list of questions and to interactions where the researcher doesn't; it's applied to data collection with and without props, about past, present, future and hypothetical settings, and numerous other beasts. Why should anyone care about this? The reason is that any idiot can collect bad (i.e. untrustworthy and scruffy) data; collecting data worth having is a lot more difficult, and means that you need to understand clearly the strengths and weaknesses of the tools at your disposal. From a sordidly mercenary point of view, no marker is going to be impressed by amateurish data collection which could have been carried out by any passer-by on the street: you get marks from collecting in a way which shows professional skills that ordinary members of the public don't have.

We'll begin by working through some of the things that are often called interviews, and then work through the things that are left.

Past imperfect, future tense

That particular line has been used before, but never mind. A lot of data collection involves either asking about past events or about future intentions. There are various techniques which have been developed specifically for collecting information of this sort, such as critical incident technique, illuminative incident technique, hard case technique and scenarios, which are described elsewhere in this book. The literature about each of these techniques includes detailed consideration of the particular problems involved in that technique, plus best practice guidelines about how to tackle those problems. With data collection about the past, for instance, you need to be aware of the literature on biases and distortions in human memory, by people such as Loftus. With data collection about the future, you need to be aware of the literature on the poor fit between expressed attitudes and subsequent behaviour.

If you're going to collect data about the past or the future, there are a lot of obvious advantages in using a technique developed specifically for that purpose. If you decide to use an interview anyway, but to include reference to the appropriate surrounding literatures about memory, etc. then you need to ask yourself whether what you are doing is actually different from one of the named techniques, or whether you're just reinventing the wheel and making it square.

The present

A lot of data collection is either about the present, or effectively timeless – for instance, asking people about their present lifestyle, or about their values and attitudes. If you're asking about activities, then you need to show why you aren't using a specific technique such as think-aloud technique or some form of observation. If you're planning to conduct an interview about activities situated in the respondent's normal environment with relevant props (e.g. the tools used to carry out the activity in question), then you need to show how this differs from think-aloud technique or observation, and what advantages it offers over them. If you're asking about lifestyle, then you need to show why asking about it is preferable to observing it either directly or indirectly. If you're interested in values or attitudes, then you can use techniques such as laddering which were developed specifically for this purpose, and which offer rich knowledge representation.

The residue

What does this leave? In some ways, not a lot. Once you know just what you want to investigate, there will probably be a specific technique other than interviews which will do a better job. For the early stages of data collection, however, interviews can be useful for getting insights into the topic. There are also various low-level craft skills which are traditionally lumped together under the term 'interview technique' and which are discussed in the section on face-to-face interactions with respondents.

In preliminary investigation of a domain, the advantages of using interviews are the same things which are disadvantages in the main data collection. Because there are no restrictions on the type and the format of questions, you can poke around in a versatile manner, doing the verbal equivalent of peering into thickets and turning over rocks. This can give you some useful insights into what's out there, and also into what appears not to be out there. It can also help with identifying important bits of terminology or etiquette. What it can't do is give you either numbers you can trust, or cross-validation on the qualitative features that crop up – for these, you'll need to use some other technique.

The next section goes into some of the nuts and bolts of asking people questions.

Face-to-face interactions with respondents: the nuts and bolts of asking questions

Then he began to chat of all things except ourselves and diseases.

(*Dracula*, p. 106)

Interviewing is easy to do badly, and difficult to do well. At its worst, it consists of some clueless soul asking whatever questions come to mind; at its best, it gives the respondent a chance to describe and explain things which might otherwise be missed completely. One reason that it is easy to do badly is that most people are very familiar with the concept through having seen interviews on television; the trouble is that being familiar with something is not the same as being able to do it well. Most people are also very familiar with the concept of scoring a goal in the FA Cup Final through having seen it done on television, but it is not likely that they would therefore conclude that they could do a good job of playing centre forward for Manchester United. When it comes to interviews, though, such sensible caution is usually thrown to the winds, and students wade fearlessly in where angels are standing around deciding what to do next.

This section is about asking people questions – what is usually known as interview technique. We've deliberately used a different name for this section, to stress the point that the same issues arise across numerous techniques, of which interviews are only one type. Watching students interview people is a good source of dark amusement to experienced researchers, partly because students appear to be endlessly creative when it comes to finding ways of screwing up. This section covers the usual ways of screwing up, but there's plenty of scope for finding more, so we don't claim to have been exhaustive.

One division used by most texts is between *structured, semi-structured* and *unstructured interviews*. In structured interviews, you decide on a structure for the interview before you start; this structure may be a list of topics, or a list of questions so tightly scripted that it's essentially a spoken questionnaire. How do you decide on the right topics and questions? That's a good question. One way is to derive them from the literature; another is to derive them from your own preliminary research. Unstructured interviews are what they sound like: you go in without any predetermined structure and fly the session by the seat of your pants, using your judgement to decide what to do next. Semi-structured interviews come in between – you have some predetermined topics and questions, but you also leave some space for following up interesting topics when they arise.

That all sounds very sensible, but it's liable to the same problems as questionnaires: if you structure your topics and questions around the literature, then the results you get will be framed within that same structure, which may or may not correspond to reality. On the other hand, if you give your respondents a free rein, then they're liable to come up with interesting stuff which is a nightmare to code, and they're also liable to shy away from all sorts of other interesting things that might have emerged if you'd been a bit more directive.

One distinction which doesn't appear much in the literature, but which is a very useful one, is the distinction between 'hard-wired' and 'soft-wired' structured interviews. In 'hard-wired' ones, the researcher decides what the precise topics and questions will be – for instance, 'the role of alcoholism in student retention'. In 'soft-wired' ones, the researcher decides on an overall structure, but doesn't specify the specific questions and topics. For instance, you might decide to ask the respondent to name what they consider to be the most important problems facing students, and then ask about the role of each of these in relation to student retention. This may look the same as a 'hard-wired' structure, but it isn't – you have no way of knowing in advance what the responses to the first question will be, and the phrasing of the follow-up questions will be completely determined by the responses to the first question. An extreme example of this approach is laddering, where the only predetermined bits are your initial question and the half-dozen standard laddering probes. With this, you're systematically uncovering the respondent's own structures, and structuring your session round that.

Another classic distinction is that between *open and closed questions*. Closed questions are ones which only allow a limited set of responses, such as 'Are you, or have you ever been, a member of a Communist organisation?' which only allows for the answers 'yes' and 'no', whereas open questions allow an unlimited set of responses, such as 'What is best in life?' which could elicit responses ranging from 'beauty and truth' to 'to crush your enemies; to see them driven before you; to hear the lamentation of their womenfolk'. The obvious risk with closed questions is that you're steering respondents towards a limited and potentially warped set of options which might bear no relation to reality; the obvious risk with open questions is that you'll get responses which are difficult to group into meaningful categories.

There is also assorted classic good advice about the phrasing of questions, so that they're clear, unambiguous, meaningful to the respondent, and so that they aren't steering the respondent towards an answer which you want to hear because of some personal agenda involving advocacy as opposed to research. For instance, tag questions such as 'don't you?' at the end of a question are an obvious cue that you're steering the respondent towards a particular answer. Most students who read such advice find it difficult to believe that anyone could be so crass; most students who listen to an audio recording of themselves interviewing some unfortunate respondent are unpleasantly surprised by the number of unclear, ambiguous leading questions which they ask, often using wording that is unintelligible to the respondent. It's a very good idea to record yourself doing some data collection, and then take a long, critical look at your performance, and you'll probably find doing this to be a good way of correcting some of those obvious faults.

There are various body language skills and interaction skills which are standard best practice and which are pretty obvious in other people (though not so obvious in our own behaviour) – for instance, maintaining eye contact, not interrupting, and so forth. There are various others which are not so obvious, and which are indicators of the professional researcher rather than the socially skilled amateur. A lot of these derive from the core concept that data collection is about finding out what's going on out there, not about trying to preach your own gospel to others, or trying to demonstrate the rightness of your cause. If your cause is that right, then the data will support it without any need for creative interpretation from you; if the data don't support your cause, then you need to ask whether your cause might be mistaken, not to try arguing away the data. What this usually translates into is listening to your respondent with an expression of genuine professional interest, without trying to judge them or correct them, even if what they are saying sounds initially abhorrent or hideously mistaken. This can be pretty hard going, but research is based on understanding what is actually happening: to take one extreme example, if you're trying to find a cause for cancer, then you need to know the reality about cancer, not a nicely sanitised version of it. Blindingly obvious? It may be for the cancer example, but if you're doing meaningful research, you'll probably run into a case sooner or later which tries your professionalism to the limit.

An example of this appeared in a documentary on French television, where the interviewee was a Frenchman who had fought in the Waffen SS. The obvious assumption was that the interviewee would be a thoroughly unpleasant individual, but he apparently wasn't. The obvious temptation for the interviewer was to try to break through the apparent veneer and show the beast underneath, but the interviewer instead took things calmly and steadily, and a very different picture emerged. What came out was a clear insight into the social milieu into which the interviewee was born, and how the anti-semitic values of that milieu predisposed him to enlist in the SS. The second thing that came out of the interview was the way that the interviewee had gradually realised the utter moral horror of the situation that he had put himself in, leading to a search for redemption. The third thing that emerged was the need to understand the social complexity and paradoxical banality of evil if we were to have any hope of preventing such horrors from recurring – simple truisms about bad people would be worse than useless, since they would divert attention from the root causes.

You shouldn't run into such extreme cases when doing a project, since from the cockroach point of view such topics would be highly inadvisable, but you do need to practise collecting data dispassionately, so that you can understand the underlying problem as thoroughly as possible. This is not to say that you should not have principles and passions; on the contrary, the world needs people who take an ethical stance. The tricky bit is making sure that your desire to stamp out a bad thing, such as cancer or war, doesn't lead you into distorting data so that it will fit with your preconceptions about the nature of the bad thing. Anyway, back to the issue of interview technique.

A problem related to maintaining calm in the face of obnoxiousness and ignorance is knowing how to respond appropriately if you hit something unexpected. What would you do, for instance, if your interviewee suddenly broke down in tears mid-interview, and told you that their life was so meaningless that they were contemplating suicide? An extreme example, but a real one, and one of the reasons that we have repeatedly mentioned the issue of ethical clearance for some topics. That particular example is unlikely to happen if you're interviewing corrosion engineers about galvanic corrosion, but if your research topic is emotional responses to divorce, then the odds will be rather greater, and you'll need to be prepared. How? That will depend on the topic, and the reason you have a supervisor is so that there's someone to help with such questions.

A lot of the guidance about interview technique is about questions and types of questions, such as questions of clarification versus probing questions. One handy way of understanding the deep structure of this is to work backwards from where you are trying to end up. It's highly instructive to try analysing the data from your pilot sessions, and even more instructive to try analysing raw data that someone else has gathered. You will probably be tempted towards physical violence or despair by the horror of the data – the number of rambling monologues, incoherent questions, inchoate responses, and general meaning-lessness of it all. The trick is to keep going beyond that reaction, and to learn from it, so that your next session collects data with some hope of validity, reliability and meaningfulness.

A closing thought about interviews: there are some specific forms of inter-view, such as the job interview or the television chat show interview, which are the topic of specialised literatures and of considerable research. If you happen to encounter this literature, remember that it's specialised and that what holds true for that particular form of interview may well be disastrously inappropri-ate for some other forms. It's also worth remembering that an interview tech-nique which works for one person will not always work for another. Again, a recording of yourself in action should be instructive, though you might find it advisable to wipe the recording afterwards, just in case some humorous col-league decides to brighten the department Christmas party with the recording where you ask the respondent a question which has a hideously embarrassing double-entendre which you had completely failed to notice.

After that extended rant, our next section is another rant, about question-naires. Most student questionnaires are embarrassingly bad, and in most cases questionnaires aren't even the most appropriate way of gathering the data. We're well aware that they're widely used in industry; we're also well aware of the amount of knowledge needed to use them correctly in industry, and we also regularly provide advice to industry people who are frustrated by the limitations of questionnaires and who want to find out about other techniques.

Questionnaires: when to use, when not to use, which questions to ask, what format to use

[They] seemed always a kind of catechism, as if Curwen were extracting some sort of information from terrified or rebellious prisoners.
(*The Case of Charles Dexter Ward*, p.173)

Questionnaires are very easy to use badly, and are very rarely used well. Because students have encountered lots of questionnaires in the course of ordinary life, they think that they know about questionnaires, and assume that (a) there's no particular expertise required to produce one, and (b) that questionnaires are appropriate for pretty much any situation. Both these assumptions are very seriously mistaken. From the viewpoints of cabinetmaking, cartography and cockroaches, questionnaires are asking for large amounts of trouble, with very little prospect of anything to show for it. Questionnaires are, like any other technique, only appropriate for some situations, and using them properly involves learning the appropriate skills. Most students don't learn these skills. The result is usually a project whose data collection method is inappropriate for that situation (bad from the cabinetmaking point of view), which provides no new methodological findings and no trustworthy data (bad from the cartography viewpoint), and which suggests that the student has not done enough homework about their methodology (bad from the cartography, cabinetmaking and cockroach viewpoints). So, when are questionnaires appropriate, and when are they not; if they are appropriate, how should they be used, and how should they not be used?

We'll start by looking at what a questionnaire is. It is, in essence, a list of questions which you prepared beforehand. Respondents can answer these questions either in their own words, or by choosing from a set of responses that you have prepared beforehand. You can ask respondents to fill in the questionnaire, or you can read out the questions to them and fill in the questionnaire yourself; for convenience, we'll lump these together for the time being. There are numerous other variations on these themes, which we'll come to later, but that is the essence.

The first problem you have to tackle is choosing the correct list of questions. How do you know that these are the right questions, and that they are phrased in the right way? If you fail to ask about the key issues, then you won't get any answers about the key issues. It sounds blindingly obvious, but it's where most questionnaires fail. Most students have a touching faith in their own ability to tell from general knowledge what the key issues are. From a purely factual point of view, most students are wrong about this. From the viewpoint of demonstrating cabinetmaking skills, most students leave themselves completely exposed to killer questions such as 'What is the evidence that these were the right questions to ask?' The correct answer involves having done extensive preliminary work to identify and validate the questions (almost certainly using techniques other than questionnaires, since otherwise you're just repeating the same problem in your preliminary work). Even if you're replicating a previous study, using their questionnaire, or using an established 'off the shelf' questionnaire, you'll need to check that it's appropriate for the context in which you want to use it. For example, imagine that you're replicating Colt and Browning's research into recreation. They developed a questionnaire which worked very well with their subject group, namely Hell's Angels. Does this mean that you can safely use the identical questionnaire on your subject group, who belong to an evangelical religious movement? (The answer, in case anyone is genuinely unsure, is a firm 'no' – although there is more social transfer between evangelical groups and bikers than you might expect, the two groups have very different preferred recreational activities, and questions highly relevant to one group would be meaningless to most members of the other – for instance, 'How much time per week do you spend witnessing?' or 'What do you think about hogs?')

The next problem, following on from the first, is how to decide which responses to allow. The best example we've seen of this comes from a humorous quiz in a women's magazine. It went as follows:

- How would you rather spend the evening?
    - (a) Stay at home and learn the tuba.
    - (b) Have dinner with Tom Cruise.

There were, to paraphrase a former politician, no alternatives. As usual, most students fondly believe that they know which responses to allow, through common sense and general knowledge, and most students are wrong. Most students are also wide open to killer questions such as 'How did you identify and validate the appropriate responses to offer for each question?' If you're to look like anything more than a raw, ignorant amateur, you need to know how to answer questions of this sort, and that's what the rest of this section is about.

Questionnaires: to use, or not to use?

The first question you should ask yourself is whether to use a questionnaire at all, or whether you should be using another method to gather your data. If you can show that a questionnaire is the best method for your purposes, that's fine, and you can happily proceed. If, on the other hand, you are only using questionnaires because you don't know about anything else, then that's a serious sign of ignorance on your part, and is just asking for trouble.

From a cabinetmaking point of view, questionnaires don't give you many chances to look good, and offer you a lot of chances to look bad, since by using questionnaires you're setting yourself up for comparison with a large body of well-established previous work. How well established? Well, the Normans based the Domesday Book on a survey which covered the whole of their conquered territories. The survey was carried out using a questionnaire very similar to those we use today. Then a second survey was carried out by an independent team, to check that the first team hadn't been bribed, corrupted or otherwise led astray. In other words, we're looking at two complete surveys of the entire population of a country, cross-validating each other. That was over nine hundred years ago. For good measure, they almost certainly conducted their data collection in more than one language (they would need to handle Norman French, Latin, English and probably Welsh). If you measure the average student questionnaire against this centuries-old benchmark, then the average student questionnaire looks pretty unimpressive. To put it another way, can you imagine someone on an interview panel saying: 'Wow, you used a questionnaire? That's amazing.' If you're going to use a questionnaire, then there's a sophisticated literature about their use, and you need to read it. This section is just a brief introduction, not enough by itself to make you look like a professional.

What are questionnaires good for? In principle, they're good for using to find out how widespread something is. Suppose, for instance, that you're interested in near-death experiences. You might have found some very interesting results in your initial work with interviews or critical incident technique, and now you want to find out how many people across the country have experienced the same things as your respondents. You know precisely what you want to ask, and why; you just want to know how widespread a particular thing is. Questionnaires can be very useful for tackling this sort of problem.

Another thing that questionnaires can be very useful for is ancillary data collection. For instance, some of our students were investigating correlations between objective features of a digitised image (such as the compression ratio) and subjective features such as respondents' opinions of how attractive the image was. Questionnaires were a perfectly sensible way of collecting information about the subjective features in a standardised format. Similarly, it's common to use questionnaires to gather feedback about, say, respondents' opinion of how well they understood the experimental task that they were asked to do. This helps the researcher to know whether the experimental results are likely to bear some relation to reality, as opposed to being meaningless gibberish because the respondents had no idea what the instructions meant.

If you're using questionnaires for ancillary data collection, then you can be reasonably sure that every respondent will complete the questionnaire, since it's an inbuilt part of the task. The situation is a bit different if you're using questionnaires as your main source of data. Most students are aware that response rates to questionnaires are low; most students are unaware of just how low response rates usually are. When Gordon was living in London, his local bus company sent out 23,000 questionnaires to get some feedback about their services. According to the local paper's feature on this, the response rate was zero – not one single questionnaire was returned. This is a slightly extreme example, but not very extreme; for a 'cold' postal questionnaire of this sort, the typical response rate is somewhere around 10 per cent. This means that if you sent out a couple of hundred questionnaires, you could expect to get perhaps twenty back. That's not an impressive number to base any conclusions on, and it's also a number which does not include 90 per cent of the people in your original sample. It's a fair bet that the people who do return the questionnaires will be unrepresentative in some way (with that way being the reason that they bothered to respond rather than ignoring your questionnaire and getting on with their life), but it's not wise to assume that you can predict the way in which they will be unrepresentative.

There are various established ways of getting the response rate up, but these all carry problems with them. You can do 'warm' questionnaires, where you contact people in some way before sending them the questionnaire – for instance, by sending an initial letter telling them about the questionnaire, and why you would like them to complete and return it. This will increase the number of people responding, but you'll still have a high proportion of non-responders, who will still probably be different from the responders. You can offer incentives to people who complete the questionnaire, but this gets you into complications about anonymity – how do you know who to reward if you don't know who the respondents actually are, and if you have some way of knowing who they are, will they answer the questions honestly? At the other end of the spectrum, it's sometimes possible to make a questionnaire compulsory (for instance, if you can persuade a manager to get all their staff to complete it). This will get the response rate up to about 100 per cent, but you're now dealing with conscripts, not volunteers, many of whom will resent being forced to spend time on the questionnaire and will give unhelpful, misleading or otherwise unhelpful answers. With any questionnaire filled in out of your sight (such as questionnaires distributed by post), you have no way of knowing who it was who actually completed a given questionnaire – it may have been the intended respondent working alone, or it may have been the respondent plus a helpful friend, or it may have been the respondent's flatmates filling in humorous answers to brighten up an evening when there was nothing entertaining on the television. The situation becomes even more interesting if you trustingly put up a questionnaire on the internet, where everyone with a twisted sense of humour can use their ingenuity to brighten your life via their responses.

Assuming that you still think that a questionnaire is the best method to use, what do you do next? If you're using the questionnaire for your main data collection, then you need to consider your survey design, which is covered in another section. Whether you're using the questionnaire for main data collection or ancillary data collection, you'll need to think about which questions to ask, how to ask them, how to structure them, and what responses to allow. These topics are the subject of the next subsections.

Which questions?

Questionnaires take time to fill in, and time to analyse. Most students ask more questions than they need to, which wastes the time of everyone involved. It's helpful to ask yourself two things about each question:

- What will this question give me?
- What literature or evidence can I use to justify the inclusion of this question?

If you don't know exactly how you are going to make use of the answers to this question, then you shouldn't include it.

It's highly advisable to derive your questions from your overall research question, and to include your intended method of analysis in this process. Most questionnaires err on the side of gathering large amounts of data using an assemblage of questions which look sensible at the time, and then dredge through the data with complex stats in the hope of finding something interesting (and/or of finding something to confirm the personal belief or hunch which motivated the questionnaire in the first place).

It's worth remembering that an indicator of quality in research is that it produces useful, interesting findings which could not have been safely predicted in advance. Before getting too far into your questionnaire design, you should try imagining what the data from your questionnaire could plausibly look like, and then asking yourself whether each of the possible outcomes is interesting, useful and something you couldn't safely have predicted in advance. If the answer is 'no' then you need to ask yourself seriously why you are proposing to spend time on something that could lead to boring, useless findings which you could have predicted in advance. It's always possible that you might get lucky and find the one outcome which is okay, but by definition lucky outcomes are rare, and basing your research strategy on hope and a belief in luck is not a good way of demonstrating your professional competence.

What phrasing?

The classic example of bad phrasing is to include a demographic question phrased as 'Sex?' If you're dim enough to do this, you'll find that a small but noticeable proportion of respondents will wittily reply 'Yes, please'. It's mildly funny the first time you encounter it, but loses its novelty once you realise that you'll need to discard all the questionnaires with this response, since if the respondent is joking about this answer, they are potentially joking about all the others as well. If you have only had 32 questionnaires returned out of the 400 you distributed, and you have to discard 3 of the 32 because of this response, then your sense of humour will probably evaporate pretty fast.

Naive souls worry a lot about 'bias' and aim for something which is 'unbiased'. This phrasing smells of trouble to the knowledgeable marker. Everyone has a viewpoint – even studied neutrality is a viewpoint – and this will be reflected in the questions that you ask and don't ask. This does not mean that all questions are equally advisable in their phrasing. A question such as 'What do you think are the causes of immoral behaviour such as pre-marital sex?' clearly has a strong set of assumptions built into it, and if used together with the three possible responses 'sin/illness/don't know' will systematically exclude a whole range of possible responses. 'Unbiased' questions are a will o' the wisp; what you can often do, however, is to produce questions where respondents are unable to tell what your personal stance is on the relevant issue. This will then reduce the likelihood that their answers were intended to make you happy (or unhappy, if they've taken a dislike to you because you've asked them to do a questionnaire when they could be doing something more fun instead).

The standard texts on questionnaire design give lots of good advice about how to phrase questions which are clear, unambiguous, etc. If you're using questionnaires, then you should heed this advice and have someone check your questions anyway, since it's much easier to spot bad phrasing in someone else's questions than in your own.

What structure?

First, length. The classic questionnaire from hell is a dozen or more pages of densely packed questions. People don't like answering these, on the whole. A useful rule of thumb is that the moment your questionnaire is more than a page long, its likely completion rate begins to plummet.

Next, layout. Most questionnaires are anonymous, in the hope that this will improve response rates. Most start with basic demographic information and sensitive information at the top, partly through convention, partly on the assumption that if someone is going to refuse to complete the questionnaire because they find a question intrusive, then it's better to have that happen right at the start, rather than needlessly antagonise the respondent by having them discover it at the end.

You'll need to collate the data from your questionnaires, which is usually done either by machine scanning, or by some human being slogging through the things and totting up the results in a separate scoring sheet. Make life easy for yourself by trying to do this collation on the draft of your questionnaire, and see which features of the layout cause you needless grief. If all the responses line up neatly against the right margin, for instance, then you can just run a finger down them to keep track of your place, while totting up the responses; if the responses are indented to various degrees, then the process gets fiddly and nasty. It's possible to do creatively efficient things like designing a template sheet with holes cut in it to show the responses in a way which makes the data collation easier.

Most student-designed questionnaires simply run through a series of questions from the first to the last. More sophisticated questionnaires may include branch points: for instance, if you answer 'yes' to question 3, then you go straight to question 5. This can be useful if you are reading the questions off the questionnaire to the respondent (for instance, in a phone survey), but will quite possibly go wrong if you get people to fill in the questionnaire on their own.

What responses?

There's a famous line about the universe not only being stranger than we imagine, but also being stranger than we can imagine. This comes across pretty strongly when you start dealing with real data. We mentioned earlier the classic witty response to the question 'Sex?', namely 'Yes, please'. Another classic example of the difference between reality and imagination involves the responses offered to the same question. When undergraduate students are learning questionnaire design, there's usually at least one would-be humorist in the group who thinks it's really funny to design a questionnaire which asks:

- Sex? Male/female/other

This is actually quite a useful way of distinguishing between someone who has potential to do real, significant research and someone who is just a clueless amateur. Clueless amateurs typically have a simplified, stereotyped view of the world, in which people fit neatly into predefined classes. The point of proper research is to find out what the world is really like, and when you start doing that, you soon discover that the world usually doesn't fit neatly into predefined classes. A huge number of problems arise precisely because of the things that don't fit neatly into predefined classes. In the example above, for instance, a surprising number of individuals don't fit neatly into the categories of male and female; in the UK, the number of such cases is somewhere between tens of thousands and hundreds of thousands of people, depending on just how you define the terms. A lot of babies are born intersex, with both male and female sexual characteristics to varying degrees; a lot of adults don't fit neatly into male/female categorisation by choice, ranging from occasional transvestism to post-operation transexuals. Age? Equally problematic, and not just for the obvious reason of people being reluctant to admit to being old; for instance, a lot of British males lied about their age to join the army in the Second World War, and now are two different ages, depending on what set of documentation you use. Name? Even worse. There are married women who use their married name, married women who use their maiden name, others who use both names for different purposes, others again who hyphenate with their partner's name, not to mention men who do the same.

So, what responses do you offer respondents? The usual options offered to respondents are:

- free text
- tick/ring/delete the appropriate option
- a number.

With free text, you allow respondents to write whatever they like. This improves the likely validity, but can drag you into horrible problems with coding and content analysis.

If you're offering a choice of options, you need to get these from somewhere. One way is to derive the responses from previous research. This allows you to compare your results directly with the previous researchers', thereby neatly increasing your data set substantially by including theirs as well, but you need to be sure that the responses which were appropriate for their respondents are equally appropriate for yours. Another is to derive the responses from the categories which emerged in your own preliminary research. For instance, if you used card sorts for the preliminary research, then you could offer responses based on the relevant categories generated in the card sorts. This allows you to be reasonably sure that the responses will be relevant and meaningful to your respondents. Beware dichotomous answers, such as 'Are you an experienced internet user? Yes/no', if possible – apart from being simplistic and difficult for respondents to answer (what do you mean by 'experienced' anyway?), they also get you into problems with stats, since you'll need a much larger sample size to test significance than if you used a finer grained set of responses.

If you're using numbers as the responses, then you get into a whole set of questions about measurement theory. Are you using cardinal, ordinal, interval or ratio values? Each of these has different implications for the types of stats that you can use to analyse the results, and it's highly advisable to think this through while you're still at the design stage. You can also use ranges of values – for instance, age groups of 6–17, 18–21, 22–24, etc. These are often used with ages because they allow people who are sensitive about their age to put themselves into a group, rather than giving an exact answer. The disadvantage is that this data format constrains the type of stats you can use on the results.

A popular format is the Likert-style scale, such as 'How athletic do you think you are, on a scale where 1 = not at all athletic and 7 = very athletic?' Again, there is a literature about this, and there are problems which have never been completely sorted out, such as whether to use a 0 or 1 as the appropriate end point for the sort of scale in the example just given. If you're going to use this sort of scale, you need to show that you know this literature, and that you know why, for instance, people usually use a seven-point scale, not a ten-point scale. We actually use Likert-style scales quite often for ancillary data collection; our preferred method is the 100 mm visual analogue Likert-style scale, which deserves some credit for its name, if nothing else. This consists of a horizontal line 100 mm long, with a label at each end (e.g. 'not at all athletic' at one end and 'totally athletic' at the other). The respondent draws a vertical line through this at the appropriate point – for instance, about halfway along if they consider themselves medium in the athletic stakes. (They're not allowed to measure the position of this vertical line – they have to do it by eye.) Once they have completed their task, you measure the distance in millimetres from the left side of the horizontal line to the respondent's vertical line, giving you a number from 0 to 100. This is a bit tedious, but gives you fine-grained ratio values (allowing you to use the most powerful forms of stats, and therefore to draw more powerful conclusions from a limited sample size), which are based on the respondent's visuospatial system (thereby bypassing the factors which limit the reliability of the usual 'choose a number' scales). The details of this are too involved to be included here, but if you're planning to use this approach, then you need to read up on it – a search on the keywords 'visual analog Likert-style scale' (with the American spelling) will lead you to a lot of relevant literature.

A neat example of what you can do with these is provided by Zoe. She asked people to rate university web pages on pairs of such scales, with one scale asking people how much a given feature would encourage them to apply for a place at that university, and the other scale asking how much that feature would discourage them from doing so. You might expect that the score on one scale was the opposite of the score on the other, but that wasn't the case. What actually happened was that for about 60 per cent of the responses the score on one scale was indeed the opposite of the score on the other. For about a third of responses, the score was low on both scales – the site neither particularly encouraged nor discouraged people. For a handful of responses, the site strongly encouraged and also strongly discouraged applications. Like most good research, this appears obvious with hindsight, but it wasn't predictable in advance. Using scales in this way allowed Zoe to put numbers on the relative frequencies of the various possible outcomes, and to show that the proportion of 'low discouragement/low encouragement' scores was much higher than the proportion of 'high discouragement/high encouragement' scores. It would have been difficult to do this using other techniques. Was she taking a gamble by asking a pair of questions in this way? No, because she had predicted this effect on the basis of relevant literature (argumentation theory and Bem's androgyny theory among others), so if she hadn't found it that would have been a significant absence.

Summary

This chapter reads in some ways like a recipe for tripe which we once encountered in a cookery book. The author began by advising the reader not to bother cooking tripe in the first place. He then went through the recipe, periodically advising the reader that they could stop now if they wanted. At the end, he described how to serve up the tripe, and concluded by recommending that they then throw it away and eat some nice pasta instead.

We don't take such an extreme stance, but we do advise only doing main data collection via questionnaires as an active, well-informed choice, and then only if you are prepared to read the literature about questionnaires thoroughly and follow best practice. You should be able to explain to the reader why questionnaires were better suited to your research question than any other method, and should be able to cite at least a couple of texts for each feature of your questionnaire design. Otherwise, you risk looking like yet another clueless, naive amateur about to waste everyone's time. This section, unlike other sections on data collection techniques, is not intended to give you enough information to use the technique adequately – we expect any readers interested in questionnaires to read up on the subject elsewhere. Our aim in this section is to make you aware of the issues involved in questionnaire use, since most students appear blissfully unaware of them.

Questionnaires are often appropriate for ancillary data collection. Even if you're just doing this, you need to read the literature as described above.

Another main use of questionnaires is at the end of a long and thorough process of research using other techniques, where the other techniques have identified the correct questions to ask, and the correct responses to offer, and where the questionnaire makes it possible to investigate the distribution of the issue in question across the population. This process of initial investigation via other techniques is usually enough to take up a complete student project in its own right, and more often will take up the equivalent of several student projects. It's not usually realistic to attempt both the initial investigation and the questionnaire within just one project. You may be able to use a questionnaire developed by someone else. This has advantages, but if you go down this route, you'll need to check whether you require permission and/or formal training to use the questionnaire, and you'll also need to check that it's valid for the use to which you plan to put it.

A closing thought brings us back to the cockroach principle. In some disciplines, questionnaires are well established, and students are taught to use them properly. This is a Good Thing. If you're in such a discipline, then by all means use questionnaires – you'll know how to avoid the mud pits that this section describes. That's probably a good note on which to end, so that's what we'll do.

The next chunk of this book is about analysing data. Most students don't think about this until after they've gathered their data. It's much wiser to think about the analysis right from the start – it can save you a lot of grief, and can let you achieve much more. There are numerous forms of analysis, ranging from qualitative description (where you say what is there) through quantitative description (where you put some numbers on what is there) to inferential statistics (where you say what the odds are of your results having happened just by chance). Most students find the thought of these a bit scary beforehand, but then are surprised by how good they feel after doing the analysis, when they can see patterns in the results that they hadn't noticed before. Since it's usually possible to analyse the same batch of data in several different ways to get different things out of it, it's worth reading the section on analysis fairly carefully, even the bits about methods that you weren't originally planning to use: you might find some useful ideas.

5

Data analysis

Content analysis: what is said in a text, how it is said, and how often it's said • Discourse analysis: who says what, about what, to whom, in what format • Knowledge representation: formats, structures and concepts for making sense of knowledge • Statistics: describing things with numbers, and assessing the odds • Descriptive statistics: giving a systematic description of the numbers you've found • Measurement theory: types of measurement and their implications • Inferential statistics: what are the odds against your findings being due to random chance?

> *'No,' he said. 'Moles wouldn't make any sense to me.'*
>
> (*People of Darkness*, p.11)

Content analysis: what is said in a text, how it is said, and how often it's said

Your first encounter with data consisting of natural language is likely to be a testing experience. Faced with the sheer quantity and the rich chaos of the data, it is very easy to feel overwhelmed. Idealistic beliefs about not showing bias in your analysis start to buckle when confronted with the number of possible analyses and the number of possible interpretations of unclear, incomplete and inconsistent data. Much the same happens to any grim resolve you may once have had to analyse the data thoroughly and systematically. So, what do you do? You may decide to give way to the dark side, selectively quoting the bits which match your prejudices and support your case, ignoring anything which suggests you might be wrong. You may comfort yourself with the thought that you are doing the same as lots of other people in the field, or with a dodgy sophistry about all truths being equally valid. Understandable, but scarcely heroic or something of which to be proud.

In case you're wondering why we go on about this so cheerfully, here's an example of what you're likely to get from someone thinking aloud while looking at a web page.

> It looks quite nice, I like the erm . . . header, it's got some cool graphics going on. The picture, I think they should have taken it on a sunny day, even though there is a rainbow. Erm . . . the side links are good, nice pale blue colour and clear. I'll have a look at the people section, doesn't have any pictures or anything, which would be nice if it did, not too much information here . . . so I'm not overloaded. Erm, there's just a long list of academic staff which is ok, the fonts are easy to read, mostly content and there's not a large amount of graphics in this bit. The Undergraduate page, there's a nice picture of the library, looks very old. I'll go on Admissions, there's how to apply and . . . it's fairly clear. It's split up into different sections and there's a different size font used for each section which is useful.

You get similar stuff from interviews and from open-ended questionnaires. It's usually ungrammatical, rambling, and, when you look at it in detail, incoherent out of context. In the example above, for instance, does the 'it's fairly clear' refer to the Admissions section, or the 'How to Apply' section, or to the site as a whole? You can guess, but that's not the same as being sure. So, what can you do with something like this?

If you have a clean research question and a good research design, then you will already know what you are going to do with it. If you have just rushed into a questionnaire or a batch of interviews without planning ahead, then you will grind to a halt about here. What we'll do is demonstrate some ways of analysing this type of data, each way appropriate for some research questions and not for others.

Basic tabulation

One thing you can do is to identify some categories, and then count how often each one comes up in each subject's ramblings. If you're investigating the reasons people give for choosing their career, you might use categories such as money, fame, power, social responsibility and fulfilment. You can then count how often each subject mentions each of these topics, and represent the results as a table like the partially completed one in Figure 5.1.

This may look simple, but even getting this far is tricky; we'll return to the reasons for that. First, though, what can we apparently tell from the table?

S	Money	Fame	Power	Social responsibility	Fulfilment	Other
1	15	6	4	0	1	16
2	5	3	6	5	4	7
3	1	0	3	12	21	14
...						
Total						

Figure 5.1 Table showing mentions of reasons for career choice

One thing is that there are some striking differences between subjects: subject 1 has said a lot about money and power, but nothing about social responsibility, whereas subject 3 appears to have done the opposite. What does this mean? It's hard to tell without seeing the original data. It might be that subject 1 has waxed eloquent about the joys of having a well-paid job, whereas subject 3 has said much about the joys of a socially rewarding path. Conversely, the opposite may be true. Subject 1 might have gone into a long rant about people who are only interested in money, and ended the rant by concluding that fulfilment is the only thing that matters, while subject 3 performed an equally eloquent rant about do-gooders, and concluded with the statement that only money really matters. Both these patterns would produce the same results in the simple table shown in Figure 5.1. The moral of this hypothetical horror story is that you need to choose and pilot your categories carefully. The other thing that an experienced reader can tell from this table is that the number of items lumped into 'other' is fairly high – it's higher than the number of mentions of power, for instance. This suggests that the categories need to be reconsidered, since they probably aren't giving good enough coverage.

This leads on to a classic question, namely, how do you choose the categories? There are various answers to this, and they lead us back towards research design.

Answer 1: use categories from the literature

This has advantages such as allowing you to blame someone else if things go wrong, while claiming credit for reading the literature and following best practice. You might, for instance, design your study as an extension of McPherson and Phibes' (2004) study, investigating a different subject population; in this case, it would make perfect sense to use the same categories as they did (and also the same briefing materials, procedures, etc.). You are then able to compare your results directly with theirs. (This is why the methodological details in write-ups are so important: they allow readers to do direct replication of the study without having to pester the authors with questions about exactly how the categories were defined.) This is fine if their categories are sound, but grim if their categories turn out to be vague, poorly defined or misleading; some time spent in piloting should show which is the case.

Answer 2: use categories derived from your research question via a clear chain of reasoning

This can be pretty efficient if you get it right. For instance, suppose that your research question is about whether people normally think of risks in terms of the probability of something happening, or in terms of the number of times that thing will happen over a given length of time. One sensible research design would involve asking people to talk about risks (without mentioning either probabilities or frequencies in your instructions), after which you could count how often each subject spontaneously mentioned probabilities and how often they mentioned frequencies. Everything else you can ignore. How can this go wrong? One possibility is that your subjects will typically use an ambiguous or vague phrasing (such as 'typically') where you can't tell whether they're thinking in terms of a probability or a frequency. Again, some piloting should tell you what to expect.

Answer 3: derive categories from the data

This sounds pure and noble, allowing the subjects to speak for themselves. In reality, it's about on a par with being hit in the groin with a carelessly swung four-inch, drop-forged WHS pointing trowel, as one of the authors can testify from experience of both cases. There are various reasons for this. One is that, no matter how conscientiously you try to reflect the subjects' words, you will still have to defend your categorisation against any barbarians who feel inclined to accuse you of bias and of choosing categories to reflect your own prejudice. You may virtuously use independent judges to do the categorisation, and then check the degree of agreement between them statistically, but the barbarians can then simply accuse the judges of sharing your underlying bias (whether that be liberalism, conservatism, reductionism or Last Tuesdayism). Another is the sheer amount of time this takes. Yet another is the risk that, as an outsider, you may be missing the significance of phrasings which are highly meaningful to the subjects. Suppose, for instance, that you are gathering data from field archaeologists and they mention in passing that something happened on a gravel site in summer. Is this just local colour, or is it an important bit of scene setting used to convey a lot of meaning without needing to specify it in full? Simply categorising everything possible isn't much help; even if it doesn't involve a prohibitive amount of time, it risks giving equal prominence to the trivial and to the important in the subjects' world views. This is one reason why we tend (a) to use methods such as card sorts quite a lot, where the subjects can do their own categorisation, and (b) to use careful research design, to avoid getting into this sort of mess unless we actively choose to.

Sometimes you need to get into this sort of mess. An example is if you're studying how students help each other with software problems. Here, you may well need to study the words they use, without being able to use a neat experimental design to get round the problem, and without a directly applicable previous study from which to borrow some handy categories. Another example is if you're comparing several standard texts to see what topics they consider important and which they consider peripheral. In both cases, you may well need to come up with your own categories. How can you do this?

In some cases, there are ways of reducing the problem space. In the case of the field archaeologists' anecdotes, for instance, you could try asking another field archaeologist to walk you through the data, explaining the significance of the various points. More often, you just need to eyeball the data for a while, seeing what strikes you, and (more difficult) seeing what is significantly absent. Once you have some first-pass draft categories, you can then try coding a subset of your data, and seeing how smoothly it goes. It's advisable to keep a running list of which phrasings you've coded into which categories so that you can be consistent. In large data sets, the running list can be pretty long. This should show you things like whether your categories are exclusive or inclusive where they need to be. (For instance, could your categorisation for the archaeologists cope with an example like 'waterlogged gravel site' using a clear criterion for whether this was a category all of its own, or one mention each of 'waterlogged' and 'gravel'?) Once you've refined this to your initial satisfaction, you can then try getting independent judges to use it, and check whether the degree of agreement between them is acceptable.

We often use a multi-pass approach, consisting of verbatim analysis, gist analysis and superordinate category analysis. This has the advantage of traceability: readers can follow your process from raw data through the various stages until your final, coarsest grained analysis.

Verbatim analysis

Verbatim analysis involves counting the instances of a particular word or phrase verbatim – that is, the identical words, as opposed to words which in your opinion are equivalent. So, for instance, if your subjects are potters and they mention 'wheel made' on one occasion and 'wheel thrown' on another, you treat each of these as a separate category because the words aren't identical, even though they may look like the same thing to you. Verbatim analysis typically involves large numbers of categories, each of which only has a few instances in it. It has the advantage of working well with software analysis – you can just do a search for instances of each term. Why bother with this layer at all? The example above demonstrates why.

Many potters make a distinction between the two terms. 'Wheel thrown' refers to pots made using fast wheel technique, whereas 'wheel made' is a generic category that includes both slow wheel and fast wheel techniques, which (despite both involving wheels) are completely different from each other. Confusing and untidy? Maybe, but your job is to cope with that, not to blame them if you get your analysis wrong because of not paying attention to this sort of detail. This is one reason that we usually use combinations of techniques when gathering data: laddering, for instance, is very handy for unpacking distinctions of this sort efficiently and swiftly.

Gist analysis

Gist analysis is the next layer up. This is where you decide which of the verbatim categories are actually synonymous alternative phrasings of the same thing – for instance, 'Windows-compatible' and 'compatible with Windows'. You can then create a gist category which includes all of the variant phrasings, add together the number of instances of each variant phrasing, and put the total in the box for that gist category. So, for instance, if you have 5 mentions of 'Windows-compatible' and 3 of 'compatible with Windows', then you can create a gist category with a name such as 'compatibility with Windows', sum the 5 and the 3, giving 8, and put that 8 into the box for 'compatibility with Windows'. At this point you can do some soul searching, if you feel so inclined, about whether you should have different names for the gist-level categories, or whether you can reuse a verbatim-level category name at the gist level. That's another story; for the moment, our focus is on the point that the gist-level terms are equivalent in meaning to each other, as opposed to being related to each other. That takes us on to the next level.

Superordinate categories

Superordinate categories are the next layer up. This is the level where you deal with categories which are 'children of the same parent'. So, for instance, 'Windows-compatible' and 'Macintosh-compatible' are clearly related to each other, but are clearly not synonymous. You might then group them into the same superordinate category, with a name such as 'compatibility'. Again, you state which of your previous categories you are lumping together into this new category; again, you add the numbers from the previous categories. So if you have 8 instances of 'Windows-compatible' and 6 of 'Macintosh-compatible' you end up with a total of 14 in the superordinate box for 'compatibility'. What if this still leaves you with lots of categories? Well, you can repeat the process of creating superordinate categories, and lump together some of your superordinate categories into a higher level set of superordinate categories. 'Compatibility' might be lumped together with the superordinate category of 'data format' into a higher level superordinate category with a name like 'formats and compatibilities'. You can keep on going up through this process for as many layers as you want.

There are various advantages to this approach. One is that it provides full traceability showing how you got from the raw data through to your five major categories at the end. In theory, if the reader wanted to, they could start with your verbatim categories (probably presented in your appendices – verbatim tables can be a bit verbose for the main body of the text) and then do their own lumping of these into gist and superordinate categories of their choice. In practice, it's a bit like offering them a chance to wrestle with your pet bear: would-be critics tend to be less vocal when faced with the prospect of having to do some brute work, as opposed to armchair criticism. It also has the advantage of making it easier for you to re-analyse your data if you decide that some of your higher level categories are wrong – you just need to amalgamate the numbers from the previous categories, without having to go back to the raw data and starting all over again from scratch. Last but not least, this approach works well with spreadsheets, allowing you (a) to get the software to do the sums for you, once you have your wizards and macros sorted out and (b) to produce pretty and impressive-looking tables showing how each set of categories is amalgamated into the next.

That's basic content analysis; as you may have guessed, there are much more sophisticated versions, if you're prepared to do the reading and the work. One sensible thing you can do is to ask yourself whether you want to get into this in the first place, and whether the answer is worth the effort. Sometimes the answer is a clear 'yes' but sometimes it's a clear 'no'. In the latter case you'll need to rethink the method that you're proposing to use and go for something cleaner. When might the answer be a clear 'yes'? One case is when you're specifically looking at pre-existing texts – for instance, in media studies. Another is when you don't know what to expect in the data and you're doing exploratory work to see what emerges. The risk in this case is that you might find an enigmatic set of apparently significant absences, or a set of rambling statements which don't make much obvious sense. That can be very useful as a starting point, where you choose appropriate methods to follow up the initial findings and make sense of them, but it has drawbacks as an end point. Readers might not be impressed by a write-up in which you say, in essence, that you don't have a clue what was going through the heads of your subjects.

The next section is closely related to this one. It deals with discourse analysis, which overlaps with content analysis. Discourse analysis tends to be more about activities and structures than content analysis: things like who interrupts whom in a conversation, or what the underlying structure of a text is. It is widely used in media studies to uncover underlying social assumptions that we often overlook precisely because they're so familiar; it can also be used in a wide range of other settings, to look at the underlying assumptions and structures in those areas.

Discourse analysis: who says what, about what, to whom, in what format

'But if you had heard him speak of wombats – oh, just in passing, and not with any sense of ill-usage – it would have brought tears to your eyes.'
(*Desolation Island*, p.69)

The boundary between content analysis and discourse analysis is fuzzy. A useful rule of thumb is that if it involves actions then it's discourse analysis, and if it doesn't then it's content analysis in the static (rather than the generic sense). The actions may be various things, including plots, narratives and conversations. As with content analysis, discourse analysis can be useful for putting some numbers on to things where you suspect that there are regularities going on (or significant absences lurking around). As with content analysis, there's a fair chance that you'll just find what you expected, and that it will be viewed sceptically by barbarians as just another batch of numbers being used to bolster your pre-existing arguments, rather than as something which contributes anything new and useful to the debate.

One of the best examples of discourse analysis that we've seen is a satirical book entitled *Planet Baywatch*. Because it's satirical, the numbers it quotes are probably invented, but the questions it asks are incisive and say a lot about contemporary society. So, for instance, it looks at which people are portrayed in which roles, and concludes that in *Baywatch* fat people are portrayed as being generally laughable, often bad and never heroic. It also looks at the storylines and finds that many of them tell the story of people who (a) are disrespectful to the Baywatch team early in the episode, (b) fall into the water, (c) are unable to swim, (d) are rescued by the Baywatch team and then (e) realise the error of their previous ways. (In case you're wondering, not all the storylines are this complex; another frequent one involves (a) someone doing something bad, after which (b) Mitch beats them up.) A more usual approach is to study something more serious looking, such as 1950s Hollywood cowboy movies. If you do this, you will probably find that if the hero falls in love with a Mexican or otherwise unAmerican woman, she will be killed before the movie ends. You might find that in those same movies a surprisingly high proportion of heroes' mothers died when the hero was young.

Moving away from the media, you might study recordings of conversations, looking at things like who interrupts whom and how often; how long each person talks for; whose suggestions are eventually accepted, etc. This can tell you interesting things about power dynamics and so forth. We've described this in two sentences, because the core concept is so simple, but its simplicity is linked with its being a powerful tool, and well worth considering in your data analysis.

There are various ways you can locate your discourse analysis in relation to the wider academic world. For instance, you can link it to a representation and/or a body of theory about discourse (as opposed to theory about the topic which you are using discourse analysis to investigate).

An example of the first of these involves using cognitive causal maps, which involve diagrams representing the network of causal assertions that the subject is making. So, for instance, if they say 'It was a wet Friday night, so I was expecting reports of a pile-up on the motorway' then you can represent this as one concept ('wet Friday night') with an arrow leading to the second concept ('pile-up on the motorway'). You can use various annotations to show whether the first concept causes the second, sometimes causes the second, usually prevents the second from happening, etc. What you end up with is a network diagram showing which concepts the subject believes to be relevant to the topic under discussion, and showing what they believe to be the way that things work in that area. This can be useful for identifying chains of causality, such as A causing B and B in turn causing C. If you're looking at teenagers' views of what affects their chances of getting a job, or politicians' views of how to bring about world peace, then this approach can give some interesting insights. The subsection on graph theory, in the section on knowledge representation, gives more detail about how to represent this kind of knowledge.

An example of linking the discourse analysis to a body of theory might be examining people's stories about job interviews from the viewpoint of transactional analysis (as in 'games people play'). You might find, for instance, that some subjects tell these stories from within a framework of 'ain't it awful?', recounting tales of doom inevitably striking them no matter how hard they try, whereas others tell them from within a framework of 'look, no hands' as examples of their ability to succeed brilliantly with no visible effort.

How do you do it? There are various ways of setting about discourse analysis, ranging from a fairly impressionistic listing of instances of the phenomenon which interests you (such as the heroes whose mothers died when the hero was young), to very formal approaches such as story grammars. If you're looking for underlying plot structures, then one simple, flexible method of getting started is as follows. You take the text and translate every specific instance into a generic class. So, for instance, where the text says 'Big Jim' you write 'the hero', and where the text says 'he shoots Snake-Eyes Pete dead in front of the saloon' you ignore the detail, and write 'he kills the villain'. You can do this at successive levels of abstraction if need be, stripping out the instances at the first level and then stripping out the subplots at the next level, and so on. Propp did this for Russian folk tales and produced elegant, abstract, story grammars; Campbell did the same for hero tales and produced similarly archetypal abstractions. A classic example is the deep structure match between Gilgamesh and Enkidu in the *Epic of Gilgamesh*, and Han Solo and Chewbacca in *Star Wars* – both heroes having powerful, semi-human companions.

As with content analysis, this can be pretty handy for spotting significant absences – things which never happen and whose absence tends to be taken so much for granted that most people never think about them. The converse of this is that the question often contains the seed of its own answer, which in turn contains the seeds of a further crop of questions: one such question is why you are looking for these particular absences in the first place. A common criticism of content analysis is that it's often a laborious way of gathering evidence to support what you expected to find in the first place. In such cases, you can end up preaching to the converted.

An underlying theme in this section and the previous one is how to represent the information gleaned from the text. The next section looks specifically at ways of representing knowledge, whether it comes from texts or from respondents. This is a topic which is not sufficiently widely known. Knowledge representation is a very useful tool to have in your box – it gives you more ways of making sense of the data.

Knowledge representation: formats, structures and concepts for making sense of knowledge

A third suspicious letter was found in an unknown tongue and even an unknown alphabet.

(*The Case of Charles Dexter Ward*, p.182)

If you're trying to trap a moose, then it's a good idea to find out a bit about how moose are put together before planning your trap – for instance, if they're put together in a way that makes them good at kicking things to matchwood, then it might be a good idea to make your trap pretty solid in its kickable bits. If you're trying to trap some knowledge, then it would appear an equally good idea to know something about how knowledge is put together, and this has been done by various disciplines, under various names such as 'epistemology' and 'knowledge representation'. Since most human beings have trouble remembering the differences between epistemology, ontology, hermeneutics and the like, we've gone for 'knowledge representation' as being easier to remember. So, what is knowledge representation, and why should you care about it?

The core idea is that knowledge is not a single homogeneous thing, but that there are different types of knowledge, and different ways of describing, classifying and representing that knowledge. Each of these offers different advantages and disadvantages; if you choose a sensible one for your purposes, then you can do better work for less effort, and look good into the bargain, without any sin or deception involved. If you choose the wrong one, then you can waste a lot of your time and other people's, and if you get it really seriously wrong, then you can divert everyone in the wrong direction for a long time. There's an interesting asymmetry, in that sometimes you can have a right (i.e. valid and reliable) knowledge representation which clearly works well, but fail to notice that there's a different and equally right representation which opens up a whole different world of possibilities.

Knowledge representation overlaps with measurement theory, described in a different section, and we'll refer to that on occasion.

We'll begin with an example involving animals. A simple distinction is between wild animals and domestic animals. That involves the concept 'animal', with two possible values of 'wild' and 'domestic'. You could, if you feel so inclined, represent this as 'wild? +/−' with the distinction between the two types represented in binary fashion as a plus or a minus. It's a start. However, there are various walks of life in which you might want to be able to make finer grained distinctions. Some animals, for instance, hang around with human beings a lot, but are not domestic animals in the same way that, say, a pet dog is: for instance, a fairly tame robin in the garden. You can't represent this sort of intermediate value on a binary system which only allows the values 'yes' and 'no'. What could you do instead? An obvious answer would be to have some sort of numeric scale, where 0 meant 'completely wild' and 7 meant 'utterly domesticated', for instance. For most purposes, this would probably be adequate, but there will be situations where you need to make distinctions of a type that won't fit neatly on a numeric scale. Suppose, for instance, that the animal in question is a moose which has just caused various damage in downtown Anchorage, Alaska. The legal implications are likely to be different if the animal is an escapee from someone's moose farm as opposed to a wild moose which has become casual about humans, so you'd want some way of representing whether the animal is and always has been wild, or is a domesticated animal which has gone wild, or is a domestic animal which escaped from the farm ten minutes ago. That clearly won't fit on to a numeric scale; you need to use a set of nominal categories to represent this. Nit-picking? Next time you try filling in a questionnaire and find yourself cursing the way that you can't work out what you're supposed to be putting in which box, you're probably a victim of imperfect knowledge representation on the part of the perpetrator of the said questionnaire.

So, what are the key concepts of knowledge representation, and how can they make your life better? The answers will vary depending on which literature you blame for your own approach; we've borrowed concepts from a variety of disciplines, so the answers are somewhat heterogeneous. (Pedantic readers may be pleased to note that this section is returning concepts to the disciplines from which we borrowed them, so the term 'borrowed' is not being excessively mangled.)

One useful concept from linguistics is the three-way distinction between entity, concept and word. (For consistency, we're using the term 'entity' to mean 'thing' in the broadest and vaguest sense. Different disciplines use different terms with roughly the same meaning as 'entity' so the terminology could get complicated if we didn't standardise here.) This three-way distinction is handy because it allows clear representation of situations where all three things exist – for instance, the term 'rhinoceros' has an entity, a concept and a word associated with it – and also of situations where only two of the three exist – for instance, the term 'unicorn' has a concept and a word associated with it, but no entity. There are numerous other permutations, such as the case of the alleged jackrabbit, where the concept and the word exist, but where the word is applied to several entities which are treated as quite different by zoologists, but which are treated as cases of the same concept by the lay public. Concrete nouns refer to physical entities, which exist whether we like it or not; abstract nouns apply to concepts, which are human creations, that we can change to whatever we like, and which we can call whatever we like. Categorisation is also an example of how concepts work, with the categorisation being a human artefact. If a category applies to physical entities, then we can apply whatever concepts and words we want to them, but that isn't the same as changing the entities referred to by the concept and the word. We could, for instance, put Russian tractors in a verbal category of 'light things that are fun to push' if we felt so inclined, but that wouldn't make the slightest bit of difference to their actual weight when we tried pushing them, and would be a good example of a remarkably dim bit of categorisation. Similarly, we can change the name that we apply to a concept if we want to – rebranding a product is often done via a name change in the hope that this will also change people's concept of the entity to which it is applied (i.e. the product). Will that change the concept, or will people just keep on using the same concept under a different name? This is a good question, which space prevents us from tackling here.

The issue of categorisation brings up another useful concept, namely the concept of 'class' in the knowledge representation sense, as a category to which entities may belong. Most categorisation systems allow classes to contain smaller classes within them, and allow the smaller classes to contain still smaller ones, and so on – for instance, the class 'bird' can contain the class 'songbird', which may in turn contain the class 'finch'. If you follow this system down to the end, you reach specific individual birds, such as the yellowhammer at Marian's bird table this morning, where you can't subdivide the class any further; this is known as 'bottoming out' and that particular yellowhammer is known as an 'instance' of the class 'yellowhammer'. (The individual instance where you bottom out is also known as 'leaf level', with the higher level classes being referred to as 'branches' or 'twigs'.) Figure 5.2 should make this clearer.

In Figure 5.2 the box at the top has two children (the two boxes on the next level down). The left-hand child has three children of its own; the right-hand child has two children of its own. The bottom level boxes (the children's children, or grandchildren), are at *leaf level*, where the graph bottoms out (i.e. goes down to its lowest level of detail). The boxes are known as *nodes*; the lines between them are known as *arcs*. This particular graph has three levels.

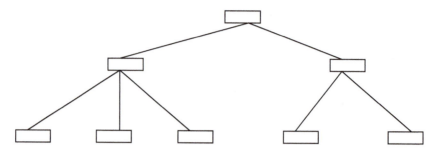

Figure 5.2 A small tree

There's an entire branch of maths relating to this, known as graph theory. 'Graph' in this sense is completely unrelated to 'graph' in the sense of something similar to a histogram. This deals with ways of representing different forms of network, and allows you to do both qualitative and quantitative representation and analysis of data in interesting ways.

The simplest form of net consists of a bunch of things (known as nodes) joined by lines (known as arcs). The line simply tells you that the things on each end of it are connected to each other in some way. A familiar example of this is the mind map. So, for instance, if your net has one node for John Dee and another one for Edward Kelley, linked by an arc, then that simply tells you that Dee is linked in some way with Kelley. So what? Good question. Simply saying that two nodes are linked doesn't get you very far.

The obvious next step is to put some labels on your arcs, so that you know what sort of relationship you're dealing with. So, for instance, you might label some arcs as 'professionally linked to' and other arcs as 'related by marriage to'. This starts getting you somewhere – for instance, if you did this for the Elizabethan power structure, you'd often find the same pair of nodes being joined by both a 'professionally linked to' arc and a 'related by marriage to' node. You can now start doing other interesting things like seeing how closely linked a given pair of individuals are, if you're analysing friendship networks and suchlike. What you typically find in such cases is that your nodes form fairly well-defined groups, with lots of links between individuals inside a given group, and with far fewer links between that group and the other groups. The individuals who do have numerous links to different groups are comparatively few, and are typically socially powerful because of their ability to act as go-betweens and mediators. Quite often the links are only obvious with hindsight; a popular recent example is the new social networks formed when smokers were obliged to smoke outside the building, and thereby started meeting people from groups that they would not otherwise have encountered.

With this sort of network, it doesn't matter which way round you read the relationship: 'Dee is professionally linked to Kelley' means the same as 'Kelley is professionally linked to Dee'. That's fine for some relationships, but there are other types where the relationship is clearly directional – for instance, 'parent of'. 'John is the parent of Katherine' is not the same as 'Katherine is the parent of John'. There are obvious advantages in being able to represent this sort of relationship, but how do you do this? You do it by using arcs which specify the direction of the relationship. The resulting graph is known as a directed graph (because it shows directions), or 'digraph' for short. Digraphs are handy for all sorts of things, such as showing causal relationships in people's world views or in social systems. Axelrod and his collaborators, for instance, used this approach to model the results from discourse analysis, producing directed graphs of the assertions that each individual made about what caused what in various political problems. Using this approach, you can trace complex chains of reasoning, and can predict possible responses that an individual might make to a given event.

The familiar hierarchy format that you may have noticed in things like organisational diagram is an example of a particular form of graph, namely a tree. In a tree, once branches have split off from a node, they never rejoin. This is different from a net, which allows any node, in principle, to be joined to any other node.

Having nodes and arcs saying 'X causes Y' lets you do numerous interesting things, but has some obvious limitations. Once you start using this sort of representation you soon want more sophisticated links, such as 'X often causes Y' or 'X occasionally causes Y'. You may be pleased to hear that there is a sophisticated literature about this, not to mention sophisticated software to support it; classicist readers may be pleased to hear that the literature on argumentation, which uses these approaches, can trace its antecedents directly back to classical rhetoric and logic. Our own work on modelling expert reasoning is within this tradition.

Scripts, schemata and sets

A handy principle in research is to take something that looks like a problem and turn it inside out, then see whether it looks like a solution or an opportunity. One recurrent problem when you're gathering information from human beings is that human memory systematically distorts what actually happened and transforms it into a neatly schematised framework of what should have happened if the universe made more obvious sense. If you're trying to find out whether A actually happened before B, as opposed to after it, then this is an obvious problem. If you turn it inside out, you get a set of questions about what the aforementioned neatly schematised framework looks like, why it takes that form, what the implications are, and so on. These turn out to be interesting questions with both theoretical and practical implications, and they take you into issues of scripts, schemata and sets, which is what this subsection is about.

The concept that much human activity falls into regular patterns is a well-established one, and has been formalised and elaborated in various ways. A traditional example is the pattern of actions in going to a restaurant for a meal, which breaks down into various subactivities in a predictable sequence. We usually don't pay much attention to these patterns until we encounter a situation where we don't know the pattern, such as our first encounter with a Chinese formal meal. Once you're aware of these patterns, you start seeing them in all sorts of places. An example is the inimitable Brian, who was looking at patterns of events in computer games. As part of his background reading, he came across *The Epic of Gilgamesh*, in which the hero has a companion who is half human and half animal. The parallel with Han Solo and Chewie in *Star Wars* struck him immediately, and left him wondering whether it was accidental; some further reading showed that it was no accident. He went on to find that the underlying plots in the games he studied were remarkably similar to the underlying plots in Russian folk tales analysed in the nineteenth century by Vladimir Propp. At one level, this was no huge surprise; the reason he was looking into this in the first place was that there was a solid body of previous research which had turned up similar findings in other areas. How can you tell, though, whether you've found something 'real' or whether you're just demonstrating the human being's brilliance at spotting patterns, even when there aren't any patterns there to spot? That depends on what you mean by 'real'. At one level, the patterns are a human artefact; we can use any framework we like to describe things. At another level, simply saying that you think two things look like each other isn't research; it's just opinion. What turns it into research is when you can make interesting, testable predictions which spring from the nature of the pattern that you're claiming to be present.

Anyway, back to the idea of underlying patterns of behaviour. There are various schools of thought which have tackled this. A popular (in both senses) school is transactional analysis (TA), which analyses human behaviour in deliberately plain language, using everyday names for the patterns of behaviour. One pattern, for instance, is known as 'Ain't it awful?' and involves the participants bemoaning the dreadfulness of a situation, regardless of whether the situation really is dreadful or not; another is 'Happy to help', which is what it sounds like. An interesting point about this approach is its claim that each individual has a set of preferred patterns, whose predictability provides certainty in an unpredictable world. As a result, individuals will manoeuvre a given situation to fit with a preferred pattern of behaviour, even if that means transforming a pleasant but unfamiliar situation into an unpleasant but familiar one.

Another approach is story grammars, which look at the abstract underlying structures of stories. You can find these by successively stripping away layers of detail, for example, by discarding the villain's name and substituting 'the villain' or by stripping out details of something that was done, and substituting a short verb phrase saying what was done. So, for instance, 'Han Solo befriends Chewbacca' and 'Gilgamesh befriends Enkidu' both become 'the hero befriends a half-animal, half-human creature'. There's obviously scope for some creative editing here, but if you're reasonably systematic, you can often find interesting similarities and differences which are likely to be fairly robust, rather than outpourings of your vigorous imagination. You might find, for instance, that all the 1950s Westerns where a cowboy falls in love with a non-American woman end with that woman dying, by way of similarities. Conversely, you might find a schism between those horror movies where the monster is killed when the authorities are finally alerted (e.g. the National Guard or the police department) and those where the monster is killed by members of the public (e.g. a crowd of peasants with torches, or an ordinary member of the spaceship's crew). More ambitiously, you can start looking through stories from different times to see whether the underlying plot elements (and the views of the universe which they reflect) have changed over time. If you link this with graph theory, you can also start looking at the complexity of the subplots and seeing, for instance, how the complexity of *Macbeth* compares to the complexity of a vintage episode of *Hill Street Blues*.

That's about patterns of actions; there are also patterns of static structure. There are various schools which tackle this. Schema theory, for instance, deals with underlying patterns (schemata) in the broadest sense, incorporating actions and static structure. So, for instance, the schema for a four-wheel drive vehicle includes large size and a high, vertical front to the vehicle; the schema for a sports car includes being low in height and having small back seats or none at all. Schemata are an important issue for measurement theory, since different schemata may have wildly different preferrred values. In the case of the four-wheel drive vehicle, for instance, then the preferred value for 'vehicle height' is as high as possible, whereas for a sports car the preferred value for this is as low as possible. If you're doing market or product research, you need to be careful that you're not lumping together several different schemata which will produce apparently contradictory results, such as asking respondents to describe 'a good car' without checking whether each respondent is using a different schema.

Experts typically have more schemata than novices, and have more richly developed schemata than novices; a classic 'fish in a barrel' research design is to compare the schemata of experts and novices in pretty much any field. This finding is so widespread that if you don't find any differences, then that's a significant absence and well worth reporting.

Schema theory leads us on to various forms of set theory, which deal with how we decide which things to fit into which categories. So, for instance, prototype theory claims that for many categories we have a prototypical value, and then assign things to that category if they're sufficiently close to the prototype. The classic example is birds, where a robin is a prototypical bird exhibiting all the classic features of a bird, and where ostriches and penguins only exhibit some of those features (for instance, they don't fly or sing). Obvious? Not really. You could argue that it's equally obvious that we categorise things on the basis of a key differentiating feature which marks the boundary between one set and another – for instance, the presence of feathers as the unique feature of birds.

An interesting feature of all of this is that people tend to tackle situations by using the schema (in the broadest sense) that looks the best match for that situation. The implication is that if someone has a large set of well-defined schemata relevant to a situation, then they have a better chance of tackling it successfully; conversely, someone with a small set of impoverished schemata is likely to hit problems. Since it's possible to teach schemata, then one way of helping people to cope with situations which cause them problems is to identify where their schemata aren't up to the job, and to teach them new schemata which will help them to do better. A classic example of this is assertiveness training, which can transform lives by teaching people a few strategies which, like many of the best things in life, are obvious with hindsight, but not with foresight.

On that edifying note, we'll end this section. The next sections deal with statistics. There is first a general overview, followed by a section on descriptive statistics, which involve putting some numbers on to your data. The subsequent sections deal with measurement theory, which involves different types of measurement, and with inferential statistics, where you work out the odds of your results having occurred just through chance. A lot of students are twitchy about stats, but the core concepts are pretty simple, and should be more widely known: properly used, they let you ask and answer much more powerful questions than non-statistical approaches.

Statistics: describing things with numbers, and assessing the odds

'They have to be perfect numbers,' the senior astronomer said. 'Numbers to make more than delusory and misleading sense need to be perfect numbers.'

(*Invader*, p.270)

Bones can be divided into four types, namely long bones, short bones, flat bones and twiddly bones; each of these can be subdivided into various types (e.g. metatarsals) and various bits (e.g. epiphyses). Statistics come in two types, namely descriptive stats and inferential stats, each of which can be subdivided into various types (e.g. parametric tests) and various bits (e.g. log transforms). What does this mean, and why should you care? Setting aside bones for the moment (a fascinating topic, but one for a different book), the big picture of statistics is as follows.

Books on research methods normally include a section on statistics. There are various plausible reasons for this. Erudite and cynical readers may harbour suspicions that each new book does it because its predecessors did the same, and may allude ironically to Gould's excellent essay on dawn horses and fox terriers. Erudite and clean-minded readers may refer to the nature of evidence and the growth of the scientific method. Readers who have seen too much of the dark side may speculate that it's because there are Bad People out there who misuse statistics to further their own twisted schemes, which means that the world needs to be warned about their ways to prevent others from being led astray. There are elements of truth in all of these, but that's another story. Anyway, statistics and the nature of evidence.

If you're just looking for supporting evidence to back up your assertion, then it's usually possible to find lots of juicy examples to support even the most outlandish claim. By carefully reporting these, and not reporting the much larger number of examples which suggest that your assertion is completely idiotic, it's possible to put together a case which looks internally consistent and strongly supported by evidence. Sometimes you'll get away with it, but more often someone will point out that you've failed to mention the counter-evidence; at best you'll look like a partisan devotee of a cult of unreason (to borrow a phrase from the literature), like the people who argue that the Moon landings were faked, or that the Nazis have secret bases at the South Pole, and at worst you'll be accused of unethical behaviour or fraud. So, what can you do to avoid such a risk? One obvious solution is to present a summary of the data in a way which shows how representative your examples are.

Let's imagine that you've stumbled across the finding that three UK prime ministers lost their fathers at an early age. You wonder whether this might reflect some interesting psychodynamics about loss of authority figures in early childhood leading to a desire for power, and you write your very first conference paper about this. You give the paper, feeling distinctly nervous, and wait for the first question. A grizzled academic in the back row points out that quite a high proportion of children in previous centuries lost a father at an early age, and that your three examples could be explained as pretty much what you'd expect from simple mortality rates, without any need to invoke psychodynamics. It's even conceivable that the proportion of prime ministers who lost a father at an early age might be lower than that for the general population, which would make you look pretty silly. So what could you do to reduce the risk of this happening?

The obvious thing is to look at all the prime ministers, not just the three you've already studied. If you do that, then you find something interesting: the number of prime ministers who lost a father at an early age is very high. That suggests that you may be on to a real effect. With that figure behind you, you're in a much stronger position. You write another article and submit it to a journal; the editor's response eventually comes back saying that it's an interesting piece of work, but one of the reviewers has suggested that the figures may be due to simple coincidence, so you'll need to answer that criticism adequately before the article can be accepted. You head off to the coffee bar in despair, where you run into an experienced colleague who listens to your tale of woe with an expression resembling sympathy, asks a few questions about your numbers, does some quick mental arithmetic, and tells you that the likelihood of your results being due to coincidence is less than one in a thousand. Armed with this knowledge, and an introduction to another colleague who can work out the precise numbers, you start revising the paper, and eventually end up with a real, live paper with your name on it in a real, proper journal.

So, how does this relate to the types of statistics mentioned before this excursion into parable began? Well, the first stage (counting the number of prime ministers who lost a father at an early age) is an example of what is called 'descriptive statistics'. Descriptive statistics describe your findings (hence the name). They include things like the highest and lowest values that you found, the number of examples that you found, the average value for your examples, and so on. Descriptive statistics are a Good Thing, but they're limited. They don't allow you to answer the suggestion that your results are purely due to coincidence. For that, you need the second stage, where you work out how likely it is that your findings were purely due to chance; this involves the field of inferential statistics (the second main type of statistics, after descriptive statistics). Inferential statistics are also a Good Thing, but likewise they are limited in ways which will become clear later.

At this point, some readers might wonder why, if statistics are such a good thing, they haven't taken over the world. There are various possible explanations for this; the most charitable one is that there are some types of research question for which statistics are not appropriate. One obvious example is the white crow effect – to prove that not all crows are black, you only need to find one white crow. If you happen across one white crow, you don't need any more examples and you don't need any statistics. Another explanation, sometimes heard among less charitable colleagues, is that a lot of people find statistics intimidating. Such colleagues tend to view a claim that a piece of research was not appropriate for statistical analysis as being a euphemism either for 'I'm afraid of hard sums' or for 'Here are the facts which support my prejudices'. Much can be said for and against these suspicions and already has been, to paraphrase a head of state who knew more than anyone should about losing a parent under tragic circumstances.

Anyway, moving on from history and the like, that's the big picture; the following sections contain more detail about the different types of statistics, and about when and how to use them. As usual, these sections are intended as an introduction; if you're using statistics in your research, you will also need to read the more specialist texts, and to take advice from knowledgeable colleagues. An important thing to remember is that you need to plan in the statistical analysis right at the start of your research plan, well before you start collecting data. This will probably save you considerable time and effort in data collection, and may also save you from tears.

Descriptive statistics: giving a systematic description of the numbers you've found

'I assure you they're perfect numbers,' Bren said, feeling out of his depth, but fearing to let the conversation stray further towards the abstract.

(*Invader*, p.270)

If you're describing your data, what do you need to describe, and why? One answer is that you need to describe the things which will assure a cynical reader that you are not a sinful person presenting a heavily edited version of events. This section discusses these things, what sinful people do, and descriptive statistics.

What have you got?

One thing that the cynical reader will want to know early on is just how much data you have. A statistic taken to three decimal places might sound impressive, but it might simply mean 'six out of my seven respondents said this', which is a lot less impressive. Experienced researchers know all about such ploys. They also know how different the first few respondents can be from the rest (there's a body of research into the characteristics of volunteers, which typically finds that people who volunteer to be research subjects are unlike the population at large, but it's generally considered bad manners to mention this in fields where research depends heavily on self-selecting volunteer subjects). You will therefore need to say how big your data set is – how many respondents, how many measurements from each respondent, and so forth. That way, the reader can form their own opinion of how much to trust the rest of your reporting. Your sample size is usually referred to using the letter n (for number), so an n of 29 means that you used a sample of 29 respondents, incidents, or whatever it was that you used.

Extremes

Once you have reported the size of your data set, you will need to say what the extreme values were that you found in your data. This is where life can start to become interesting, and to present you with opportunities to practise applied ethics. Why? Two stories illustrate a couple of the main reasons.

Suppose that you have been testing your new method for teaching history, to prove that it helps primary school children learn more Facts. (We have capitalised this word as a sign that we are using it in an ironic sense, and are well aware of the epistemological arguments that have raged over this concept for the last few centuries.) You discover that one child in the group taught with your method learns 17 per cent more Facts than any of the children in the comparison group taught using the traditional method. However, all the others in the group taught using your method have learned considerably less than the children in the comparison method, with one unfortunate child knowing 28 per cent fewer Facts than they did when they started the course, having forgotten them through boredom and traumatic amnesia. What can you do? If you are a sinful person, you can report that children taught using your method can learn up to 17 per cent more Facts. That would not involve any active falsehood: an increase could occur (even if it was only in one student), and the upper limit for that increase was indeed 17 per cent.

If, however, the perpetrator of this method had to say what the lowest values were as well as the highest, then a more honest picture would emerge, and would establish that this method was not all that it appeared. So, in consequence, a virtuous person describes the range of values that they found. That is a good start, but there is more to learn, which leads us on to the ethically debatable case of the unanaesthetised chimpanzee.

Suppose for a moment that you have been doing some research into chimpanzee reactions to anaesthetics: a virtuous and worthy thing for science to investigate (especially from the viewpoint of a sick chimp). For the research, chimps which are about to undergo medical treatment are put into a small room containing objects which chimps like; the anaesthetic gas is then pumped in surreptitiously, and the chimps fall asleep without trauma. You are measuring how long it takes for a typical chimp to be anaesthetised and you find a beautifully consistent set of figures, except for one chimp, which is cheerfully conscious long after it should by your figures have passed into unconsciousness. When you look more closely, you discover that the chimp has heard the gas and has stuffed a large and unhelpful finger up the gas inlet, blocking it completely. Can you exclude this chimp from your data set? The answer is a fairly clear 'yes', though you might want to include the episode in your next submitted article in the hope that the reviewers will be amused enough to overlook any shortcomings in the rest of the article.

At the other extreme, what if you're investigating the number of alleged coven members in witch trials, to prove that a disproportionate number contained either 7 or 13 members, and you find that these numbers are in fact not disproportionately common: is it okay to exclude some reports which don't fit your theory, so that the remainder do fit? The answer here is a fairly clear 'no'. If all choices were this simple, then the world would be different, but they aren't: you often have to make judgements about grey areas. For instance, what if one of your subjects performs slightly worse than any of the others, and you afterwards discover that they had a migraine just before the data collection session – would it be appropriate to exclude their data? If they were the only subject who was affected in this way, then that might be acceptable. However, to be justified in doing that you'd need to know whether or not the other subjects were in a similar situation, and that leads into questions such as whether they'd be willing to tell you, and whether you can ethically ask them, and so on.

Extreme values of this sort are known as outliers; removing them is part of what is often called data cleaning (less charitably known as data massaging when it is done by someone you dislike). You might be relieved to hear that there are standard statistical techniques which you can use to exclude outliers in most cases without getting into difficult ethical dilemmas (in brief, you're allowed to chuck out any which are more than three standard deviations from the mean, though you should check with someone knowledgeable whether this is okay in your specific case). The account above is probably a bit longer than strictly necessary, but it gave us an excuse to use the chimp story, which is based on an allegedly true incident which we quite like, and it does help to make the point that research requires judgement as well as consistency.

So, at the end of all this process you end up with two clauses in your first sentence, one saying what the n is, and the other saying what the extreme values were. It's a solid start.

Mean, mody and magnificent

Yes, that's a pretty bad title, but once in a while temptation becomes too strong – anyway, back to the plot. We know how much data you have; we know what the extreme values are. Is that enough? It isn't (otherwise this would be a much shorter section), for a variety of reasons. Imagine that you are deciding between two books in the bookshop; you have enough money to buy one, but not both. Both promise that applying the skills described in their pages will increase your salary by up to 90 per cent. Both may be telling the truth. Truth, however, is seldom plain and rarely simple. Consider these figures for salary increases among readers of Kelley's book and Phibes' book on how to prosper financially:

Kelley's book has eight readers whose salary increased by 1 per cent, and one whose salary increased by 90 per cent. It is therefore true that there was an increase of up to 90 per cent, but this case was a distinct minority.

Phibes' book has one reader whose salary increased by 1 per cent, two whose salary increased by 80 per cent, three whose salary increased by 85 per cent, and three whose salary increased by 90 per cent.

Which book would you prefer to buy? It is pretty clear that Phibes' book has a much better set of outcomes overall, but these are not visible if you only report the extreme values. The obvious thing to do is to report the average values, which leads us towards some important concepts well known among advertisers and statisticians, but not so well known among students: namely, the three very different things which are lumped together in everyday English under the name 'average'. These are the *mean*, the *median* and the *mode*. What are these? The next paragraphs deal with this question.

Mean

The mean is what you get when you add all your values together and describe them by the number of values you have. For instance, suppose you are studying the number of pets that postgraduate students have. Your sample consists of 5 students (to make this example simpler). Student A has 2 pets; student B has 2 pets; student C has 3 pets; student D has 5 pets, and student E has 30 pets. The total number of pets is 42 (2+2+3+5+30); the total number of students is 5. If we divide the number of pets by the number of students, the mean value is 42 divided by 5, which is 8.4.

At this point you may be suspicious, and rightly so. One reason for suspicion is that pets normally come as complete units, not as fractions. This could be fixed by rounding off the mean to the nearest proper number, namely 8. The second reason for suspicion is that the mean value has been raised by the student with 30 pets; if we excluded that student, the total number of pets would be 12, and dividing this by the remaining number of students (4) would give a mean of 3 pets, which looks much more realistic (setting aside temporarily the issue of what 'realistic' means in this context).

Median

The median value is one way of getting round this problem of distortion by extreme values, without resorting to removal of the outliers. The median value is the one exactly in the middle of a range. To calculate the mean, you arrange the numbers in order from smallest to largest, and then choose the one midway along that list. If your list is five items long, then you choose the third (which has two items before it and two after it); if it is eleven items long, then you choose the sixth (which has five items before it and five after it) and so on. In the case of our students and their pets, for instance, the list consists of five items, namely 2, 2, 3, 5 and 30; the median value will be the third of the five in this list, which is 3.

Medians are not particularly bothered by extreme values: in the example of the pets, for instance, even if student E had 300 pets instead of 30, the median would still be the third value on the list, and would still be 3. This is useful if you're using statistics for any sort of planning. Another feature of the median which can be useful is that it will consist of a proper number, rather than an abstraction such as 0.2 of a pet.

Mode

The mode is the third thing which can be described as an 'average'. It is the value which occurs most frequently in your sample. So, for the long-suffering students and pets above, 2 students each own 2 pets, 1 student owns 3 pets, 1 student owns 5 pets, and the last student owns 30 pets. The most frequent value for 'number of pets' is therefore 2, since this is the most frequently occurring number of pets (even if it does consist of just two instances).

This may not strike you as the most useful concept that has ever graced the world with its presence, but it has its part to play, as will become apparent later, when we encounter bimodal and multimodal distributions. That, though, is another story.

Anyway, that's a quick overview of averages. You might wonder why we have worked through all this in such detail – surely eyeballing the data would give you a pretty good idea of what was going on? The answer is that with data sets this small, eyeballing the data would indeed give you a pretty good idea. It's a very different story, though, if you're dealing with more normal data sets. These typically range from a few dozen up to hundreds of thousands, and eyeballing complete data sets at the large end of the scale is not a wise thing to try. In such cases, it's better to summarise the data down to a manageable size. Summarising it without distorting it, though, is not always simple, as we've seen with something as small as our data set of five pet-loving students. The next sections continue this process, and discuss what to do about some of the problems which you will probably have noticed in the examples so far.

Variance and standard deviations

One thing that you will probably have noticed in the example above is that the values were not evenly distributed – for instance, there was a big jump in the number of pets between the fourth and the fifth student. In case you're wondering whether you might get a Nobel Prize for maths for spotting this, the answer is that you won't, for two reasons. One is that this issue has already been spotted and dealt with at considerable length by statisticians; the second is that there isn't a Nobel Prize for maths. (The story about Nobel's wife and the mathematician is an urban legend, in case you encounter it on the internet, but that's yet another side-issue.) So, with that diversion put neatly aside, let's return to the issue of data scatter.

Representing data: graphs and the like

Imagine that you see two data sets. The first consists of the values 5, 6, 6, 6, 7; the second consists of the values 3, 4, 6, 8 and 9. By one of those fascinating coincidences that litter introductions to statistics, both sets have the same mean (6) and the same median (again 6). The first set has a mode of 6 (which occurs three times); the second set does not have a mode, since every value occurs only once. It is immediately apparent to the meanest intellect (to use a phrase no longer as common as it used to be in introductory texts) that the first set is more tightly clustered than the second, but how do we represent this? The extreme values of the two sets give a partial indication of this scatter but, as we saw earlier, extreme values need to be treated with caution. Is there some other way that we can show the distribution of values so as to bring out the degree of scatter? The answer, unsurprisingly, is that this is indeed possible; there are several ways of doing it.

Measures of deviation

Measures of deviation do not involve private lives (well, not usually); they are ways of showing variation within a data set. The underlying idea is beautifully simple. If you know the mean value for your data set, then you can see how far each of the individual data points is from the mean. In the example above, for instance, the first data set consists of the values 5, 6, 6, 6 and 7. The mean is 6; the first measurement varies from the mean by 1, the next three measurements don't vary from the mean at all (variation of 0), and the last measurement varies from the mean by 1. In the case of the second data set (3, 4, 6, 8 and 9), almost all the figures for variation are noticeably higher: 3, 2, 0, 2 and 3 respectively. You might wonder at this point whether it's possible to add these numbers together to get a numerical measure of the amount of difference. The answer is that it's not quite that simple, but you're thinking along the right lines.

Sums of squares: a slight detour via a simpler path

What you can do is to take each of the individual values, multiply it by itself, and then add all the resulting values together. (There are good reasons for this, but they're too long to fit neatly into the margin of this page, to misquote someone whose knowledge of mathematics was somewhat greater than ours.) So, for the first set, we take the variances from the mean (1, 0, 0, 0, 1) and square them, giving us 1, 0, 0, 0, and 1; when we sum these results we have the grand total of 2. For the second set, we take 3, 2, 0, 2 and 3, and square each number, giving us 9, 4, 0, 4 and 9; summing these gives us the noticeably larger total of 26. This process is known as calculating the sum of squares (short for 'sum of squared deviations from the mean'). In this example, the values for the sums of squares tell the discerning reader that the two samples are very different in their distributions, even if their means and medians are the same.

Standard deviations

Standard deviations are a concept closely related conceptually to sums of squares. Like sums of squares, they tell you how much variation there is in the whole body of the data, as opposed to how much of a difference there is between your extreme values. Why should you need something more than sums of squares? The answer is that sums of squares tell you only part of the story. Being sums, they are affected by your sample size: other things being equal, the larger your sample size, the larger the figure for the sum of squares, even if the larger sample doesn't have a greater degree of variance than the smaller one. You might by now be wondering whether it's possible to calculate something like a mean value for variance, and if so you'd be thinking along the right lines. If you simply take your sum of squares and divide it by your n, then this gives you something called the *mean variance*. In the example above, the first sum of squares is 2, and the second is 26; if we divide these by the n of 5, we get values of 0.4 and 5.2 respectively for the mean variance. (Nearly there now.) But, you might ask rhetorically, what about the fact that one of the processes in the sum of squares involved squaring numbers: do we need to make some allowance for that? The answer is that we do, for various reasons (such as that squaring numbers exaggerates the distance between small and large numbers). We can make this allowance by using the opposite process to squaring, namely using the square root of the mean variance as our measure of variance. The result is the *standard deviation*, which tells you how much variance from the mean value occurs in your data. In our example, the mean variation of 0.4 has a square root (and therefore a standard deviation) of 0.63, and the mean variation of 5.2 has a square root (and therefore standard deviation) of 2.28. So, for our two data sets, both have a mean of 6, but one has a standard deviation of 0.63 while the other has a much larger standard deviation of over 2, telling us that the second sample contains much more variance than the first.

At this point, you may feel the urge to rush off and calculate some standard deviations on your newly purchased calculator. If so, you may find that there is a key marked *sd* (for standard deviation) and another marked *sd-1*. Why the multiplicity of keys? The reason is that the usual practice with standard deviations is a bit different depending on whether you're dealing with a complete population or with a sample set. A complete population, to remind you of that useful concept, consists of all the specimens of the population that you're studying (for instance, all the herrings in the North Sea, or all the year 3 children at Grimsley Junior School). Sometimes you can get data for the complete population (a fairly realistic prospect for Grimsley Junior School), but more often this is not a realistic ambition (as with the North Sea herring), so you need to use a partial sample instead. If you're using a complete population, then you can use the ordinary sample deviation; if you're using a sample of a population, then the usual practice is to include some allowance for the likelihood that your sample won't be perfectly representative of the whole population. A simple way of doing this is to subtract 1 from your n when calculating the standard deviation, which gives you a more conservative figure. That's what the *sd-1* button is for.

Normal distributions

Once you start plotting real data, you'll almost certainly see some classic patterns emerging. This is discussed in more detail later, but there's one pattern which we'll mention here because it's so useful. The standard distribution (also known as Poisson distribution, Gaussian distribution and bell curve, though these terms aren't perfect synonyms) is one where your data plot looks like a cross-section of a bell: a high bit in the middle, curving away symmetrically to a low bit at each side. In data terms, it means that most of your sample are somewhere near the average, with extreme values being relatively rare. A real, proper, normal distribution has several distinctive properties. In brief, these are as follows.

The curves are symmetrical, with the mid-point being the mean; the median and the mode are the same as the mean. If you plot the values for one standard deviation above the mean and one standard deviation below the mean, then you'll find that 68 per cent of the area of the bell lies between these points; if you do the same for two standard deviations above and below the mean, you'll find that 95 per cent of the area of the bell lies between these points. This comes in very handy if you want to use inferential statistics on your data.

Here are some illustrations of distributions. We have assumed that most readers will already have enough experience of graphs and charts to understand the figures below, but if you've escaped that experience, then you might like to read the section on graphs and charts before proceeding further. We've erred on the side of exaggerating any points that the illustrations are intended to show, and we've also erred on the side of realism, rather than producing beautifully smoothed curves, since we've found that this helps many students understand the underlying principle

Figure 5.3 shows roughly what a normal distribution looks like. It is symmetrical and bell-shaped. The mean, median and mode all occur at the same point, the highest point, in the middle. You can predict the proportion of your sample which will occur at a given point, if the data form a normal distribution.

Figure 5.4 shows a graph superimposed over the corresponding bar chart, to produce the familiar bell curve graph. If you imagine that the histogram bars are rectangles of cardboard, then you should be able to imagine calculating the

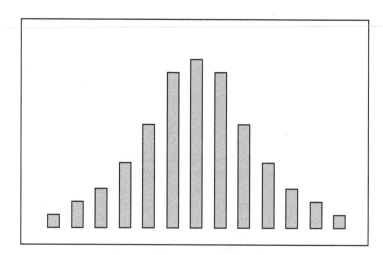

Figure 5.3 A normal distribution

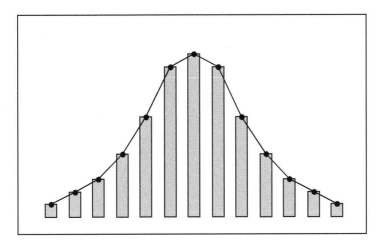

Figure 5.4 A normal distribution shown as a graph superimposed over a histogram

area of each rectangle, which will allow you to measure the proportion of your data at a given distance from the mean point on the histogram.

Figure 5.5 shows a curve looking a bit like a normal distribution, only flatter. It's symmetrical, like a normal distribution, but the distance between the lowest scores and the highest scores is quite small.

Figure 5.6 shows something looking a bit like a standard distribution, only steeper. Like a normal distribution, it's symmetrical, but the distance between the lowest and the highest scores is greater than in a normal distribution.

Figure 5.7 shows a bimodal distribution – it has two modes (most frequent values), as shown by the two humps in the graph. Distributions like this are sometimes caused by two overlapping groups within your data, as in Figure 5.8, which shows two different groups overlapping to form a bimodal distribution.

Figure 5.9 shows a distribution a bit like a normal distribution, only lopsided

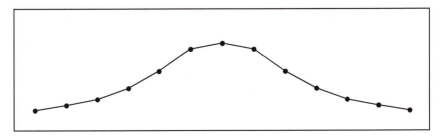

Figure 5.5 A flat symmetrical distribution

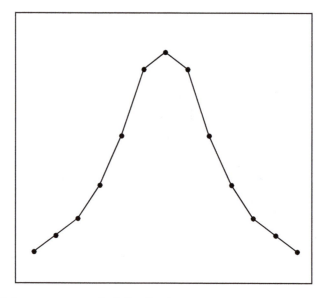

Figure 5.6 A steep symmetrical distribution

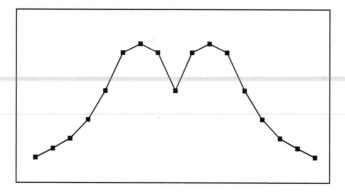

Figure 5.7 A bimodal distribution

('skewed' in technical terms). Here, most of the values are low overall, with only a few high ones, which are towards the right side of the graph; the graph isn't symmetrical around the middle of the horizontal axis.

Descriptive statistics let you say what you've got, but they don't tell you whether you've found something remarkable, or just something which has probably happened through random chance. To work out the odds of your results happening through random chance, you'll need to use inferential stats,

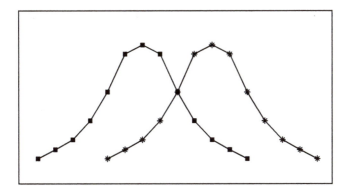

Figure 5.8 A bimodal distribution caused by two overlapping groups

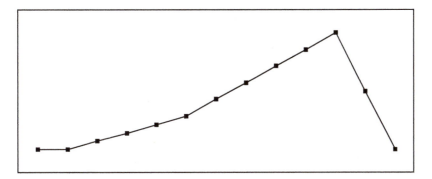

Figure 5.9 A skewed distribution

and to use those you'll need to know something about measurement theory. The next section deals with measurement theory, and the section after that deals with inferential stats.

Measurement theory: types of measurement and their implications

> *It was hard work keeping our personal emotions out of this matter – and we did not mention numbers or say exactly how we had found those which we did find.*
> *(At the Mountains of Madness, p.49)*

Measurement theory is one of those things that distinguishes the professional from the well-intentioned amateur; it not only allows you to get more out of the same amount of work but also gives you credibility as an academic heavy-weight. A lot of people end up very attached to the topic, though that may be for the same reasons that some people end up attached to cross-country running through British weather in November. Why does it play such an import-ant role in research? The answer is that it's one of the foundations on which statistics are based. Because it's an important foundation, it has received a lot of attention from assorted schools of thought; and because it has received attention from assorted schools of thought, there are various areas of profound disagreement about it. For our purposes, fortunately, that's not a problem, since there's agreement about the bits that we need to cover, but you do need to be aware that different textbooks will divide up measurement types into different categories from the ones that we use. They will, however, explain with detailed examples just what they mean by each category, just as we are about to do, so there shouldn't be any ambiguity.

One of the central concepts of measurement theory is that there are different types of measurement; another central concept is that you can do different things with the different types. This in turn affects what sort of statistics you can use with each type of measurement, which in turn means that (a) if you use the wrong sort of measurement, you'll screw up your intended statistical test, but (b) if you use the right sort of measurement, you'll need to do less data collection to get to a given point (sometimes drastically less data collection). So, what are the types of measurement, and what can you do with them?

Nominal categories

The first type are not really measurements at all, and are included in the stand-ard texts partly so that you know how to watch out for them. We've used the phrase 'nominal categories' by way of overkill – many texts refer to 'nominal values' or 'categorical data'. The 'nominal' bit means that these involve names of categories, as opposed to measurements (handy mnemonic: nominal cat-egories deal with names). So, for instance, if you record someone's name as Chris or Jean, then 'Chris' and 'Jean' are nominal categories. It's meaningless to ask to what extent someone is 'Chris', whereas it would be meaningful to ask to what extent someone was tall or hot. The 'Chris' bit simply says what category someone or something belongs to.

That looks pretty straightforward, and if the rest of life didn't get in the way then it would be pretty straightforward. You can do some stats with nominal categories, but as you might expect, they're not terribly fancy, and you'd normally need pretty big sample sizes before you could start drawing conclusions. The reason that we can't proceed cheerfully to the next type of measurement is that it isn't always immediately obvious when something is a nominal category, and if you're not careful, you can make an unfortunate mistake. Some wordings are ambiguous, and may appear to be nominal cat-egories where in fact they are not, or vice versa. So, for instance, if you record someone's nationality as British or French, then that's a nominal category.

Unfortunately, many people also use words like 'British' or 'French' in a different sense, corresponding roughly to 'stereotypically British' or 'stereotypically French'. When the words are being used in this way, then it is meaningful to make statements such as 'he's very French', whereas it would not be meaningful to say 'he's very Jean-Luc'. As a useful rule of thumb, if you can meaningfully say that someone or something is very X, then X is not a nominal category. It's also useful to remember that the answers 'yes' and 'no' on questionnaires are nominal values, so designing a questionnaire which asks for yes/no answers is a bad idea, unless you have absolutely no option – yes/no answers require a lot of data before you can find anything out.

Another frequent cause of misunderstanding is when nominal categories are given an arbitrary number as a label. Suppose, for instance, that you find three separate populations of fish in a pond, and you label them 'group 1', 'group 2' and 'group 3'. It's then all too easy to have a tick-box labelled 'group' into which you enter a number such as '2'. Why do we say 'all too easy'? The reason is that the numbers in this example are not real respectable numbers that you can do things to; they're just arbitrary labels. You could instead label the groups as 'group A', 'group B' and 'group C', or something more imaginative such as 'group Godzilla', 'group Mothra' and 'group Rodan'. It's highly unlikely that you would be tempted to try calculating the average of group Godzilla and group Rodan and produce a result like 'group Goddan', but it's horribly easy to try something meaningless like calculating the average value for the group number when you're dealing with numbers like 1, 2 and 3, and end up with a mean group value of 1.47. As a rough rule of thumb, if you can substitute a group name based on Japanese monster movies for a group number, then you're dealing with nominal categories, and you should consider giving the groups nice sensible names like 'A' and 'B' to reduce the risk of accidental sin.

Ordinal values

Ordinal values involve things that form some sort of a scale, even if you don't have a clue how big the gaps are between the things on that scale. So, for instance, you might know that Mercury is nearer to the sun than Venus, and that Venus in turn is nearer to the sun than Earth, even if you don't know the actual distances – astronomers were in precisely this position until just a couple of centuries ago. (Mnemonic: ordinal values deal with the order things are in.) You can do more powerful stats with ordinal values than with nominal values; the stats look at the extent to which different things tend to occur in the same order. People are often able to rank things in this way, even if they can't begin to agree on numbers for them – for instance, young people might agree that New Order have more street credibility than Abba, even though they might not be able to put any specific numbers on to the street credibility of either. This can be handy when you're dealing with very squishy, subjective concepts (not a phrase which you should consider using in your write-up, but it gets the idea across).

You can use numbers for the ranks (so, for instance, the music charts are simply a ranked set of ordinal values for a subset of music sales), but you need to remember that these aren't real proper respectable numbers that you can do things with – you could replace them with words like 'most', 'next most', and so on without any loss of meaning. Trying to do any sort of calculation with them as if they were real numbers (e.g. working out the average value) is meaningless, so resist the temptation. (Yes, you can do stats on them, but that involves using stats tests that are specifically designed to be used with ordinal values.)

Interval

When you have a shiny new spreadsheet or stats package waiting for you to use it, the novelty of categories and ranked orders soon wears thin – you start wanting to put in lots of numbers and do something impressive look-ing with coloured charts and suchlike. This moves you inexorably towards using some proper numbers that are so respectable that if they were people you could invite them home for tea to meet your family. Interval values are a good step in that direction. They're a bit like ordinal values, only more sophisticated. With ordinal values, things are ranked from most to least, and it would be meaningless to have a value inserted between a couple of those ranks – so, for instance, saying that something was 3.7 on the indie chart would be meaningless. If you meant that something belonged between the items that were currently ranked third and fourth, then with ordinal values you'd just insert the new thing in the slot below the third slot, and move everything else down one (so that the thing that was originally ranked fourth would be shifted down one by the new item, and would become ranked fifth).

There are some situations where you might want to shove in an intermedi-ate value without moving the existing ones out of the way, and this is what interval values are about. With interval values, you'll typically have an agreed set of fixed reference points, and you can then put things into the spaces between them. The classic example is the old Moh scale of mineral hardness, which works on the basis of what scratches what. Diamond is hardest, and is given the fixed value of 10; talc is the softest, and is given the fixed value of 1. Each of the intermediate exact values is assigned to a specific mineral on this scale. Suppose that you find a mineral which is harder than mineral number 6, but softer than mineral number 7; you can then give it a numeric value such as 6.5. As more minerals were found, geologists slotted them into a pecking order, with numbers such as 6.2 and 6.4. These numbers weren't completely arbitrary – a mineral with hardness 6.4 was predictably harder than one with hardness 6.2, for instance – but they weren't quite respectable numbers either, since the '.4' bit essentially meant 'we know it's harder than the one we put at .3, and softer than the one we put at .5, but we haven't a clue whether it's bang in the middle between them or nearer one than the other'.

Time passed, and geologists developed more sophisticated ways of measuring hardness; it then became apparent that the gaps between points on the Moh scale varied widely. The gap between diamond (the hardest mineral) and the next hardest on the scale was much, much wider than the gap between the mineral ranked fifth and the one ranked sixth, for instance. At one level, this didn't matter – the Moh scale allowed geologists to do various things much more systematically than would otherwise have been possible. At another level, though, it meant that they couldn't use their fancy spreadsheets on Moh hardnesses – trying to calculate a mean between two hardnesses on that scale would have been like trying to calculate the mean between two car registration numbers. However, there was the consolation that it was possible to do more powerful stats with interval measurements than with ordinal values, which in turn allowed more powerful stats than with nominal values.

Ratio

The key problem with interval values was that the gaps between the numbers were systematic, but they weren't regular. Ratio values have the advantage of regularity: they have a regular ratio between one value and the next. So, for instance, the gap between 54 and 55 will be exactly the same size as the gap between 89 and 90 (which isn't the case with interval systems). This means that you can get your calculators and spreadsheets out and start producing some pretty artwork; whether or not that artwork is statistically sound, though, is another question, and depends on how well you grasp the principles of statistics.

The rest of this section is devoted to some classic errors made by novices, in no particular order.

Some classic errors

Calculating averages is a classic minefield. If you're calculating means, as opposed to medians or modes, then what you do is to add up all the numbers, and then divide the total by however many numbers you had to start with (the section on descriptive statistics has a more sophisticated explanation of this). That only works, however, if you have proper numbers, i.e. ratio values, to add up. If your numbers are not the right type, then you can't calculate a meaningful mean, and you will provide a source of mildly sadistic pleasure to numerate colleagues for some time to come. Classic examples of things that you can't use as input for calculating means include the following:

- percentages – you can't take a percentage of 52 and a percentage of 58 and conclude that the mean is 55; instead, you have to add up all the numbers that went into producing the '52 per cent' and all the numbers that went into producing the '58 per cent' and then calculate the mean from that grand total. (If you're not sure why, imagine a situation where the 52 per cent was the mean of one response of 51 per cent and one of 53 per cent, whereas the 58 per cent was the mean of 23,000 responses.)

• nominal values – easy to do by mistake if you set up your spreadsheet to do stats on one column too many, such as the column of group code numbers (group 1, group 2, etc.).

Using excessively crude measures is a favourite error in questionnaire design. A classic phrasing is something like 'Are you an experienced internet user? Yes/no.' This means you're using nominal values, which in turn means that you'll need a much larger sample size to get to the same place. So, for instance, if you were trying to find out whether experienced internet users could perform a specified task faster than inexperienced ones, you would need a much larger sample of subjects to answer this question than if you phrased the question so that you got out a numerical value (via e.g. asking them how experienced they were in internet use).

With a knowledge of measurement theory, you're ready to do inferential statistics, which are the topic of the next section. There are various different types of inferential statistics, but the core concepts are pretty simple.

Inferential statistics: what are the odds against your findings being due to random chance?

. . . He didn't know what he was going to do when the numbers began to describe processes of an imperfectly perceived universe.

(Invader, p.200)

Inferential statistics, as you may recall from the introductory section, allow you to infer how likely it is that your findings are the result of nothing more than random chance. This section is about the underlying concepts that you need to calculate this likelihood.

Most stats books follow pretty much the same well-established format: there's a division into parametric and non-parametric stats, and a chunk about normal distributions, plus lots of examples showing you how to do the sums and calculate the probability values. It's a well-established format, but we haven't followed it. Low, cynical persons might wonder whether this was because we weren't numerate enough to work out the sums; such thoughts are unworthy, since our first draft contained enough hard sums to stun a walrus. There are two reasons that we've used a different format.

One is that the traditional format is worthy, neat and attractive to mathematicians and statisticians. However, most other people find it dull beyond belief, and in consequence read as little as they think they can get away with, resulting in only a partial understanding at best. The other is that the vast majority of researchers use stats packages which do the sums for them. These packages are a wonderful idea in theory, but in practice they tend to be used as a fast, efficient way of doing the wrong thing. A depressing percentage of published research involves statistical analysis which used the wrong test, usually because the researchers didn't make the right choice when they used their stats package. What we've done therefore is to focus on the choices you have to make when choosing a stats package, and the reasons behind those choices. We haven't aimed this at any particular package, but the underlying concepts are pretty much the same across packages.

What are the concepts? We've focused on what we consider to be the key concepts, as opposed to an exhaustive list. The concepts covered in this section are:

• probability – what it is, how you can calculate it, how you can use it
• factors affecting which statistical tests you can use
• how statistical tests interact with research design.

It ends with a list of common concepts and common pitfalls. We'd have liked to cover inferential statistics in considerably more detail, but something had to give as a result of space limits, and this was one of the things that gave, since it's a topic well covered in numerous other books.

Probability

Probability lies at the heart of inferential statistics. It's a useful concept: if you can say to someone that there's only a one in a thousand chance that your results can be explained as the result of random chance, then that's a pretty strong position for arguing that you've found something solid and worth closer attention. So, how do you set about working out what that probability is? This question leads into a batch of follow-on questions, which we'll clear out of the way first.

Significance

You might wonder what level of probability is considered worth bothering with, and why. The answers are rooted in the past. In the old days, you had to calculate probabilities by hand, and very boring it was too. To speed up the process, helpful souls created tables of values, so that once you were most of the way through your calculations, you could use the tables to help work out the remaining bits. The tables contained columns of precalculated values, and you looked up where your part-way values came on the table. You might find, for instance, that your part-way value was high enough to get into the 'at least one chance in twenty' column, but not high enough to get into the 'at least one chance in a hundred' column; you would therefore know that your final result would be somewhere between one chance in twenty and one chance in a hundred. Understandably, people soon stopped calculating exact values and started quoting the 'at least' figure from the table instead. The convention arose that results with a probability of one in twenty were treated as 'statistically significant'. This doesn't mean the same as 'important' – it just means that they've reached the point at which you can conventionally assume that your results probably reflect some real underlying causal factor rather than just chance. There are three conventional levels of significance, each of them with its own wording, which can lead to problems for any-one who uses those wordings without realising that they have a specialist meaning:

• 'significant' means 'one chance in twenty or beyond that this happened by chance'
• 'highly significant' means 'one chance in a hundred or beyond that this happened by chance'
• 'very highly significant' means 'one chance in a thousand or beyond that this happened by chance'.

'Probability' is usually referred to as 'p' and pronounced 'pee'; the values are usually stated as decimals, so 'one chance in twenty' becomes 'p = 0.05' and 'one chance in a hundred' becomes 'p = 0.01'.

At one level, these are arbitrary human conventions. At another level, they mean that there's a shared set of conventions which allows researchers to communicate with each other. That's a brief description of statistical signifi-cance; the next question is how to calculate probabilities, and this involves the concept of randomness.

Probability calculation and randomness

One of the key concepts in estimating probabilities is that if two events are independent of each other, then you can calculate the likelihood of both of them happening by multiplying together the likelihood of each one happen-ing. So, for instance, whether or not your watch stops on a given day should be completely unconnected to whether or not your car refuses to start in the morning. If the chance of your watch stopping on a given day is one in a hundred, and the chance of your car failing to start on a given day is one in a hundred, then the chance of your watch stopping and your car failing to start on the same day as each other is one in a hundred multiplied by one in a hundred, namely one in ten thousand. If the chance of rolling a six on a die is one in six, then the chance of rolling two consecutive sixes is one in six multiplied by one in six, namely one in thirty-six. You can extend this to any desired number – for instance, the likelihood of rolling four consecutive sixes is 1/6 times 1/6 times 1/6 times 1/6, which works out to 1/1296.

This core concept is simple, but there's a complicating factor which often confuses novices. In dice games, you're usually looking at the total score that the dice show, and some scores can be achieved via numerous permutations, whereas others can only be achieved through one or two permutations. For example, a total of seven can be achieved with a six and a one, a five and a two, a four and a three, a three and a four, a two and a five, and a one and a six, whereas a total of twelve can only be reached via one combination (a six and a six), so a total score of seven is six times more likely than a total of twelve because it can be reached via six permutations as opposed to just one, even though each of these individual permutation is equally likely. Figure 5.10 gives an illustration of this. It shows the total score generated by each possible combination of two dice, with the scores from one die shown in bold and the scores from the other in italics.

Figure 5.10 shows that some total scores are more frequent than others, for the simple reason that there are more ways in which they can be generated. For example, a score of twelve can only be generated in one way (a six on the bold die and a six on the italicised die), whereas a score of seven can be generated in any of six different ways – for instance, a five on the bold die and a two on the italicised die, or a four on the bold die and a three on the italicised die, or a three on the bold die and a four on the italicised die. If we plot the results as a histogram, then it forms a neatly symmetrical shape, with its highest bit in the middle and its lowest bits at the ends, which may stir memories of normal distributions, and rightly so.

You might be wondering about that assumption of events being independent, and if so you're right to wonder: it's a big assumption, and one that has implications for your research design. We'll return to it later. The next concept

	1	2	3	4	5	6
1	2	3	4	5	6	7
2	3	4	5	6	7	8
3	4	5	6	7	8	9
4	5	6	7	8	9	10
5	6	7	8	9	10	11
6	7	8	9	10	11	12

Figure 5.10 Total scores from combinations of two dice

on the list is randomness, which underlies the concept of 'fair dice' specifically and probability theory in general.

Students often ponder the issue of what randomness actually is: it tends to be treated as some sort of mystical entity which sits in ubiquitous omnipresence making sure that dice around the world behave themselves and form proper statistical distributions. This image causes understandable unease among people in general when they first encounter stats. It also causes considerable theological unease among people of various religious persuasions, since it implies that there are things which are not controlled by an all-powerful god. (Yes, we're serious: trying to teach stats to people who refuse on religious grounds to believe in randomness is a non-trivial challenge, and an increasingly frequent one.)

One way of making sense of the concept of randomness is as follows. It may or may not be true, but it's a useful approximation either way. Let us assume that everything is caused by something else and in principle is completely predictable, *if only we had all the relevant information*. In the case of rolling dice, for instance, if we knew exactly what all the forces were which were acting on the dice, then we could predict the outcome of every roll correctly. Now we do a bit of subtle labelling. If these forces are not distributed evenly, so that one number comes up more often than others on the dice, then we say that there is an underlying factor involved, and we might go on to do experiments to find out what that factor is. If, on the other hand, the forces are distributed evenly, so that all the numbers come up about equally often, then we say that we are witnessing randomness, and we don't bother to look into what the factors were, or into whether there was some reason that they were distributed evenly. (This isn't an original model which we dreamed up, so we can't claim credit for it – it's been floating around for some time – but it might help some readers to rest more easily with their consciences when they use analysis of variance for the first time.)

So, where does this leave us? It leaves us with the concepts of randomness, and calculating probabilities. It's fairly easy to see how to calculate probabilities with dice, but what about more mundane examples, such as working out whether or not there's a statistically significant difference between the contents of the two Iron Age rubbish pits that you've been excavating, or the incomes of people who went to two different schools in the same town? That, as you might suspect, involves a greater amount of mathematics, but the core ideas are fairly simple. The next subsection deals with the core ideas for the main types of inferential statistics.

Factors affecting which statistical tests you can use

The best advice about choosing a statistical test is to involve a competent statistician in the decision before you finalise your research design. It's such good advice that we repeat it throughout this book, just in case any reader misses it the first couple of times.

The next bit of advice isn't strictly about choice of test, but it's still import-ant. Once you've got your data, it's highly advisable to check it, eyeball it and double-check it. Checking and double-checking data are not the most entertaining of activities, but they can save you from a world of grief. It's difficult to spot your own errors, so one effective strategy is to bribe a friend to do an independent check for you, with an agreed reward for each error that they find.

Eyeballing your data involves looking at the overall pattern of the data (or absence of pattern), without using anything much more sophisticated than the naked eye. For instance, if you think there's a correlation between two factors in your data, you can feed the data into a scattergram and see whether there's any hint of a pattern. If the results from the eyeballing don't correspond with the results from your use of the stats software, then you'd be wise to double-check whether you've used the stats software correctly. Another advantage of eyeballing is that it can alert you to the presence of particular patterns in the data which might correspond to particular statistical tests. For instance, most people think of correlations as a steady process, in which the value of one variable corresponds fairly systematically to the value for another. The full story is more complicated: for instance, you might have data which show a nonlinear correlation, in which one variable starts off increasing slowly in value relative to the other, but suddenly starts increasing much more rapidly. If you're aware that you might be dealing with a nonlinear correlation, then you can use appropriate stats; if you missed this possibility, then you would probably get misleading results as a result of using the wrong sort of test.

Once you've checked, eyeballed and double-checked your data, then you need to answer a small number of questions, described below.

The first question involves the type of measurement you're dealing with – nominal, ordinal, or whatever it happens to be. Most tests can only be used with one or two types of measurement. As a rough rule of thumb, the coarser the type of measurement, the weaker the tests, and the more work you'll have to do in terms of things like sample sizes.

The next question involves what type of association you're investigating. One option is correlations, as described above. The other option is testing whether groups' scores are different from each other or not. For instance, you might be testing whether or not the group of children taught using the Learning Acceleration Method™ differs significantly in test scores from the group of children taught using the Boring Old Traditional Method™.

The last main question involves whether your data are from a normal distribu-tion or not. Since a normal distribution involves a highly predictable distribu-tion of values, you can tell much more easily what the likelihood is that your findings arose through sheer chance; this means less effort required on your part in terms of sample sizes and the like. If your data don't involve a normal distribution, then they won't be so amenable, and you'll need a larger sample size to assess the likelihood of your results arising through sheer chance.

These questions will let you decide which family of tests you can apply to your data. After that, there are some further questions which will tell you which members of that family you can legitimately use. Statistics books normally include a flowchart which takes you through these questions – for instance, whether your data are in groups of equal size, etc. These questions look straight-forward, but in practice this is a point where novices are particularly likely to make mistakes. We toyed with the idea of explaining each decision point in great detail and decided not to try: the best advice, as usual, is to discuss the issue with a competent statistician before finalising your research design, since they're likely to spot issues which you might have considered too trivial to mention, but which would have far-reaching implications for choice of test.

How statistical tests interact with research design

The first way: tests that you can use with nominal data

These are normally used when you have several categories, and when you're testing whether the number of instances in each category is what you'd expect from chance. For instance, you might be checking whether a particular ethnic group is underrepresented in some social roles, or whether the number of people who describe themselves as 'internet-literate' on your questionnaire is different between two professions. Since the statistics used to handle nominal data can't make many assumptions about the distributions of the data, and are dealing only with very limited raw material (i.e. counts of how many things are in each box or pot or pit), they're limited in what they can do, and they require a comparatively large sample size to reach a given level of statistical significance. The obvious implication is that you only use nominal data if you have no option. A lot of students, however, voluntarily condemn themselves to needless extra effort by plunging headlong after nominal data even when there are better options. The classic example is the needlessly crude 'yes/no' question in a questionnaire, where the 'yes' and 'no' are nominal values, instead of a question that allows an answer on a scale.

A more debatable issue is what type of measurement is involved if you collect data on numeric scales (for instance, a seven-point scale on a questionnaire). The convention in many fields is to treat these as interval or ratio measurements, and not to ask too many questions about this assumption. We tend to use 100 mm visual analogue Likert-style scales where possible, since there are strong grounds for treating the results as respectable ratio values, but this opinion is not shared by everyone, so it's worth checking the convention for your area.

The second way: tests of correlation

These are used when you have two or more variables which can be measured on some sort of scale, and you want to see whether two or more of them vary in a systematic way (for instance, both getting bigger, or one getting smaller when the other gets bigger). For instance, you might want to see whether the more assertiveness classes that a person attends, the more their self-esteem grows.

There are three main flavours of correlation: positive, negative and non-existent. In a positive correlation, the variables in question get bigger together and get smaller together. In a negative correlation, if one variable gets bigger, the other gets smaller, and vice versa. In a non-existent correlation, the size of one variable is unrelated to the size of the other variable. If the variables are so strongly correlated that you can predict the value of one perfectly through knowing the other, then this is given a numeric value of 1 if it's a positive correlation, and a value of −1 if it's a negative correlation. Intermediate strengths get intermediate numbers: for example, a value of .7 shows a fairly strong positive correlation, a value of 0 shows no correlation at all, and a value of −0.3 shows a weak negative correlation.

There are various tests for correlation, and your choice of test will depend on things like the measurement types involved, and whether you're dealing with a linear or a nonlinear correlation. You can correlate ordinal values, but as usual the more precise the measurement type you're using, the more powerful the test you can use. There can also be issues if you're trying to correlate variables which involve two different measurement types – for instance, one variable which is ordinal and another which is interval.

It can be useful to know that it's possible to do multiple correlations, where you're testing correlations between several variables. For instance, you can correlate someone's weight with their height, their waist measurement and their hip measurement. You'll probably find that all of these correlate with each other to varying degrees: waist measurement and hip measurement will probably correlate strongly with each other, moderately strongly with weight, and less strongly with height. It's also useful to know that if you do this with enough variables, then one combination will probably achieve statistical significance through sheer chance, so it's worth asking a statistician about how to allow for this in the analysis, if you're planning to use a multiple correlation analysis.

You might be thinking that if you know both someone's height and their waist measurement, then you can probably predict their weight more accurately if you can factor them both in somehow. You can indeed do this, and the resulting stats will show you how much each variable contributes to the accuracy of the overall estimate. The details of this go beyond the level of this book, but if you want to know more then you can ask your neighbourhood statistician about it, having first done some background reading on multiple regressions, factor analysis and principal component analysis. You should be aware that there is a polite feud between proponents of factor analysis and principal component analysis, so you may get different advice depending on which flavour of statistician you approach.

The third way: tests you can use with controlled experiments to see whether the intervention makes a difference to the groups' scores

This differs from the first way because you're looking at the scores from the group members, as opposed to simply counting how many members there are in the group. For example, you might use this to investigate whether the group members who have attended your class in mnemonics score higher on vocabulary tests than students who did not attend the class.

The classic experimental design involves taking one or more groups, treating them in different ways, and seeing what happens to one or more variables. In medicine, for instance, you might give each group a different drug treatment and see what happens to the recovery rates for members in each group.

As you may remember from earlier sections, some designs involve doing more than one thing to each group (a within-group design), whereas others involve doing different things to the different groups (a between-group design). Normally within-group designs allow stronger statistical analysis for a given group size, but it's often logically or logistically impossible to use a within-group design because of the type of problem you're investigating.

Stats tests for group-based experiments assess how much of the variation in the groups' scores appears to be random noise, and how much of the variation is associated with group membership – for instance, some of the variance may be random noise, but most of it may be associated with group membership, if there's a strong effect.

One last thing on the subject: the software will probably ask you about degrees of freedom. We'll resist the temptation towards witticisms, since this is too easy a target. The underlying concept for this is that you're analysing a set of scores which you're tabulating in various ways. It's a bit like a spread-sheet with totals for the rows and columns and for the grand total. Once you know all but one of the values in the individual cells, you can work out what the value for the remaining one is. Since it's completely predictable, it's not contributing any new information. The precise interpretation of this will depend on your particular experimental design, but that's the core concept.

Some closing thoughts

One thing to keep in mind is the reason for using inferential stats in the first place: testing whether or not there is an association between two or more things, at a level beyond what you'd expect from chance. The 'whether or not' bit is important: your mission is to find out whether or not there is an association, not to prove that there is one or to prove that there isn't. Finding that there isn't an association can be just as important as finding that there is one – for instance, finding that a particular substance isn't associated with the incidence of cancer is a useful addition to our knowledge, particularly if there were once grounds for suspecting that it might be associated.

It's important to remember that hitting that magic 0.05 significance level doesn't 'prove' that there is an effect. What it does is to establish that there's a prima facie case for an effect, so the effect is provisionally admitted into civilised society as something worthy of further investigation. Conversely, if you don't hit the 0.05 level, that doesn't prove that there isn't an effect – using a larger sample size, or a different design, might uncover a significant effect. As a rough rule of thumb, the more controversial the area you're working in, the more solid your probability values, sample sizes and experimental designs need to be before anyone trusts them very much.

Novices usually have a touching faith that larger samples are better than smaller samples, and that very large samples are best of all. The reality is more complex. Setting aside the issue that needlessly large samples are a waste of resources, there's also the issue of the power of an effect. Some effects are hulking great monsters; others are tiny. For example, a newborn baby is more likely to be a male than a female. This is a solid, reliable effect, and you can demonstrate it at pretty much any level of significance you want, if you have a large enough sample size. However, it's also a very weak effect: the difference between the percentages of males and females being born is less than 1 per cent. From the viewpoint of proud parents-to-be wanting to choose a name for their unborn offspring, this effect simply isn't worth bothering with. If you use a huge sample size to demonstrate statistical significance at the 0.05 level for a weak effect, this is known as 'inflating your p value', and is viewed as somewhat tacky by those who know about such things.

Some useful concepts, in alphabetical order

Fair dice

Dice are often used to illustrate statistical points; a lot of the early work on probability theory and statistics was motivated by a desire to calculate the odds in upmarket gambling. Pedantic statisticians know that the singular of 'dice' is 'die', which causes some confusion and much irritation on introductory stats courses, particularly for students whose first language is not English and who do not know this.

Dice are useful for illustrating what happens when there is some non-random effect going on, and the usual illustration of this involves working out whether or not a given set of dice are loaded, i.e. tampered with so that they show a particular score more often than they would otherwise do. A fair die is one which has not been tampered with, and which is equally likely to show each of the numbers when thrown. Detecting loaded dice is sometimes easy. For instance, if someone has loaded the dice so that they always show a six, that's pretty easy to detect. What happens, though, if they've loaded the dice more subtly?

One favoured way of loading dice is to drill a hole through the dot showing a one, which is on the opposite side to the six, then insert a weight and fill up the hole so it looks like a normal dot showing a one. The extra weight will make the one disproportionately likely to settle at the bottom of the dice, which will mean that the six will be at the top. If you put a very heavy weight very near the surface, then the dice will almost always end up showing a six. If you put in a lighter weight, and it's nearer the centre of the dice, then you'll get a six more often than one roll in six, but not on every roll. This is a lot harder to detect – you'll need a bigger sample to detect it. This sort of thing is known as the power of an effect: the crudely loaded dice would show a very powerful effect that was visible even in a small sample size, whereas the more subtly loaded dice would show a weak effect that was only visible in a large sample size.

Most stats books spend a lot of time explaining how to calculate statistically whether a die is loaded. The best method in a realistic setting such as a gambling den is actually to drop it into a convenient body of liquid, such as your glass of shandy: if the die is loaded, it will sink with one number persistently uppermost, and you can then discuss applied ethics with its owner. That, however, doesn't help this section very much, so we'll assume that you go for the statistical method instead.

Evenness

This is not the same as randomness. Random results are usually not even, except for some cases involving very large numbers, so treat evenness and departure from evenness with caution. This is particularly important when dealing with rare events; if events are rare and random, then some of them will probably form clusters purely as a result of chance.

Independent events

Calculating probability by multiplying individual likelihoods is a neat and very useful concept, but it runs into problems when the things aren't actually independent of each other. For example, if you're trying to calculate the likelihood of your suffering both from a stopped watch and being late for work on the same day, then it's pretty obvious that the stopped watch could have some influence on whether or not you're late for work. It's depressingly easy to come up with plausible arguments for even the most unlikely things being causally associated in this way, which creates inspiring challenges for ethically conscious researchers.

Other things being equal

The phrase 'other things being equal', is much beloved of stats textbooks. Other things often aren't equal, but stats textbooks are trying to explain the principles to you starting with the easiest cases, which deserves at least some sign of appreciation. We see no reason to depart from this honourable tradition, and will either implicitly or explicitly assume that other things are equal in the examples below, unless otherwise stated. The rest of this book is about what to do when other things aren't equal. There's a classic story of other things not being equal which isn't sufficiently widely known outside Scandinavia, so we'll mention it before returning to the main plot. According to legend, two Scandinavian kings were settling a territorial dispute in a commendably peaceable way, by throwing dice for the territory. The first king rolled two sixes, and looked understandably smug. The second king rolled (perhaps rather vigorously, though history does not record this), and one of the dice showed a six, while the other split in two (which sometimes happens with bone or wooden dice), and came down showing a six and a one. (Terry Pratchett uses a similar story in one of his books.) It's worth remembering that such improbable things can happen, so you don't get too complacent, especially if you're working in a safety-critical field. It's also worth remembering that it's the only instance of this kind that we've met in the literature, and that it dates from several hundred years ago, so anyone considering using this as a reason for dodging out of the Introductory Statistics course should think again.

Precise phrasing

Students sometimes complain about the insistence in academic writing on precise phrasing. Such students would be well advised to stay away from gamblers. Two similar sounding things may differ enormously in probability. Suppose that you are at a cocktail party and some sharply dressed individual proposes a wager on the likelihood that two people at the party share the same birthday. A gullible soul might glance at the forty-odd people in the party, multiply 1/365 by 1/365, and take the wager. That gullible soul would probably lose the bet: for forty people, it's more likely than not that two people will share the same birthday. The reason is that the sharply dressed person didn't wager on the likelihood that two people at the party shared the same, *specified* birthday (note the italics). The wager was about the likelihood that two people at the party shared the same birthday, *without any specification about what the date of that birthday was* (again, note the italics). In other words, any old date would do, and that gives you a lot more scope. The precise detail of the sums gets a bit fiddly, and tends to bore some readers, but the outcome is that if you have forty people in a room, probably two of them will have the same birthday.

It's extremely important in statistics, and in research generally, to be careful and precise about just what question you're actually asking: it can make an enormous difference.

Probability theory

Probability theory is a branch of mathematics which deals, as you might expect, with issues relating to probability, such as whether likelihoods are better expressed as frequency estimates rather than probability estimates.

Sample sizes

Most non-statisticians are easily seduced by large sample sizes and by statistical significance, and then callously abandon any concern with the power of an effect, like some Victorian reprobate tempted away from a worthy true love by a person of superficial charm, high sensuality and low principles. Large sample sizes are much more likely to find effects than small sample sizes. However, you need to ask yourself whether an effect which only shows up on very large sample sizes is powerful enough to be worth bothering with. It's usually wiser to look for the most powerful effects first, since these are likely to give you most understanding of what's going on, and only deal with the weaker effects after you understand the more powerful effects.

This looks pretty obvious when phrased this way, so why would people want to mess around with fickle, weak effects which will do the statistical equivalent of trifling with them, spending their money, and then abandoning them to a life of shame and penury? One answer is that it can be difficult to find strong effects – it often requires a deep understanding of the domain and of research design so that you know where to start looking – whereas if you gather a large enough collection of data in a crude and horrible way, you'll probably find at least some weak effects in it if you drag it through a stats package. Finding weak effects via a tastelessly large sample size in this way is known as *inflating your p value*, and is viewed as somewhat tacky by knowledgeable statisticians. (Yes, we know we've gone on about this elsewhere in the book, but it's an important point, and worth reiterating: there's also the consideration, which might appeal to those of weaker moral fibre, that it's a valid reason for not collecting enormous quantities of data in all circumstances.)

That concludes the chunk on analysis. The next chunk is about writing up your results, and about what to do after your degree is over. It's a good idea to plan the write-up right from the start: if you know what form the write-up is going to take, then you can gather the type and quantity of data you need in an efficient manner. For instance, if you're writing up your project as a demonstration of method, then you don't usually need a big sample. We've included a section about the rest of your life, since it's all too easy to lost sight of that, and then to realise after the project is over that you could have angled it in a different way which would have helped you towards your future goals.

Conclusion: the end game

Indeed, I flatter myself that even in the midst of our distress, utter bewilderment and soul-clutching horror, we scarcely went beyond the truth in any specific instance.

(*At the Mountains of Madness*, p.47)

Writing up: demonstrating your excellence efficiently, and practical points to remember

Most students do the research and then start thinking about writing up afterwards. Most students make life needlessly tough for themselves. We're not suggesting that you should do the write-up before the research (which would lead to the prospect of dispensing with the research altogether), but if you plan backwards from the finished product, then you can avoid a fair amount of needless slog, and can add a fair amount of pixy dust with no visible effort. We've started with the end product and with the sordid practicalia, and worked back to the broader issues.

There are several main schools of thought about writing. One is that writing is used to conceal how ignorant you are. A second is that writing is used to show how clever you are. A third is that it is used to persuade other people that you are right, which has some strong points if you happen to be right, but has corresponding disadvantages if you happen to be wrong. A fourth, and one which is useful in dealing with The System, is to cover your back in case of future hassles, by documenting that you have done that which you ought to have done, and have not done that which you ought not to have done. The fifth, and the one on which we will focus here, is that writing is used to convey information accurately, honestly and efficiently. Academics in general, and people marking your work in particular, are well aware of the first school of thought, and typically don't show much mercy to it. If the reader can't understand what you're saying, then that's your fault, not the reader's, and you will be awarded a mark which reflects this. The second school of thought is a trickier challenge for the marker, since it can be hard to distinguish between a brilliant application of a radically new approach and a flashy pile of vaporous waffling with lots of impressive-looking words in it. You may get away with it, but it won't win you any friends, and will send out a signal similar to the famous job reference stating that to the best of the writer's knowledge, the candidate had not stolen anything yet.

The fifth school of thought (writing to convey information accurately, honestly and efficiently) is generally considered a Good Thing, though it requires knowledge and skill. One classic problem is to get the balance right between accuracy and clarity. Most writing has to fit into a word limit. To achieve clarity within a tight word limit usually involves having to leave out complicating detail, which in turn means writing a simplified version. The more you simplify your account, the less accuracy it contains. This interacts with the problem of writing for your intended audience. A useful rule of thumb is that you explain any concepts which you can't reasonably expect your intended audience to understand. If you're writing for professional geomorphologists, for instance, then you shouldn't need to explain what is meant by 'periglacial'. If you're writing an article for your local newspaper, then you will need to explain what you mean by 'periglacial'.

A second classic problem with writing accurate, clear text is that as a student you are trying to do two things. One of these is to tell the reader about your chosen topic. The other is to show the reader the cabinetmaking skills you have acquired as a student. These should not come into conflict, but there may be times when you need to make a detour to ensure that the cabinetmaking skills are properly visible in your writing.

That's the background; we'll now look at the various tasks involved in writing up, ranging from low-level practicalia to strategic planning.

201 WRITING UP 201

Sordid practicalia

Even if your work is miserable grot, you can at least scrape together a few marks by ensuring that it's well-presented miserable grot. More positively, attention to practicalia can lift a good piece of work into excellence, and the prospect of a distinction. Most of the issues involved are pretty obvious with hindsight, but are easy to overlook when you're stressed and working to a tight deadline.

The first thing to do is to plan backwards from the date when the work is due in. You should then aim to submit at least two days before the real deadline. There are various reasons for this. One reason is that you will probably over-run. Over-running one day past your personal deadline will still get the work in by the official deadline, if your personal deadline is a couple of days before the official one. Over-running by one day is a different proposition if your personal deadline is the same as the official one. The second reason is that everybody else will be leaving things till the last minute, so there will be huge queues for printers, photocopiers, binders, and suchlike; at least one device is likely to break down because of the increased load.

How do you do the actual planning? A simple way is to list all the tasks you will have to do, such as printing off the final version, copy-editing it, and so forth, then allocate a pessimistic amount of time for each of them, working back from the deadline. If the official deadline is 21 April, then you might make your personal deadline 19 April; you might allow one day for printing the final version, a couple of days for your long-suffering lover/best friend/semi-literate drinking companions to scan it for typos, and one day for you to clean up the typos and print off the really final version. That means that you'll be printing off the really final version on the 18th, having a break on the 16th and 17th during the copy-editing, and spending the 15th sweating over a hot printer which will run out of ink and/or paper just after the shops shut. What happens if your printer does run out of ink at this point? It's not a pretty thought. That's why you need to be pessimistic with your planning, and build in plenty of spare time and fallback strategies. It's worth thinking about co-operation: for instance, you could pool resources with some friends, so that one of you did the last-minute run to the shops for paper and printer cartridges, while another figured out the arrangements for getting things bound, and so on. (Don't extend this to co-operation by writing text for each other: if you do this, then you'll suffer the academic equivalent of being lined up against a wall and shot – collusion and plagiarism are really serious offences, and academics are pretty good at spotting the tell-tale changes in writing style.)

The important thing to remember is that your supervisor is the person most likely to have a personal supply of pixy dust, so it's extremely advisable to give them a chance to comment on the pre-final draft – a couple of suggestions from them at this point can make a substantial difference to the quality of your final draft, and to the marks that you'll get. Remember that all their other students are also likely to be showing them drafts just before the hand-in date, so allow a reasonable amount of time for this – most supervisors ask for two weeks. (How would you feel about having four 50-page dissertations handed to you on the same day, with a request to read them by tomorrow?) Wise students show drafts to their supervisor throughout the research, which speeds up the process considerably, and usually leads to a much better product for less effort.

Remember to allow lots of time for printing off the final version, and remember to do the right number of copies – the regulations will tell you how many. You usually have to do more than one copy so that two people can read and mark it in parallel. Some departments return a copy to you; others don't. It's a good idea to print off a copy for yourself while you're about it. You may feel that you never want to see the thing again, but a year or two later you may feel differently, and by then you'll probably have misplaced the soft copy. Remember to check the regulations about font, margins, word counts, etc. Remember also to obey them, even if you think they're silly. In later life, you may have to produce reports, etc. as part of your job, and you'll find that the rest of the world is just as uncompromising as academia about adherence to house style.

You should read through the final version carefully to check for errors. The spell checker in your word processing package will catch most errors, but not all (such as whether you have two tables both entitled 'Table 1'). It's difficult to spot your own errors, which is why it's a good idea to have a friend check the final version. If you can't persuade anyone to do this (it's a fair-sized job), then persuade someone to check the pages up to and including page one of the introduction, and the first page of references: that's where the first impressions are made. Remember cabinetmaking: your dissertation is your cabinet, and you don't want to leave it with big oily thumbprints all over it.

Some really inadvisable ideas

- Writing it up the way we do back home in Texas/business/symbolic interactionism – you should use the format and style recommended in your current department or discipline, or you'll look clueless at best, and like an arrogant idiot at worst.
- Writing it in 'plain simple English' by throwing away any evidence that you've learned anything (such as technical terms, references or facts).
- Plagiarism or anything that smells of plagiarism (for instance, references in inconsistent formats, which suggests you've just downloaded a batch of references off the internet without bothering to read the actual articles).
- Using big words that you found in the dictionary and wouldn't use normally (the resulting howlers bring some entertainment to the lives of overworked markers, but won't do anything positive for your marks).

Structure, content and strategy

Some bits of the structure are supplied to you by your department – the required chapter titles, conventions about appendices and references, etc.

Within this, you need to sort out various things relating to structure which are explained in this section: narrative spine, red thread, signposting, flagging, keeping to the plot, snagging, etc. These make the difference between a rambling assortment of vaguely connected words, and a piece of work that makes the marker think good things about you before slapping on a high mark. The first thing to remember is that you're telling a story, with a plot and an outcome. A good story pits you against a large dragon, and ends with a happy resolution; a bad story pits you against something which is never clearly identified, and ends with something different which is also never clearly identified. This is what narrative spine and its approximate synonyms 'the red thread' and 'the plot' are all about. What is the problem that you're tackling in your research? Why is it difficult, and why is it important? What has been tried unsuccessfully before? What did you do to tackle it? Why that approach? Have you demonstrated clearly that you have moved us a step closer to the solution, even if it's via telling us that the approach you tried is a blind alley? Each new section of your write-up should unfold another part of the story, and keep the readers wanting to find out what happens next. One handy way of doing this is to start off by writing the key point of each chapter as a single sentence. This can be irritating, since you're aware of all sorts of complications which have to be left out when you produce that single sentence. You then tweak these sentences so that they tell an interesting story. After that, you expand each sentence by adding the things that you had to leave out when you were creating your sentences. They'll still be pretty much the same things, but they'll hang together much better in the new structure.

There are various other structural things that you need to do. Remember that readers are human beings, and unlikely to try reading your whole dissertation in one go – they'll have breaks to notice the family, go to the toilet, sleep, and do other mundane things which help to keep the human world going round. When they pick up your dissertation again, they'll probably have forgotten large chunks of your carefully crafted argument. This is where signposting comes in. Signposts remind the reader where they've just been (i.e. what you've said in the chapter that you're now ending) and tell the reader where you're going next (i.e. what you'll be doing in the next chapter, and why). It's usual to put signposts at the beginning and end of each section, with big signposts for big sections and small ones for subsections. A closely related concept is 'bridging text', which is text used to join together chunks of text about different topics. For instance, if you're researching the application of semantic prototype theory to concepts of nature, then you'll have one chunk of text telling the reader about semantic prototype theory and another telling them about previous work on concepts of nature. If you just stop writing about the first topic and go straight on to the next, the transition will come as an unexpected jolt to the reader; a better plan is to write some text between the two sections, reminding the reader how these concepts are connected to each other.

Flagging is another structural concept, and can involve looking tens of pages ahead. A classic use of flagging is when you find something very interesting, but quite unexpected, in your results. If you wrote up your research in strict chronological order, then the unexpected finding might not be discussed until near the end of your dissertation. Trying to explain why this finding is significant will take space, and can seriously unbalance the structure of your discussion section. A better strategy is to mention the topic early on (i.e. plant a metaphorical flag on it to show that you've been there), so that readers are prepared for it. It also implies, without telling any outright lies, that you were discerning enough to have considered this in advance as a possible finding (though don't push your luck on this – not blurting out the truth is okay, but telling lies isn't). Readers of a literary bent may use the analogy of the detective story convention that when the villain is stabbed in the study during the dénouement on page 203, it is done with the Afghan dagger used as a paperknife that was first described on page 27.

On the subject of flags, there are also various tactical things that you should remember for the write-up. One is to show that you're aware of surrounding territories, and have not rambled through your topic in innocent unawareness of the dozen relevant areas that surround it. For instance, with the example of semantic prototypes and perceptions of nature, there's a lot of literature on semantics in general, and you can't be expected to know it all. You can, however, be expected to show that you know that this literature exists, even if you don't know the details. You can do this with a couple of well-crafted sentences. For instance, you could say early in your introduction: 'There is a substantial and well-established literature on X (e.g. de Ville 1853; Smith 1986; Jones 2006). The approach used for this study is Y, as used by . . .'. That's a bit brief, but it gives the general idea – name the relevant territories, cite a couple of relevant references which you have read, and then move on. You hit diminishing returns pretty quickly with mentioning relevant territories, so don't waste effort. Incidentally, this is where you may be able to use references which turned out to be less relevant than you had hoped – you can mention them in passing, and say briefly why they were off-topic. That way you get a brownie point for your apparent erudition, from something which would otherwise have been a waste of your time.

You need to bound and scope your study – to say where you're going to stop, and what you're not going to cover, and preferably why. Giving reasons such as 'I ran out of time' is not advisable. You can just say that something is an interesting topic, but outside the scope of the present study. Remember that there are some things that you can't put outside your scope though, such as reporting what you found, or doing something properly.

Yet another use of flags comes at the end of the write-up. Most disciplines end dissertations with a section which contains conclusions and further work. The conclusion should say what you found, and should not spout on at length about how much you have learned about programming in Java, or whatever it was that you did. Spouting on about how much you have learned will draw attention to your previous ignorance, and will put the issue of your ignorance on to the agenda. Telling someone that you think you know a lot about something is not usually very persuasive; any idle braggart can do that. Showing someone your knowledge is a very different proposition, and much wiser.

The 'further work' section should contain at least one sensible, thought-through suggestion for what could be done to follow on from your research. Shrewd markers will look at this section to see whether you're the sort of person who looks no further forward than the end of the dissertation. Shrewd job interviewers may ask you questions about this to see whether you're the sort of person who might be promotable material if they employ you. Weak students typically produce a 'further work' section which says that their work needs to be tested on a larger sample; this simply raises questions about why they didn't or couldn't use a large enough sample themselves in the first place. Strong students produce some interesting, useful suggestions where the reader thinks: 'Now that's a neat idea.'

One simple way of producing a reasonable 'further work' section is as follows. If you've planned your research sensibly, with a set of core tasks and a wishlist of subtasks to do if time permits, then you may find that there isn't enough time to finish one of the subtasks on the wishlist. If so, you can shove a description of it into the 'further work' section, where you can talk knowledgeably about how this problem might be tackled by someone following in your footsteps, and about what obstacles would confront that person. Another thing that you can do with the 'further work' section, if you're a professional academic, is to use it to plant your own flag on an idea, and show that you got there first.

Most dissertations have to include an abstract. Abstract writing is a valuable skill for later life and well worth learning. Most people don't learn it, and then wonder why their brilliant document has been ignored by higher management in favour of something by somebody far less competent. The answer probably lies in the abstracts of the respective documents. People higher up the food chain than yourself are likely to be seriously overworked, and are unlikely to read entire lengthy documents unless they absolutely have to. What they do instead is to read the abstracts (broadly equivalent to 'business summaries' in business language). If an abstract looks promising, they might then go on to read the entire document; if not, then they'll consign it to history. So, what is an abstract, and how do you write a good one?

An abstract is a summary (usually one page long) summarising what you did, why you did it, what you found, and what the implications are. It is short enough to fit into the required word/page count, but detailed enough (and therefore long enough) to cover the most important specific points. How do you get that balance right? There isn't a single simple answer, which is one reason why most people don't write brilliant abstracts. One useful approach is to decide what the main points are which you will cover, at the highest level – for instance, what you did, why you did it, what you found, and what the implications are. You can then allocate one paragraph to each of these. Within each paragraph, you now work out what the most important subpoints are, from the viewpoint of your intended reader. For instance, if you are tackling a problem which is legendary throughout your discipline, then you won't need to go into as much detail about the nature of the problem as you would if the problem was an obscure one. You then write down a brief, clear account of those subpoints. Disciplines vary as regards whether or not you should include references in the abstract; a useful rule of thumb is to leave them out unless they're a central part of what you're doing.

Once you've done this, you can see which sections need to be comparatively long, and which can be pretty short. You may then be able to combine a couple of the short ones into a single paragraph, or otherwise rearrange the text so that it's clearer.

Another useful rule of thumb is to imagine that you're a harassed middle manager who was supposed to have read a lengthy document before an important meeting, but who wasn't able to because life got in the way. What you're hoping is that reading the abstract will give you enough overview and specifics to let you bluff your way through the meeting while giving the appearance of having read the entire document. What would you want, and what would you not want, in those circumstances? You would want a clear overview, and some specific details where relevant; you would not want a lot of content-free truisms about the internet being the fastest growing media (sic) in the history of the world, or about human motivation being difficult to investigate, nor would you want 400 words of impenetrable technical detail that left you unclear whether the thing worked or not. Similarly, you would not want a lot of self-glorifying claims about how the writer had revolutionised the field unless there was some pretty solid evidence to back it up. One exercise which might help you is to wade through the abstracts of some previous dissertations in your field, and note which ones gave you a reasonable idea of what to expect in the dissertation as a whole, and why. Practice also helps – this is one topic where you can usefully practise on other students, exchanging abstracts in a spirit of constructive mutual criticism.

Last in this subsection, but far from least, there's snagging – catching all the little minor errors that have crept in. It's useful to keep a separate snagging list as you go through (one way to avoid losing it is to have it as the first page of the draft dissertation, though if so remember to remove it before submitting the final version). Why have a list, rather than fixing the problems as you find them? Sometimes you can't fix them at that point: the snag may be something that you spot at midnight and which involves access to an obscure document in the library, which is now shut. Sometimes they're better done as a coherent batch at the end: for instance, if you're doing a lot of cut-and-paste with tables and figures, it often makes sense to number them after you've made the final decision about which ones will go where, otherwise you will spend a lot of time repeatedly renumbering them with each successive version.

Cabinetmaking

Remember that the dissertation is your cabinet, and that it's your job to make your skills and knowledge visible. As with cabinets and much else in life, first impressions are important – make sure that the general look and feel is good even before the reader starts on the words (so get layout, etc. right, and don't have handwritten corrections on the first page). Once the reader gets started on the actual words, they're likely to look at the pages up to and including the first page of the introduction, and then to have a look at the reference section. This is the equivalent of pulling out a drawer from a piece of allegedly antique furniture and seeing whether the joints in a seldom-seen area are as good as they should be. Yes, people will look at your 'Acknowledgements' section in detail – they're likely to check whether you've spelled your supervisor's name right, for instance. If you don't even get that right after months of supervision, then this suggests that other bits of your work may be iffy, and may merit closer inspection.

How do you send out good cabinetmaking signals? One important issue is avoiding blood in the water (yes, that's a seriously mixed metaphor, but its vividness may help potentially lost souls to remember it). Blood in the water attracts sharks, so if you're in shark territory, you don't spill blood into the water. In terms of writing, this translates into not doing things that will make you look like a clueless amateur or an active sinner. Clueless amateurs and sinners tend to do things in the most immediately obvious way, without bothering to check whether this is the best way; they seldom bother to do any proper homework, and rely heavily on the internet as a source of information. Any uninformed member of the public could do this, so the likelihood of producing something decent this way is minimal. What you're being assessed on is how much more you know than an uninformed member of the public, so you need to do things that they don't know how to do. Supplementing internet sources with textbooks and set texts from the course reading list is not much better – it sends out a signal that you're too lazy to read anything except the bare minimum.

One thing that gets you off to a good start is showing that you've done your homework by reading the relevant literature and by learning the relevant technical terms and concepts. Something that gets you off to an even better start is showing that you've done homework above and beyond the call of duty, such as reading more advanced literature than your peers. The usual way to demonstrate this is in the first page of your introduction, where you lay out the main issues that you will be tackling in the rest of your dissertation, and where you include appropriate citations for each issue as you mention it. Appropriate citations include the seminal ones that originated the approach you're using, and the bang-up-to-date ones that you're using as the starting point for your own research, plus one or two advanced ones to show that you're a real professional. Don't overdo it – your supervisor should be able to advise you on the appropriate number for your field – but half a dozen well-chosen references in the first couple of paragraphs can get you off to a flying start. This book contains an entire section about referencing, which shows how serious a topic it is. This may sound daunting, but it's not as much work as it looks – we're only talking about half a dozen texts, most of which will probably be short journal articles rather than full-sized books. By focusing efficiently on the right texts, and not wasting time on less useful ones, you end up making much better use of the same amount of time (or less time, if you really get your act together).

We've taken it for granted that your spelling and grammar will be as faultless as you can manage, and that your tables and figures will be impeccably produced. We're not big fans of prescriptive grammar for pedantry's sake, but like most professional researchers, we get pretty annoyed when we encounter language which is vague, misleading, ambiguous or otherwise sloppy. The physicist Pauli once crafted a neat insult about research so bad that it wasn't even wrong: one of the ways in which this can be true is that nobody can work out exactly what you did, in which case your work was a complete waste of your own time as well as the reader's. Many students who have learned English as a foreign or second language are actually pretty good at expressing themselves clearly and unambiguously even when their formal grammar is a bit iffy – if they've learned about the importance of a clear conceptual structure in their writing, then they can force the bits of English that they do know into a clear structure.

On the subject of tables and figures, idle and clueless students often try to deflect attention from their dreadful work by including humorous clip-art and colourful pie charts in abundance. Trying to be funny breaks the second golden rule of presenting information in public (don't try to be funny), and is a really dim idea – you don't become a cabinetmaker by demonstrating your skills as a clown. Colourful charts are fine if you're in a discipline which is keen on them, but many disciplines take a deliberately austere view of such things. The risk is that you'll use a format which betrays your ignorance of an important concept – a classic example is producing a graph for discontinuous data, instead of using a histogram.

Returning to structure, the plot and structure of your dissertation should mirror the research question that you ask. If your research question produces three hypotheses in the introduction, then the reader will want to know what happens to these hypotheses. The sensible way to handle this is to plan your structure so that each hypothesis has a corresponding subsection in the results and in the discussion sections. That makes sure that you don't leave any loose ends lying around in a way that might suggest that you're trying to distract the reader away from an embarrassing finding or failure. Academics have plenty of experience in spotting such ploys and shortcomings: Herodotus' *Histories*, for instance, are several hundred pages long, were written well over two thousand years ago, and contain a grand total of four loose ends. That's from someone so uncritical that he thought the Spartan kings had two votes each, and that there was a Spartan company called Pitanate, though no such company had ever existed; academia has had quite a long time to refine its skills since then, so such sloppiness is now unlikely to go unnoticed.

There are various schools of thought about when to write up which bits of your work. The method that we favour is to begin by writing a draft of the introduction, and drawing a thick red line through it so that you're not tempted to keep it in that form. This draft forces you to think clearly about what you're doing. You can then do the method section, which is unlikely to change much as the write-up progresses. The results section needs to be done after you've finished analysing all your data (remember to collect all of the data before you start the analysis, so you don't subconsciously cue yourself to nudge the remaining data collection in a particular direction). You can then write the discussion, the conclusion and the further work. At this point you rewrite the introduction from scratch. This may seem like masochism, but it means that you're in a much better position to do things like flagging issues which will arise later, and emphasising points which have turned out to be important. With the hindsight of having done the research, you'll also be able to see your original research question in a much clearer perspective. What about the references? It's usually a good idea to update the reference section continuously as you go through. If you're having a bad day and aren't up to anything requiring creative thought, you can tidy up the references a bit, so that by the deadline they're all beautiful and polished.

A recurrent theme in this book, and one which is particularly important when writing up, is the sources of evidence you can use. The usual way of demonstrating these is via bibliographic references, with the number and the types of reference demonstrating how knowledgeable and brilliant you are. This is something of an art form, and one which most students don't know, so the next section is about this topic. There's also the practical consideration that finding and using the right references can let you stand on the shoulders of giants (or at least prevent you from reinventing the wheel).

References and referencing: using and citing the right texts to demonstrate your excellence

I was rather sorry, later on, that I had ever looked into that monstrous book at the college library.

(*At the Mountains of Madness*, p.16)

What are references? The word is, helpfully, used in two quite separate senses. One relates to references for jobs: these involve someone writing things about you to help prospective employers decide whether or not to take you on. Most prospective employers don't trust the average reference very much, since the law in this area has tightened up recently to the point where most references are pretty anodyne and content-free. If you write a glowing reference to get rid of someone, and that person is as dreadful in the next job as they were working with you, then the next employer can sue you for writing a misleading reference; conversely, if you write a scathing reference because you despise the individual's politics and taste in bow ties, then the individual can sue you for lying about them. Some references are a bit more informative: if the reference is glowing and contains lots of specific, impressive and easily checked facts, rather than opinions, then the candidate is likely to be genuinely good, and it's likely to be worth looking more closely at their application. (Most job applicants write pretty dreadful covering letters and CVs, so it's surprisingly easy to overlook a good candidate at first glance if they've covered their light with a large bushel and if there's a large set of candidates.) This sort of reference is important, and is something you need to prepare for early in your course – you need to convince someone with an appropriately impressive title that you are worth writing an outstanding reference for, and you can't do this in the last two weeks of your course. That, however, is not the sort of reference that this section is principally about.

This section is about bibliographic references, sometimes known as citations. What are these, and why do they matter? They matter because they're one of the most important bits of cabinetmaking in your research. There's a huge difference between the referencing skills of top-grade researchers and clueless amateurs; an experienced academic can tell a great deal about the quality of your work from your referencing. Most clueless individuals either don't believe this, or believe it but fail dismally to do anything about it, either through a nihilistic desire to snatch defeat out of the jaws of victory, or because nobody has ever told them what references are about. That's why we've devoted an entire section to this topic.

The core concept is pretty simple. Whenever you make a significant assertion of fact which is not taken for granted by your intended readership, you include some text which tells the reader where you got that fact from. This is the reference (or citation; most people use the terms interchangeably). So, for instance, you might mention, as part of your chain of argument about mammalian locomotion, that sloths can swim surprisingly well. This is not something which most readers will take for granted, so you'll need to include the source for this assertion – the article, book or whatever it was in which you found the evidence for this statement. You don't need to do this for statements which your intended readers will take for granted – for instance, that Paris is the capital of France, or for trivial statements, since otherwise the number of references would become unmanageable. As you might guess, there's a grey area where it's debatable whether or not you need a reference; for instance, if you're writing an article about knowledge representation and you use the example of swimming sloths as a random example, where any other example would do equally well, then you probably won't need a reference, as one of us can thankfully testify from personal experience. If in doubt, either ask your supervisor or err on the side of including a reference.

Why do you need to cite references in this way? One reason is that it provides a chain of evidence, so that if someone for whatever reason wishes to check what you're claiming, then they can look up the reference in question and check the full details. Sometimes people want to do this because they find an assertion hard to believe: there are Bad People in the world who make false and misleading claims, so good referencing makes it clear to readers that your claims are solidly based. On other occasions, people want to follow up your references because the references might give them a useful new source of information which might help them to solve problems of their own. Professional researchers do this a lot.

From a sordid Realpolitik point of view, references can do many other things. They show the reader that you have done all the homework that you should have done, so you're not reinventing the wheel and making it square. They're also useful for deflecting the blame if things go wrong: if you've based one of your assumptions on a virtuous reading of McPherson's (2002) article on the topic, and it later emerges that his article was not as reliable as it might have been, then that's McPherson's problem, not yours: you've acted in good faith, and nobody can blame you if he got something wrong.

This leads us on to a couple of important points about references. One is that they're a functional tool, not an ornament. It is incredibly irritating to spend ages in a dreary corner of the library trying to track down a reference, and then discover that the perpetrator of the article where you found that reference has given its details incorrectly. A classic example is writing that something was in issue 13(3) of a journal, whereas it was actually in issue 31(3) – a simple trans-position of digits makes a difference of 18 years and dozens of intervening issues. For this reason, people assessing your research (whether markers of your dissertation, or reviewers of papers that you have submitted to a journal or conference) are extremely picky about the formatting of your references: if they're sloppily presented, with obvious typos in the authors' names and suchlike, then it's quite likely that there will be factual errors elsewhere.

On the subject of marking, markers are well aware that a depressingly high proportion of dissertations contain references which the author of the disser-tation has downloaded from the internet, without ever reading the articles themselves. This usually results in inconsistent formatting: for instance, some of the references in the dissertation will have the authors' names followed by their initials, whereas others will have their initials followed by the names. In consequence, if you've virtuously read the original articles but been sloppy about your formatting, then you may be suspected of academic sin worse than simple sloppiness.

Moving further down the depressing slope of sin, there are various other manifestations of human weakness which may appear in references. We could go on about this at some length, but we won't, because it gets too depressing. Instead, we'll work through the nuts and bolts of referencing, and then say a few things about the strategy of referencing.

The nuts and bolts are pretty simple from a functional point of view. You're writing down all the information required for someone else to find the same source that you're quoting. Innocent souls often believe that simply giving the title of the book is enough; unfortunately, it isn't, and that's why this topic merits a section all of its own. Beginning with books, successful books are periodically revised, updated, and generally changed, then republished. Very successful books, such as *Gray's Anatomy*, will continue this process over tens or even hundreds of years. The result is that any two editions published in different years may contain very different material. Quite often, the earlier edition contains errors which are corrected in the later edition. The consequence for you is that you need to specify which edition you used. Even that isn't enough, for numerous reasons, all of which have happened to hapless researchers over the years. For instance, an edition may be published in one year, and then republished in a different year, with one year's version of that edition containing typos which were not in the other year's. If the typo involves a figure, such as a date or an equation, then the implications are obvious (and yes, precisely this has happened on at least one occasion).

The assumption that only one book will have that title is also sweetly innocent and wrong. There may be large numbers of books with the same title, or with very similar titles, particularly on popular topics – how many sensible titles are there, for instance, for a book which is an introduction to Microsoft Windows? You therefore need to specify the authorship of the book, and you need to get the details right, because there are often different people with identical surnames working in the same field (for instance, husband and wife teams, whose names are differentiated only by initials, and sometimes not even by those). You may also encounter pairs of researchers who often publish together and who alternate first authorship, so that some publications are by Smith and Jones, whereas others are by Jones and Smith.

Those issues involve simply making it clear which publication you meant. If you're on the other side of the fence, trying to track down a particular book, then you'll soon run into the practical question of who published it, since you might need to contact the publisher to track down a copy. These days, this is less of a problem than ten years ago, but it's still not safe to assume that you can find any book on internet booksellers, especially if it's an obscure or old one (and therefore particularly likely to contain information that you couldn't find elsewhere). Deborah Harkness, for instance, tracked down the long-lost *Book of Soyga* via a physical card index system in a library, where it was filed under one of its alternate titles – the internet would have been of no use whatever in this case (no, we're not making that one up, and the full story is even more improbable).

So, where does this leave us? It leaves us having to specify full and unambiguous details for everything we cite – the authors' names and initials, the publisher, the title of the work, the year of publication and the edition. There are different conventions for citations, such as the Harvard system or the American Psychological Association system, each of which requires slightly different details. Yes, that's not perfectly logical, but that's a problem for someone else to sort out, not us or you; an important cabinetmaking skill is meticulously following whatever system is required by whoever is publishing your work, however silly you privately consider that system.

The situation is similar for journal articles, except that you need to remember to specify the volume number (journals usually have a new volume number each year) and the issue number (journals typically publish several issues each year). The usual convention is that the volume number comes first, in bold, followed by the issue number in parentheses and not in bold, such as **18**(3) for volume 18, issue 3. You usually also need to specify the page numbers for that article. Why? Try tracking down a reference whose details are slightly incorrect, and you'll discover why; every bit of information in a reference helps specify unambiguously which reference is really involved.

That's nuts and bolts. Strategy is a longer story, and boils down to demonstrating as many cabinetmaking skills as possible – reading seminal, milestone and foundational literature, reading complex uncompromising journal articles where appropriate, rather than gently simplified textbooks, showing initiative in your reading rather than only reading what's on the list, reading bang-up-to-date references as well as older ones, and so on. Careful consideration of the cabinetmaking skills described throughout this book should help with this.

The next section of this book is also the last main section. It's about the next steps after your degree is over. It's a good idea to read this section before choosing your project topic. Students are often unaware of the number and quality of options open to them after they graduate, and tend to underachieve as a result. Most people are capable of more and better things than they realise, so it's well worth spending some time on thinking ahead: it improves your chances of looking back on a life full of the experiences and achievements that you've always wanted.

What next? thinking forward about what you really want your life to be

There are no limits, literally none, to what she can think of when she gives her mind to it. The imagination boggles at the thought of what she might be cooking up.

(*Stiff Upper Lip, Jeeves*, p.120)

There are two main views of projects among students. One is that the project is analogous to being thrown into a wolf pit: you focus all your energy and concentration on getting out alive, and leave long-term planning until after your escape. The other is that the project is analogous to doing greasy washing up in cold water when you have a hangover after a wild party: something to be done, and then to be expunged from your memory as thoroughly as possible. Both these views are understandable, but they're a bit limited in their ability to make your life better: they tend to get you out of one problem and straight into the next – the existential equivalent of clambering over the wall of the wolf pit, and realising that your escape route has just dropped you into the tiger pit next door. So, how can you achieve a happier outcome?

Usually, a sensible strategy is to work backwards from where you want to end up, and work out what you need to do to get there. Unfortunately, this encounters problems when deciding what to do after your degree, for the sound reason that you probably don't know where you want to end up. This is usually because you can't know what might suit you until you've tried it; you also can't know all the possible life paths and job possibilities in the world. This isn't as big a problem as it might appear. The world changes; you change; life isn't an exam where you lose marks for not choosing the right job. It's up to you whether you want to be head of the company that buys out Microsoft, or a primary school teacher, or a beach bum or a monk. Having said that, there are various things that you can do to reduce the likelihood of ending up in a job that makes you so unhappy that even we hesitate to mention an apposite metaphor.

One thing you can do is to imagine yourself on your deathbed, looking back on your life. What things would you want to have done, or at least to have tried? Is there anything that you would bitterly regret not doing, or not trying? Once you have a shortlist of such things, you can sketch out a life plan which includes them. You can change that plan at any time, or abandon it completely; that's up to you. However, having a sketch plan of this sort will improve your chances of making the most of your life. So, for instance, you might want to go scuba diving in the Bahamas at least once before you die, and you might want to be a management consultant. The scuba diving is pretty simple to plan: you just need to save enough money, book the holiday, and do the preparatory work that will let you get the most out of the trip, such as learning to scuba dive before you leave. The management consultant role takes a lot more preparation, and it might be ten or twenty years before you have the experience and the reputation to earn a living from it. Knowing this, you can decide whether you really want to be a management consultant, and are prepared to pay the price of preparatory work, or whether you can live without it.

A related thing that you can do is to look through the things on your list, and ask yourself why you want to do them, and what you would do after you had done them. Suppose, for instance, that you want to win a Nobel Prize before you die. What would you do with the rest of your life after you had won it? If the answer is that the rest of your life would be a pathetic anticlimax which you filled by waiting for death, then you might want to rethink your ambitions and the reasons for them. If the answer is that you would use your prestige to foster good works around the world, that's a much healthier prognosis, and you can start doing your homework with an untroubled soul. (A useful tip which might save you from social embarrassment: if you win two Nobel Prizes, remember that you only shake the hand of the King of Sweden on the first occasion when you meet; it's bad manners in this context to try to shake it on the second occasion.)

You can't know all the possible life paths, jobs and careers which exist, but you can at least work out what sort of life you want. One simple way of doing this is to collect two highlighters of different colours and a large pile of job adverts and/or brief biographies, including some that you know you will like and others that you will loathe. You then go through each of the documents, highlighting things that you like in one colour, and things that you hate in the other colour. Once you have done enough of this, you then write two lists, one for the things in the first highlighter colour, and the second for the things in the other highlighter colour. You can then, if you're feeling ready for some introspection, go through each list, writing by each item what the reason is for your feeling the way you do about it. So, for instance, your hate list might contain things like 'working in a cubicle' and 'doing an administrative job'. Your reason for hating working in a cubicle might be that you like to work in attractive surroundings, and your reason for hating an administrative job might be that you like having discrete projects that you can complete, rather than an endless stack of tasks. Taken together, these things suggest that you should be looking for a job involving discrete projects in attractive surroundings.

You might wonder why you can't simply write down what you want to do. You can try, but this hits problems with the nature of human memory. We're better at recognising things than at recalling them (hence the use of job adverts or biographies, so you can recognise things that are important to you). We're also liable to overlook things that are so familiar we take them for granted (hence writing down the reasons for each feeling, since otherwise you might completely overlook some of the most important things).

Once you have a sketch plan of what sort of life you want, you can start to plan ahead, and to make your own luck. Most people take a reactive approach to life planning: a typical example is that you want a new job, so you start looking in the job advertisement part of the paper, and thereby reacting to the jobs which happen to be advertised in that paper at that time. There are other ways, and better ways. For instance, if you want a job as a forest ranger in Canada, then you're unlikely to find one advertised in the *Shropshire Star*. One option is to complain that life is difficult, and to settle for a job in lower management at the local supermarket which happened to be advertised when you were looking. A better option would be to work out how to hunt down that job as a forest ranger. This would involve things like finding out what qualifications and experience you needed, what residency and visa requirements were involved, and where the jobs were advertised. It would take time and effort, but any interview panel would be impressed by someone who put in that time and effort, and you would have a sporting chance of getting that job. If you didn't get it, then you could make some more luck for yourself by the way you handled the rejection: being courteous and constructive and asking what you could do to improve your chances next time a job came up would be a good start. Most people underestimate how much they can achieve if they put in some sensible homework and some time and effort. It's surprising how much you can achieve, and you're likely to have a much better life if you take control of it in this way.

Whatever route you take, you'll need to pay the bills, and to go through some sort of selection process. This usually involves applying formally for the job that you're hunting, and then being inverviewed if you're shortlisted. Three important concepts here are triage, haloes and blood in the water. One useful viewpoint is that of the people on the interview panel. From their point of view, the selection process is a lengthy set of hassles, when they already have far too much to do (if you're senior enough to be on an interview panel, you'll almost certainly be hideously overloaded). In an ideal world, they would carefully read every word of every application form sent in by every candidate. In reality, they are likely to start with a process of triage. This involves glancing at the applications, and chucking them on to three piles. One pile is for the applications which look completely unsuitable; another is for the really promising ones; the third is for the ones who may be okay, if there aren't enough really promising ones. This is where haloes and blood in the water come in. If your application contains highly visible indications of excellence, then it's likely to go on the 'promising' pile, with its halo gleaming; if it contains highly visible indications of trouble, then it will probably go on to the 'unsuitable' pile, and meet the fate of anything with an open wound that falls into shark-infested seas. The key phrase here is 'highly visible'. If your application has brilliant things from page two onwards, that's too late; its fate will be decided before anyone reads that far. It's up to you to get the indicators of excellence on to the covering letter, on to the application form, and on to your CV – and to make sure that those indicators are visible as early as possible.

Things that make haloes gleam include attention to detail (for instance, getting the name of the company right, and including the reference code for the job if there is one – large organisations often advertise several similar jobs at the same time, so just saying you are applying for 'the job' is not a good start). Another good thing is homework: surprisingly few candidates read the 'information for applicants' that goes out with application forms, and hardly any do any proper research about the organisation that they're applying to work with. Tangible evidence of excellence is also a good thing – any awards, achievements, etc. that you may have notched up. Notching these up is your responsibility, not anybody else's. The earlier you start thinking about this, the better your chances of having something decent to show. Any evidence that you are a safe pair of hands is also a good thing: capable, dependable people are a rare commodity, so if your account of yourself demonstrates good judgement and professional reliability, then that's a good start.

There are numerous ways of getting blood into the water. One thing which is a particular problem for most students is that they are young, and have therefore had relatively few chances to do anything remarkably good except for achieving high exam grades. They are therefore tempted to make subjective statements about themselves, such as 'I have great communication skills and have a professional approach to my work'. These statements are at best meaningless, since nobody in their senses would claim the opposite as a reason for employing them, and at worst suggest that you are a boastful brat with serious delusions of adequacy. It's much better to show than to tell. If your project led to a paper at the TLA2007 conference, that shows that you did good work – the paper is a fact which can be shown, not an opinion. There are also various things which suggest that you would be a positive liability or a serious risk. For instance, if your CV has a gap starting six months after you graduated and ending a year after you graduated, most potential employers will wonder whether this means that you were unemployed, or whether you were in prison for six months. Most students think we're joking when we mention this. However, a surprising number of panel members will have encountered candidates with CV gaps which did conceal time in jail (we've met a couple of these cases ourselves). If you were unemployed, say so, and then reclaim some credit by saying how you used that time to develop yourself and your career plans (for instance, by teaching yourself some useful skill). Most of the sins can be avoided by remembering the three golden rules: don't lie, don't try to be funny, but above all, don't panic and blurt out the truth. If you're not sure why the first and the third rule aren't contradictory, then you would be well advised to ask someone wise, since there's a serious point behind those rules.

Most employers are looking for someone who is a safe pair of hands, who will be pleasant to work with, and who might be promotable with time. Most panels have to assess these qualities by ticking boxes (often literally) to show which of the criteria you meet from the person spec and the job spec. Make life easy for them in your job application by saying how you meet each criterion, preferably with some tangible evidence for each bit. If you have enough sense to do this, then they're likely to think that you'll have enough sense to do a good job once you're hired.

When you do start a job, remember that everyone is entitled to courtesy, but respect is something that is earned. You'll probably be at the bottom of the status heap. Don't be tempted to bend rules and conventions which more senior colleagues bend, for instance by turning up late to meetings: you haven't earned the right to do this yet. You'll probably get a lot of unpleasant tasks to do in your first year. This is partly because that's how the world is, and partly to see how well you respond to this treatment. If you handle it professionally, without either complaining endlessly on the one hand, or being a masochistic victim on the other, then you'll be treated better later. It's a good idea to see how the longer serving staff are treated, if your first year is bad: if they're also treated badly, then it's time to think about building up the CV and moving on.

Some readers may wonder about a career in academia as a lecturer. If you're thinking along those lines, then you'll probably need a PhD, and it would be worth talking to wise, approachable staff sooner rather than later. There are also various good books about doing a PhD, and it would be wise to read some of those.

There are various clichés about careers which are clichés because they're true. One is that a moment spent in reconnaissance is seldom wasted. Another is that your life is what you make of it; the more you steer it, the more likely you are to end up where you want. On that cheering note, we'll end this book; we hope you've found it useful and enjoyable.

Bibliography

Of his vast collection of strange, rare books on forbidden subjects I have read all that are written in the languages of which I am master.
(*The Statement of Randolph Carter,* p.354)

We've deliberately kept this bibliography short – a list of our usual suspects, in no particular order, rather than an attempt to give systematic and encyclopaedic coverage of all the topics in this book. The last few years have witnessed a huge increase in the number of good texts about research, and this looks likely to continue, so any list of leading research resources is likely to become out of date very rapidly. The texts below are classics which we find both readable and useful; we hope you will find them a useful starting place.

Phil Agre's website:
http://polaris.gseis.ucla.edu/pagre/
There is a lot of useful material here for students at all levels.

Lynne DuPre, on writing skills:
DuPre, L. (1998) *BUGS in Writing, Revised Edition: A Guide to Debugging Your Prose*. Reading, MA.: Addison-Wesley
A good, hands-on guide to writing; clear, skilful and highly readable.

Sir Ernest Gowers, on effective writing:
Gowers, E. (revised by Greenbaum, S. and Whitcut, J.) (2003) *The Complete Plain Words*. Harmondsworth: Penguin.
A classic guide to clear writing.

George Pólya, on problem solving and reasoning:
Pólya, G. (1971) *How to Solve It: A New Aspect of Mathematical Method*. Princeton, NJ: Princeton University Press.
Not just about mathematics, despite the title: a fascinating guide to strategies for tackling and solving research problems.

The Skeptic's Encyclopedia, on reasoning and evidence:
http://skepdic.com/contents.html
An invaluable source for information about logic, reasoning and use of evidence.

William Strunk Jnr. and E. B. White, on writing style:
Strunk, W. and White, E. B. (1979) *The Elements of Style*. New York: Macmillan.
Another classic, which complements the other books we've mentioned on writing.

Robert H. Thouless, on reasoning and logic:
Thouless, R. H. (1995) *Straight and Crooked Thinking*. London: Macmillan.
An excellent introduction to reasoning, and to common errors (deliberate or inadvertent) in reasoning. Contains a useful list of 'thirty-eight dishonest tricks which are commonly used in argument' which you can use when assessing literature about your chosen topic.

The urban legends FAQ:
http://www.urbanlegends.com/afu.faq/
Sometimes gruesome, always interesting, and very instructive in terms of the number of things which you assume to be true and don't bother to check.

The Wikipedia sections on rhetoric and logical fallacies:
http://en2.wikipedia.org/wiki/Rhetoric
http://en.wikipedia.org/wiki/Fallacy
Very useful for helping you spot errors in your own and other people's reasoning – particularly handy when you're working through the chain of reasoning that underlies your research design.

Darrell Huff, on descriptive statistics:
Huff, D. (2003 reissue) *How to Lie with Statistics*. London: Norton.
Generally agreed to be the clearest and most entertaining introduction to descriptive statistics.

Andrew Siegal and Charles Morgan's 'gentle introduction' to statistics:
Siegel, A. F. and Morgan, C. J. (1996) *Statistics and Data Analysis: An Introduction*. New York: Wiley.
It is what it says on the cover, with lots of examples and gentle explanations. This is the one we recommend to students with a fear of statistics.

Chris Chatfield on statistical thinking:
Chatfield, C. (1995) *Problem Solving: A Statistician's Guide*. London: Chapman & Hall/CRC.
For years we searched for a book that gives a good overview of *statistical thinking*, rather than just recipes for statistical techniques. This is the book.

Hays on statistics:
Hays, W. L. (1988). *Statistics*, 4th edn. New York: Holt, Rinehart & Winston.
This is *the* classic statistics reference book. There's probably a fifth, if not a sixth, edition by now.

Dr Bram Oppenheim on interviews and questionnaires:
Oppenheim, A. N. (1992) *Questionnaire Design, Interviewing and Attitude Measurement*. London: Pinter.
A famous, detailed introduction to methods that includes principles, rigour and sense. Based on Oppenheim's decades of experience teaching methods.

Norman Denzin and Yvonna Lincoln's heavyweight collection on qualitative methods:
Denzin, N. K. and Lincoln, Y. S. (eds) (1994) *Handbook of Qualitative Research*. London: Sage.
This weighty collection attempts to represent qualitative research in its entirety. As such, it's a terrific source book and an authoritative volume to cite. It is also a book with many voices, and many viewpoints, and so it should be read discerningly.

Jonassen and Grabowski on individual differences:
Jonassen, D. H. and Grabowski, B. L. (1993) *Handbook of Individual Differences, Learning, and Instruction*. Hillsdale, NJ: Lawrence Erlbaum Associates, Inc.
If you do studies of human beings, then individual differences is an issue. Although set in the context of learning and instruction, this book has broader relevance. It is an excellent overview and reference book on how individual differences are viewed and assessed.

William Trochim's online Research Methods Knowledge Base:
Trochim, W. M. *The Research Methods Knowledge Base*, 2nd edn. http://www.socialresearchmethods.net/kb/ (version current as of 16 August 2004).
Lots of useful information online, accessible and not too heavy (also not too deep).

Sir Ronald Fisher set the agenda for experiment design:
Fisher, R. (1935) *The Design of Experiments*. New York: Hafner.
Well, if you're looking for a classic, this seminal book shaped our notion of experimentation.

Two classics on designing experiments and field experiments:
Campbell, D. T. and Stanley, J. C. (1963) *Experimental and Quasi-Experimental Design for Research*. Chicago: Rand McNalley.
Cook, T. D. and Campbell, D. T. (1979) *Quasi-Experimentation: Design and Analysis Issues for Field Settings*. Boston: Houghton-Mifflin.
These are both classics, for good reason.

There are plenty of basic introductions to experimentation, and this is one:
Field, A. and Hole, G. J. (2002) *How to Design and Report Experiments*. London: Sage.
Students like this very introductory guide, especially students who are daunted by the notion of experimentation.

Robert Yin on case study research:

Yin, R. K. (2003) *Case Study Research: Design and Methods*, 3rd edn. London: Sage.

Yin has written a number of books on case studies; this is one of his widely used textbooks.

Glossary

Dr Johnson, sir, was capable of very inaccurate statements . . . what do you say to a man who defines the mainsheet as the largest sail in a ship, or to belay as to splice, or a bight as the circumference of a rope? And that in a buke that professes to be a dictionary of the English language? Hoot, toot.

(Post Captain, p.268)

This glossary deals with some of the idiosyncratic terms which we have used in this book. We haven't tried to deal with all the standard terms used in this book, for the simple reason that if we had the glossary would be almost as long as the book.

Bad People Students often forget that there are students who lie, cheat and plagiarise. New researchers often forget that there have been researchers who lied, cheated and plagiarised. If you accidentally send out signals which make you resemble such individuals, then this will ring alarm bells, and The System will scrutinise your work very carefully. You need to make sure that you don't look like one of these Bad People.

brownie points Credit for good deeds. Allegedly used by Brownies (like Girl Guides, only younger), but we can't swear to this.

cynical readers Many students believe that their writing should be simple, clear and enjoyable to read. Most markers have seen too much work which is simple because the writer doesn't understand the complexities of their field, which is clear because the writer's understanding of the topic is clear but wrong, and which is enjoyable to read because it is pleasant fiction. They will, in consequence, be unlikely to think charitably about any unusual features of your writing; they will be more likely to think that these features are just a way of concealing sin.

doing a Raquel In one episode of *Coronation Street* (a popular British soap opera) Raquel the barmaid marries Curly the supermarket manager. The next morning, he sets off to work, and she finds herself alone in the house. She looks around, and wonders aloud: 'Now, what do wives do?' Many novice researchers do a Raquel by asking 'What do researchers do?' when confronted by a problem of research design: in other words, they copy the outward manifestations of what they think real researchers do, as opposed to focusing on the reasoning processes and deep structures which real researchers use. A frequent analogy is that it's like noticing that doctors wear white coats and stethoscopes, so if you wear a white coat and a stethoscope that makes you a doctor. Copying the outward appearance is a bad idea. In the case of Raquel and Curly, it ended in a traumatic divorce, and in the case of research, it usually ends with findings which are at best harmless but useless, and at worst help drag other researchers into a pit.

Elbonia   A fictitious country which features in Scott Adams' 'Dilbert' books. Some software warranties now include Elbonia in the small print (presumably because some hard-pressed software engineer has tried to introduce some brief humour).

eyeballing the data   Inspecting the data by eye for any obvious patterns before doing systematic analysis. Useful as a sanity check in case you make a mistake with your stats.

Facts (with a capital F)   Ironic allusion to a naive view of reality, particularly prevalent in popular beliefs about history. In this view, there are simple, uncomplicated fixed points which can be used as a basis for objective, apolitical teaching – for instance, the date when the American Civil War ended. The reality is more complex – in the Civil War instance, there were several different dates on which different bits of the hostilities ended, and there wasn't even an agreed name for the War at the time.

giggle test   When you describe an idea for research to a capable researcher, do they giggle? If they do, then you might need to rethink the idea. Note the 'might' phrasing: sometimes they'll giggle, but then say that it's actually a good idea. In such cases, you need to be pretty careful with the phrasing of your write-up, so you don't look like a clown.

Last Tuesdayism   The belief that the entire universe, including records, fossils and our memories of the past, was created last Tuesday. You may encounter it in introductory logic, philosophy or research methods courses, where it is used as an example of an unfalsifiable belief. Conspiracy theorists may like to know that nobody has ever succeeded in disproving Last Tuesdayism, so it might be true. It can be divided into smaller sects such as Last Tuesday Morningists and Last Tuesday Afternoonists.

The Past (with a capital P)   ironic allusion to widespread and mistaken beliefs about history. The Past is often used as something on to which people can project their beliefs, rather than as something which people investigate.

pixy dust   A concept which the excellent Michèle suggested to us. In *Peter Pan*, pixy dust is something that you sprinkle over everyday objects to give them a magical glamour. You can do something similar in research by including indicators of excellence which, like pixy dust, don't take up much space, but which make a disproportionate difference to the final product.

reliability (contains a scary bit at the end)   The extent to which you get the same answer when the same question is asked repeatedly. This is defined differently in different disciplines, and there are different types of reliability, just to add some spice. For example, test–retest reliability measures the extent to which you get the same answer if you test the same person on two different occasions; inter-rater reliability measures the extent to which you get the same answer if two different raters rate the same thing. Reliability deals with how closely the answers agree with each other, as opposed to how closely they agree with reality (which is what is meant by *validity*, also known as external reliability). Just because you have high reliability on a large sample size, that doesn't prove that your results have high validity; if you asked 10,000 British adults to describe Father Christmas, there would be a lot of highly reliable responses describing a genial old man in a red coat and white beard, but these would have no validity because (*scary bit starts here*) Father Christmas is fictitious.

three golden rules of public speaking Don't lie, don't try to be funny, but above all, don't panic and blurt out the truth.

three ignoble truths FIRST IGNOBLE TRUTH: hardware breaks and software crashes. SECOND IGNOBLE TRUTH: resources are never there when you need them. THIRD IGNOBLE TRUTH: people fail you, get sick and die.

Three more or less noble principles (with apologies to the three noble truths) THE COCKROACH PRINCIPLE: when the dinosaurs died, cockroaches were watching them. When the last mammoth died, cockroaches were eating iffy fruit somewhere much warmer. When the Black Death devastated Europe, cockroaches were not too bothered: they'd seen much worse. Cockroaches didn't make it through so much without knowing something sensible. The answer might involve eating leftovers, but is more likely to involve a desire not to stray too far from a nice, dark, safe bolt-hole. If a cockroach wanders into the middle of a high-visibility, well-lit space, then its life is likely to take a significant turn for the worse. Much the same is true for novice researchers who stray too far into the limelight and too far from their bolt-hole. THE CABINETMAKING PRINCIPLE: back in The Past, would-be cabinetmakers served an apprenticeship. At the end of this, they were assessed to see whether they had the skills required to be formally accepted as a master cabinetmaker. A key part of this involved the apprentice making a cabinet to demonstrate the required cabinetmaking skills. A sensible apprentice would ensure that this cabinet displayed as many joints, marquetry and general difficult bits as possible, so that the required skills were easily visible to the examiners. It's much the same if you're a novice researcher (for instance, someone starting a PhD): your work needs to demonstrate the skills required of a professional in your area. It's your job to find out what these skills are, and to make them visible. THE CARTOGRAPHY PRINCIPLE: research is a lot like map-making. Your research should extend the previous maps of our knowledge, either by mapping areas which have not been mapped before, or by creating more accurate maps of known territories. If you work sensibly, then you can normally expect to have something useful to show for your efforts, and to return to fortune and glory.

Truth, the™ Ironic allusion to various absolutist schools of thought.

validity   how closely your results map on to reality, as opposed to some consistent but fictitious version of reality (see also *reliability*). Novices tend to spend a lot of time fussing about reliability, which is comparatively easy to measure, and to pay less attention to validity; they also tend to assume that high reliability must mean high validity.

Sources of quotations at beginning of each section

At the Mountains of Madness
By H. P. Lovecraft. In *H. P. Lovecraft Omnibus 1: At the Mountains of Madness*. Grafton Books, London, 1989.

Blue at the Mizzen
By P. O'Brian. HarperCollins, London, 1999 edition.

Desolation Island
By P. O'Brian. HarperCollins, London, 1996 edition.

Dracula
By B. Stoker. Arrow Books, London, 1979 edition.

Forbes's Hindustani Dictionary: A smaller Hindustani and English dictionary, printed entirely in the Roman character, conformable to the system laid down by Sir William Jones, and improved since his time.
By D. Forbes. Sampson Low, Marston & Company, London, 1861 edition.

The Fortune of War
By P. O'Brian. HarperCollins, London, 1996 edition.

Geology and Settlement: Greco-Roman Patterns
By D. P. Crouch. Oxford University Press, Oxford, 2004.

History of the Peloponnesian War
By Thucydides the Athenian, son of Olorus. Penguin, London, 1972 edition.

Invader
By C. J. Cherryh. Legend, London, 1996.

Night Winds
By K. E. Wagner. Coronet Books, London, 1978.

People of Darkness
By T. Hillerman. Sphere Books, London, 1988.

Post Captain
By P. O'Brian. HarperCollins, London, 1996 edition.

Stiff Upper Lip, Jeeves
By P. G. Wodehouse. Herbert Jenkins, London, 1963 edition.

The Case of Charles Dexter Ward
By H. P. Lovecraft. In *H. P. Lovecraft Omnibus 1: At the Mountains of Madness*. Grafton
  Books, London, 1989.

The Definitive Tarot
By B. Butler. Rider and Company, London, 1975.

The Statement of Randolph Carter
By H. P. Lovecraft. In *H. P. Lovecraft Omnibus 1: At the Mountains of Madness*. Grafton
  Books, London, 1989.

The Walls of Air
By B. Hambly. Unwin Hyman, London, 1989.

Index

Related books from Open University Press
Purchase from www.openup.co.uk or order through your local bookseller

---

THE PhD APPLICATION HANDBOOK

Peter J. Bentley

> . . . snappy and informative; it's a must-buy and there's nothing near it on the market at the moment.
>
> *Stephen Hart, University College London*

> I found it very informative and helpful. There was loads of useful detail that wasn't covered by the other PhD books I've been reading.
>
> *Miki Grahame, prospective PhD Student*

A PhD is one of the most ambitious and exciting things you can do in your life. Upon successful completion you will be a doctor – and a world authority in your chosen area.

Each year several thousand graduate students apply to do a PhD at universities in the UK. Many are not successful – they are unable to find a suitable university, or a supervisor, or decide on a suitable research project, or they cannot obtain funding to pay their fees and bills. Most students fail to obtain a PhD because they have one of these aspects wrong at the start.

The PhD Application Handbook is the first ever comprehensive handbook for people wishing to apply for a PhD in the UK. It provides a step-by-step guide to PhDs, explaining:

- What a PhD is
- How to apply for your PhD
- How to find the right university, supervisor and project

It also provides detailed information about funding, eligibility, deadlines for different awards, and which funding is best for which student. Examples of research proposals, application forms and interview technique are given, helping you to secure your PhD place with the minimum of problems.

The PhD Application Handbook is designed to help prospective PhD students achieve their ambition. If you want to do a doctorate in the UK, This book is essential for you!

Contents
Acknowledgements – Before you start – What is a PhD? – Funding – Finding the right university – Finding the right supervisor – Finding the right research project – Securing an offer – Accommodation – Beginning your PhD – Resource guide: Current funding opportunities – Index.

192pp   0 335 21952 7 Paperback   0 335 21953 5 Hardback

THE UNWRITTEN RULES OF PhD RESEARCH

Gordon Rugg and Marian Petre

A breath of fresh air – I wish someone had told me this beforehand.

PhD student, UK

If you are contemplating a PhD, buy the book and read it straight through to get the larger picture; then re-read each section in greater detail as you tackle each stage of your work.

I did the basic research for my PhD in about twelve months, then spent two years writing up the results – and producing possibly too much. It succeeded, but I think I might have made a better job of it if I had read a book like this first. But they didn't exist in those days.

Mantex

This book looks at things the other books don't tell you about doing a PhD – what it's really like and how to come through it with a happy ending! It covers all the things you wish someone had told you before you started:

- What a PhD is really about, and how to do one well
- The "unwritten rules" of research and of academic writing
- What your supervisor actually means by terms like "good referencing" and "clean research question"
- How to write like a skilled researcher
- How academic careers really work

An ideal resource if someone you care about (including yourself!) is undergoing or considering a PhD. This book turns lost, clueless students back into people who know what they are doing, and who can enjoy life again.

Contents
Preface – A challenge! – About this book – Acknowledgements – So you want to do a PhD? – Procedures and milestones – The system – Supervision – Networks – Reading – Paper types – Writing – Writing structure – Writing style – The process of writing – Presentations – Research design – The viva – Conferences – What next? – Useful principles and the like – Useful terms – Some further reading.

240pp   0 335 21344 8 Paperback   0 335 21345 6 Hardback

HOW TO FIND INFORMATION
A GUIDE FOR RESEARCHERS

Sally Rumsey

- What's the best way to find the information I need for my thesis / dissertation / project?
- How do I evaluate the relevance and quality of the information?
- How can I keep up to date in my subject?

Anyone setting out to research a topic, whether undertaking a project, report, dissertation or PhD, needs to find appropriate resources to inform their work and support their arguments. This book enables researchers to become expert at tracking down, accessing and evaluating information.

The book works systematically through the information-seeking process, from planning the search to evaluating and managing the end results:

- Formulating a search strategy to find and evaluate the most relevant resources
- Guidance for using online bibliographic databases and the Web
- Includes referencing, copyright, plagiarism, and keeping up with new developments in your field

This concise and contemporary book covers all major areas of information seeking and selection for researchers. Written by an information professional, it is invaluable for anyone researching a topic including academics and students, public and government researchers and researchers in the private sector.

Contents

List of figures – List of tables – List of abbreviations – Foreword – Preface – Acknowledgements – The information gathering process – Using a library – Formats of information sources – Finding information about existing research – Identifying the information need – Resource discovery – The online searching process – Citation searching – Resource location – Using the World Wide Web for research – Accessing materials – Evaluation of resources – Citing references – Keeping records – Intellectual property and plagiarism – The research community and keeping up to date – The changing landscape of research – Glossary – References and bibliography – Web addresses – Index.

288pp   0 335 21428 2 Paperback   0 335 21429 0 Hardback

Open up your options

 Education

Health & Social Welfare

 Management

 Media, Film & Culture

Psychology & Counselling

 Sociology

Study Skills

for more information on our
publications visit **www.openup.co.uk**

OPEN UNIVERSITY PRESS
McGraw - Hill Education